The Glory of the

The Glory of the Garden:
English Regional Theatre
and the Arts Council 1984-2009

Edited by

Kate Dorney and Ros Merkin

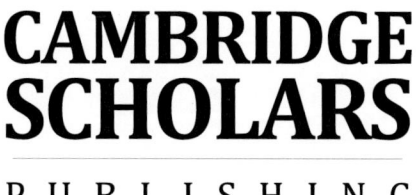

The Glory of the Garden:
English Regional Theatre and the Arts Council 1984-2009,
Edited by Kate Dorney and Ros Merkin

This book first published 2010. The present binding first published 2010.

Cambridge Scholars Publishing

12 Back Chapman Street, Newcastle upon Tyne, NE6 2XX, UK

British Library Cataloguing in Publication Data
A catalogue record for this book is available from the British Library

Copyright © 2010 by Kate Dorney and Ros Merkin and contributors

All rights for this book reserved. No part of this book may be reproduced, stored in a retrieval system, or transmitted, in any form or by any means, electronic, mechanical, photocopying, recording or otherwise, without the prior permission of the copyright owner.

ISBN (10): 1-4438-2059-8, ISBN (13): 978-1-4438-2059-2

Contents

Acknowledgements vii

Foreword ix

Introduction 1
Kate Dorney and Ros Merkin

Chapter One 15
From Rep to Regional: Some Reflections on the State of Regional Theatre in the 1980s
Anthony Jackson

Chapter Two 29
'Guarding Against the Guardians': Cultural Democracy and ACGB/RAA Relations In The *Glory* Years, 1984-94
Ian Brown

Chapter Three 55
The Gang of Forty: A Response to *The Glory of the Garden*
Glen Walford

Chapter Four 69
Devolve and/or Die: The Vexed Relationship between the Centre and the Regions: 1980-2006
Ros Merkin

Chapter Five 103
Touring and the Regional Repertoire: Cheek by Jowl, Complicité, Kneehigh and Eastern Angles
Kate Dorney

Chapter Six 125
Opening Up the Garden: A Comparison of Strategies for Developing Intercultural Access to Theatre in Birmingham and Nottingham
Claire Cochrane

Chapter Seven 139
I Bet Nick Hytner Doesn't Have to Do This: The Role of the Artistic
Director in the Regions
Gwenda Hughes

Chapter Eight 151
Salisbury Playhouse: Anatomy of a Theatre in Crisis
Olivia Turnbull

Chapter Nine 173
Strange Bedfellows: Making a Commercial Success of a Subsidised
Theatre
Ros Merkin

Chapter Ten 189
Enjoying and Achieving: The Future of Participation in Building-Based
Theatre
James Blackman

Conclusion 197
"What's Possible and Who Cares?": The Future of Regional Theatre
Kate Dorney

Appendix A 209
    Revenue Funding to ERPT 1984/85
Appendix B 211
    Revenue Funding to ERPTS 2008-09
Appendix C 213
    Arts Council Spending in the Regions 1984-1988
Appendix D 215
    Summary of Subsidy per head by region 1999-2000
Appendix E 217
    Ministers and Arts Council Executive 1984-2010
Appendix F 219
    Arts Council Drama Advisory Panels 1984 – 2002

Bibliography 229

Contributors 235

Index 239

Acknowledgements

The editors would like to thank the Arts and Humanities Research Council, the staff of the V&A Theatre and Performance department, the library and archive team at Liverpool John Moore's University, Laura Cockett and all the contributors, both to the conference and the book.

Particular thanks to Revinder Chahal for designing such a cover that so eloquently sums up the challenges of writing, researching and working in regional theatre.

FOREWORD

This book is the result of two Arts and Humanities Research Council funded projects. The first, was a resource enhancement grant which enabled Ros to salvage the archive of the Liverpool Everyman, re-house them at Liverpool John Moores University, employ an archivist to catalogue it, and then an interviewer (Kate) to create an oral history of the theatre. From the stories told to us over the course of the project, it became clear that there were many other stories to be told and we decided to organise a conference, 'The Glory of the Garden? Regional Theatre Since 1980' at Liverpool John Moores University to explore them. That was back in September 2006. Since then regional theatre has seen a number of highs and lows, the Arts Council has been through two restructurings, and a second AHRC funded project began, this time on the relationship between subsidy, policy and practice in British theatre. This project focuses on the archive of the Arts Council of Great Britain housed in the V&A, and is a joint venture between the University of Reading and the V&A We have been lucky in our colleagues and contributors, both to the book and to the conference, and extend our thanks to them all.

This book however, is dedicated to those who work in regional theatre, and strive to support it.

INTRODUCTION

KATE DORNEY AND ROS MERKIN

Asked to sum up their perceptions of the history of regional producing theatres in England since 1984, most people would characterise it as an era of crisis. Unquestionably, crises run like a sore through the period, and inevitably through this book. From William Rees-Mogg warning in 1984 that many of the Arts Council's clients would "find their existence jeopardised" to Dominic Cavendish's 2008 assertion that "uncertainty hangs over some of the country's biggest regional houses", the sense of impending doom, destruction and devastation runs deep.[1] During this time other voices have clamoured to confirm this. In 1990, Philip Hedley, artistic director of Theatre Royal, Stratford East, had become so weary of reading scare-stories and signing petitions for endangered theatres that he established a national campaign to save them. Journalists rushed to confirm this view: "Curtains Up for the Last Act", announced John Davison in *The Times* in 1986. By 1997, *The Observer* proclaimed that the litany of troubled companies was "as lengthy as some Wagnerian operas" and ten years later, Philip Hensher could start an article on yet another regional theatre facing a crisis by saying:

> When the same old story seems to be wearily repeating itself, it's tempting to put the whole thing in a box marked "Dog bites man" and ignore it. "Doubts over regional theatre's future" is just one of these stories; type the four key words into Google and it effortlessly produces nearly 2 million results.[2]

As Hedley pointed out in a letter to the *Guardian*, it was like working in a hotel in Scarborough, poised to fall over the cliff and into the sea.[3]
One of the dangers of categorising the period in this way is that we quickly become immune to the crises and the closures. We forget that each of these stories is, as Hensher argues, a very individual story of "tragedy and neglect". We don't just become immune to so many crises, we also forget that "regional theatre is not a unified thing. Each theatre will have its own flavour, its own history and its own place in the community".[4]

This book, then, tells some of those stories and some of those tragedies. This introduction and the chapters that follow aim to fill in the gaps between the cracks that the crises inevitably produced and to argue that the picture is a complex one (as well as, at times, a bleak and confusing one).

This book also serves to argue that the local matters. Paul Kingsnorth recently made an impassioned plea for the local and the destruction being wrought by globalisation. We are, he argues, discovering:

> that a global market requires global tastes – that it needs us to want the same things, feel the same things, like or dislike the same things, see in the same way. Only that way can demand cross, and break down, cultural boundaries. And we are discovering that an advanced post-industrial economy is symbiotic with mass production, the smoothing out of edges, uniform and characterless development – the standardised manufacture of places as well as things.[5]

In order for this global economy to progress, we must, he continues:

> cease to be people who belong to neighbourhoods, communities, localities. We must cease to value the distinctiveness of where we are. We must become consumers, bargain-hunters, dealers on a faceless, placeless international trading floor. We must cease to identify with our neighbourhood, our landscape and our locality, or to care much about it. We must become citizens of nowhere.[6]

The danger of this in theatrical terms is self-evident – as citizens of nowhere with "the same chains in every high street; the same bricks in every new housing estate...the same menu in every pub" we are also to have the same shows in all our theatres.[7] This tide of McDonaldisation is something that regional theatres can stand out against. For Michael Billington theatres are "as much part of a city's identity as the local soccer team", and there is a strong social case for keeping them:

> wander around our increasingly desolate city centres at night and they are often the only real source of communal life. Kill them off and you might as well shut up shop.[8]

These theatres then can, at their best, provide a sense of life, a sense of who we are in all its complexities and contradictions, a sense of our community. One example, from many, can be drawn from West Yorkshire Playhouse's work in 1999/2000 on the Ebor Gardens Estate in which the theatre laid out its aspirations to become a hub in "a sophisticated set of relationships between institutions in the city" and in which it saw itself as having responsibility for "providing the communities in its neighbourhood with ways into a wider world".[9] At the same time, while staff at the National were involved in "soul-searching" about the age and whiteness of their audience, at West Yorkshire:

> an over-55s debating society was sorting out media sex coverage, craft groups were making bobbin lace, and two Leeds accountants were investigating the Business Circle deal for corporate entertainments.[10]

There are numerous other examples that suggest a local theatre can forge links in the community, as Blackman's chapter seeks to show in discussing the educational role of theatres, and can also provide a communal space in a city, something which is increasingly coming under attack with the privatisation of our public spaces. And this says nothing about the work on stage that can reflect and refract the community. At Liverpool Everyman, the arrival of Gemma Bodinetz and Deborah Aydon in 2003 led to a focus on plays "Made in Liverpool". These have included: Tony Green's *The Kindness of Strangers* (2004) which looked at the question of asylum seekers; Esther Wilson, John Fay and Lizzie Nunnery's *Unprotected* (2006) a verbatim piece about street sex workers and the question of a safe zone; Jonathan Larkin's *Paradise Bound* (2006) focused on a community that felt as though the Capital of Culture was shutting them out; and an updated version of Chekhov's *Three Sisters* by Diane Samuel and Tracy-Ann Oberman (2007), set on Hope Street, where the theatre is located.

But it is seen as being rather old fashioned, small-minded, politically reactionary and nostalgic to defend or champion the local, that somehow we want to "shore up the stockades of little England"[11] We are either global and urged to be less provincial (a word which itself has loaded connotations) or, more recently, cosmopolitan: all members of a single moral community.[12] This book seeks to argue that in our rush to abandon the local we are in danger both of missing its importance and missing the subtlety, complexity, diversity and colour it can bring to theatre, as Cochrane shows in her chapter on intercultural performance in Birmingham and Nottingham. The fractures between local and global or local and cosmopolitan are also refracted in the split that runs through the story between London and the regions, the local and the metropolitan. The two sides have often been at each other's throats, quick to apportion blame for wrongs perceived to have been done. As Peter Hall points out:

> If an actor in Wrexham rep cannot afford a new pair of tights, it is all the fault of Hall and his sybaritic cronies who spend their days lolling on beds of down puffing on opium pipes and making bonfires of public money.[13]

As Artistic Director of the National, Hall had his own axe to grind. And the grinding of axes dominates the discourses around regional theatre, exacerbated by decreasing amounts of cash and divisive policies that pit one organisation against another

We have tried to pinpoint here some of the key ideas and themes in the history of English Regional Producing Theatres (ERPTs) between 1984 and 2010 and to trace the troubled relationship between the Arts Council (the centre) and the regions. Inevitably it is partial and draws on existing work.[14] The theatres and companies examined here are just a small sample of England's regional producing theatres, and although some of them are the bedrock of the regional theatre ecology, there are some obvious omissions: the Festival Theatre in Chichester; Stephen Joseph Theatre in Scarborough, the Sheffield Crucible, and Manchester Royal Exchange included. There is also a ring of neighbourhood theatres that surrounds the West End including the Lyric Hammersmith, Hampstead Theatre, Theatre Royal Stratford East, the Young Vic and the Tricycle who serve the same function as their regional counterparts. But their work is already documented: extensively in case of the Tricycle and Stratford, less so in case of the others, and their relationship to the centre is not the same as that of a regional theatre. For one thing, it's easier and cheaper to get actors to work in London ERPTs and, for another, it's far easier to get national critics to review the work there. What is also mostly absent from this book is any detailed account of the work produced. But that is a story that will have to wait for another day. This story starts in 1956 with the Arts Council closure of its regional offices.

From its outset, the Arts Council always had an eye to the regions with Maynard Keynes seeing nothing more damaging than "the excessive prestige of metropolitan standards" and delighting in a vision of every part of Merry England being "merry in its own way."[15] But despite taking over the 14 regional offices of CEMA in 1946, in 1951-2 these became six regional offices and between 1952 and 1956 all regional offices were closed, despite a Select Committee suggesting that the provinces "where the Arts are not so readily available to the public" provided a more "valuable field than the metropolitan area for the activities of the Council."[16]

In response the regions started to organise, with a deputation from the South West arriving at the Arts Council's headquarters in January 1956 and leaving with funding and the agreement to set up an association. Other associations appeared somewhat haphazardly between 1956 and 1973, receiving support from Labour's 1965 White Paper *A Policy for the Arts,* until the entire country (with the exception of Buckinghamshire) was covered by 12 associations.[17] Since then, the relationship between the centre (Arts Council in London) and the regions has been vexed, fraught and often poisonously reductive. As Jackson, Merkin and Brown discuss, the 1984 report *The Glory of the Garden* was designed to change this relationship by devolving responsibility for regional theatres to the RAAs. Ever since, the Arts Council and government have been commissioning new reports, reorganising and ushering in new policies to manage this relationship and vowing to ensure greater equality between London and the regions in terms of funding allocated and critical esteem.

But it's not just structural reorganisation that has rung the changes in the regional theatres since 1984. A series of significant shifts in ways of working, expectations and language also shaped the life of these theatres and they have been faced with a barrage of new possibilities. Commercial terminology overwhelmed the subsidised theatre: plural funding, product, marketing, efficiency, cost-effectiveness, business incentives, performance indicators, challenge funding, sponsorship, private sector partnerships, enhancement funding, challenge funding, parity funding, incentive funding and a constant push for plurality in funding sources. Plural funding is not in and of itself a new feature. Rowell and Jackson noted its growth in 1984, but the distinctive development since that date has been the emphasis placed on it and the speed with which theatres have had to turn this policy into practice.[18] Local authority funding was one pot to be plundered but there were other sources to be tapped – and, fundamentally, new ways to define what theatre was about. Although the incentive for this clearly comes from Thatcherism and the desire to wean everyone from what was seen as an over dependence on the welfare state, in terms of theatre funding the key shift was made through the Policy Studies Institute (PSI). In 1985, Myerscough and the PSI were commissioned to undertake the first rigorous research into the economic benefits of the arts. Starting with a pilot study in Merseyside, they followed this with a more detailed study of Glasgow and of Ipswich and Suffolk (for rural comparison) culminating in a survey of the entire country. Published in 1988, *The Economic Importance of the Arts in Britain* estimated that £10.5 million was spent on the "cultural leisure market" between 1974 and 1984, about 5.4% of total consumer spending, that it gave direct employment to some half a million people and that the arts were fourth "among the top invisible export earners".[19]

His work was presaged and accompanied by a series of arguments, booklets, pamphlets and speeches made by the ACGB itself which highlighted the benefits of a mixed economy. At the Fortune Theatre in September 1985, and complete with steel band and string quartet, it launched *A Great British Success Story*. It was a clear attempt to appeal to the business sense of the government. Described by Rittner as "a change in presentation but not of policy" (and complete with a glossy cover featuring torn up tickets), it was the brainchild of the council's new finance director Anthony Blackstock, a 35-year-old accountant. It arrived complete with tables and statistics which made the point that the arts in Britain were not only thriving but economically successful and putting money back into the government's pocket to the tune of £75 million in taxes from its £106 million grant – or investment. They were also attracting tourists, Luke Rittner observing that the arts "are to Britain what the sun is to Spain" and creating jobs. An accompanying briefing paper concluded that:

> The money spent from the public purse on the arts is a first-rate investment, since it buys not only the cultural and educational elements, but also a product with which we compete on equal or superior terms with the rest of the world. To provide job opportunities, invest in business expansion and stimulate production and exports, the government could do no better than to put our money into the arts.[20]

Alongside making the case for the economic worth of the arts, theatres were also increasingly expected to look to business for sponsorship. The Association of Business Sponsorship (ABSA) had been founded in 1976 but received a twofold boost in the early eighties when its chairman, Luke Rittner, moved across to become Secretary General of the Arts Council and when Gowrie introduced the Business Sponsorship Incentive scheme in 1984, with the government offering to match selected new sponsorship in the arts (later to be succeeded by challenge funding). Richard Luce, Minister for the Arts, maintained that in 1986 business was contributing some £20 million which by 2007 had become £153.4m.[21] But sponsorship could lead to a variety of problems, as Sheffield's Crucible Theatre found out in 1986 when ABSA withdrew £3000 of match-funding for a production. The original funding had come from the council workers union NALGO which was sponsoring the production and using the foyer to mount an attack on Government cuts. ABSA wrote to the theatre arguing that NALGO's support "goes beyond the proper boundaries of business sponsorship" and ABSA were backed up by Richard Luce who agreed it "would be quite unacceptable for taxpayers' money to be used to support party political purposes in this way."[22] This is a one off example, but sponsorship has raised continuing problems not least in its reach. In 2007, it was shown that 3% of the arts received 75% of the sponsorship money and, as Turnbull points out, the bulk of sponsorship went to more 'prestigious' companies (she cites the RSC's £3.3 million deal with Royal Insurance between 1988 and 1994) and to the more commercial activities. In 1994-5, Equity claimed that business sponsorship was worth, on average, about £7,500 per theatre and questioned whether the investment of time and scarce resources justified the sums raised. They too were concerned about the problems regional theatres found in attracting sponsorship, citing the Swan Theatre in Worcester where it only accounted for 2% of their overall income.[23] On top of this, as Andrew Sinclair notes:

> Commercial sponsorship was also fickle and impermanent, usually for a single event; and it tended to play safe, putting its money on the known and the fashionable rather than the new and the experimental. It paid for good and cheap publicity.[24]

But, the biggest problem was that it was "not serving as the icing on the cake for many companies, but as the necessary bread and butter". At the Theatre Royal in Plymouth, where, in 1990, the artistic director Roger Redfarn could claim they had been "the very model of a Thatcherite theatre", raising £4.25 million the previous year from box office, sponsorship, catering and other sales, they were still facing a deficit of £384,000 and considering the closure of the studio. Given commercial investment of over £431,000 (making its turnover third only to that of the RSC and the National), it did not bode well for other ERPTs.[25]

If *A Great British Success Story* argued for the economic value of the arts, then *Partnership: Making Arts Money Work Harder* (1986) argued for the use value of them as well. The partnerships in question were working to bring new life to the inner cities, to expand and develop cultural industries (and consequently the number of jobs) and to improve the quality of arts provision outside of London. *An Urban Renaissance* (1989), subtitled "Sixteen case studies showing the role of the arts in urban regeneration" set out to demonstrate how the arts were making a substantial contribution to the revitalisation of cities and to urban renewal. The case studies, none of which directly included an ERPT, showed how arts development could not only attract tourists and business to an area but also act as a catalyst for regeneration, enhance the quality of the built environment, help build self-confidence in individuals and provide a focal point for community pride and identity.

But if all these publications attempted to speak the language demanded by government, it didn't follow that the Council were not above pointing the finger at the government or demanding higher subsidy. They were quite often a lever to apportion blame or demand more. In *Partnership,* the finger was pointed at the lack of central resources which had "sadly" brought the Housing the Arts programme to a halt and at the fact that further progress could be achieved with devolution if there was "renewed commitment from central Government".[26] It also warned quite starkly what might happen to sponsorship if the Government's expenditure plans raised fear rather than hope:

> Insufficient funding directly affects the quality and number of events which an arts organisation can produce. This in turn, threatens box office targets and deters sponsor; it leaves companies with idle assets and surplus capacity, limiting the range of products which can be offered for partnership and leading to disillusion and distrust. There is a quick and modest antidote to this spectre of waste and failure: a proper uplift in basic funding.[27]

It seemed that Myerscough had spawned a new industry though he was widely criticised on a number of counts for both his wide definition of what constituted culture and what constituted a benefit. As Sir Alan Peacock pointed out, if one city were to attract business through its arts policy, another city would logically be the loser, warning as well, that the economist "might become a hired gun for the cultural establishment".[28] The Arts Council seemed not to want to heed the warnings about hired guns and instigated their own economic impact survey in 2004 and their own social impact survey in 2006, both by Dominic Shellard.[29]

Executive directors began to appear alongside or above artistic directors (although Ian Brown warned they should be seen not as dry bureaucrats but as impresarios)[30] and theatres hired and had to find the money for fundraisers, a move which didn't always pay off in financial terms. The scope of the changes and demands is well summed up in Equity's 1996 report, designed as a look at subsidised theatre 10 years after the Cork Report. Not only did they find that any sense of overall strategy had been rejected in favour of a "collection of misdirected, uncoordinated, ill-defined and short term initiatives" but that the number and speed of these initiatives was truly "impressive". There were seven different Ministers for the Arts and Secretaries of State for National Heritage between 1986 and 1996, each pursuing their own policy priorities. They go on to point out "the most startling development of the decade has been the sheer volume of administrative and legislative changes – numbering over 35 – that have been heaped upon the sector".[31]

One example serves to illustrate the story – others are included in the chapters that follow. The Swan at Worcester, opened in 1968, had the dubious privilege of being one of the least well-funded producing theatres throughout its entire 40-year history. It was one of the theatres moved in *Glory's* devolution drive of 1985/6, becoming the responsibility of West Midlands Arts (WMA). In 1998, WMA announced their intention to withdraw funding in April 1999, as Michael Foster, MP for Worcester, explained in a parliamentary debate in October 2002:

> West Midland Arts announced its intention to remove completely its funding…because it was under funded and needed to make savings. The Swan was chosen as the sacrificial lamb because historically the local authority had funded the theatre poorly. West Midlands Arts took the view that if the local council did not value a theatre then there was no reason to put money into it.[32]

The council responded by agreeing an extra £83,000 a year, on top of their annual grant of £54,000, for three years. The theatre developed a three-year plan for 1999-2001 called *Creative Connections* and WMA agreed to three years worth of funding. In 2001, a city council working party recommended that the grant was maintained at the full level after the agreement expired but in the same year, the Swan discovered it was one of only four theatres not to benefit from the £25 million windfall.[33] WMA, through the lottery programme, funded a report by Andrew McKinnon. This concluded that the main problem faced by the theatre was under funding. The Swan urgently needed an extra £77,000 a year and work needed to start even more urgently on building a new arts centre for the city. It had already been identified in 1998 that vital work needed to be undertaken on the forty-year-old theatre and in investigating its relocation away from the flood plain on which it had been built. Whilst WMA and the county council were prepared to find the much needed £77,000 identified by McKinnon, at the same time the county council announced its decision to withdraw the 'top-up' money of £83,000. It had its own financial problems and was facing a £1.4 million shortfall. The Swan (along with youth services and the Museum of Local Life) was to be its sacrificial lamb, one councillor claiming, "it is highly expensive and labour intensive", and a "costly drain on resources". If they could remove the professionals and run the theatre through amateur groups and volunteers things looked much rosier. "It leaves us with an uneasy feeling that the Swan will be a glorified village hall" bemoaned one local paper.[34] No amount of petitioning (they collected over 13,000 signatures) or arguments about tourism and lost revenue (one study suggested the city stood to lose £2 million, including immediate loss from the pay and display car park by the theatre) or support from Alan Ayckbourn, who donated to the theatre's fighting fund, could change the councillors' minds. They thought being asked for money, in the words of the theatre's artistic director, Jenny Stephens, was a sign of weakness, not an investment in the city and its people. They were:

> that rare thing in today's Britain; a local authority which has not bought the idea that cultural investment is a cost-effective way of building a vibrant and prosperous town.[35]

Nor were they moved by the theatre's production of local work. Although the theatre had developed as a base for local amateur and writing groups, an integral part of their strategy had been new writing on local themes. In the recent years, commissions had included *The Worcester Century Plays*, Alex Jones' *River's Up* about flooding in Worcester and Lance Woodman's *Red Sky Over the Severn*, exploring the impact of the foot-and-mouth crisis on the area, which had attracted a large audience from the farming community and which was described as speaking urgently and directly to its audience.[36] Indeed, at the time of the crisis, Woodman was the recipient of the Pearson Group Scholarship as writer in residence for the Swan and had a second local play, *Growing Old Disgracefully*, ready for the autumn 2003 season.

Without a production team and production budget, the Swan found itself in competition as a receiving house with the recently refurbished Malvern Theatre and The Courtyard Arts Centre in Hereford, which had opened in 1998 with lottery funding and which had received a massive 417% increase in the £25 million windfall.[37] The fact that The Courtyard had been such a large beneficiary in the handout suggested that the Arts Council were favouring what they saw as more 'go-ahead' venues, with more mixed programming, a point made by WMA's Kate Organ who claimed they were trying to bring the theatre more in line with contemporary life, not just spend £25 million "trying to bring the world back to 1970".[38] The Swan was seen as old-fashioned and in the end, closed its doors as a producing theatre at the end of January 2003, leaving no producing theatre in the country between Birmingham and Bristol.

The Swan was not the only theatre to close in the period covered by this book. As Turnbull has noted, during the Conservative's eighteen year period in government, the number of regional producing houses in Britain fell by a quarter – and more have gone since, either closing permanently or moving out of the subsidised or producing sector.[39] These include Chester Gateway, finally closed in January 2007 to make way for a shopping precinct (although the developers are promising to replace it with an arts centre). The Cheltenham Everyman closed as a producing house in 1993, to re-open as a receiving house. The Redgrave in Farnham closed in 1995 and the Thorndike in Leatherhead closed in 1997. Others closed for a short period, to reopen again; despite Glen Walford's ambitious response to *The Glory of the Garden* (reproduced in this book), in 1993 the Liverpool Everyman was closed for six months while the Arts Council attempted to save it by turning it into a receiving house. The story of Liverpool Playhouse (closed between 1998 and 2000) is explored by Merkin in this book and in 2007 both Derby and Bristol closed their doors mid-season, as discussed by Dorney in the conclusion.

But not everything has been doom and gloom. New theatres have opened including West Yorkshire Playhouse in 1990, one of the last theatres built as part of the Arts Council's Housing the Arts Policy, The Curve in Leicester, a £66 million ground-breaking design by Rafael Viñoly and Hull Truck who have finally moved from the converted church hall opposite the morgue which has been their home since 1983. Others have been refurbished - in part thanks to money from the other big development – the National Lottery. Some of the most recent of these include the Belgrade, Coventry, the Northcott, Exeter and the Sheffield Crucible and current projects include those at Liverpool Everyman and the Lyric Hammersmith, the latter building the country's first "teaching" theatre.

What is clear is the feeling that regional theatre is on the threshold of a new renaissance. Many would have been surprised to hear Stephen Daldry, interviewed on Radio 4's *Front Row*, responding to a question about running the National Theatre one day. He replied that what he really wanted to do was take on a regional theatre "because the relationship you have with a town can be so dynamic" The post-Boyden windfall has led many to feel that we are, as Kate Kellaway asserts, "on the brink of a new era" with the arrival of new artistic directors determined to reinvent regional theatre.[40]

Nor should we think that optimism about the health of the ERPTs is simply a current thing. There are also many reminders that theatres which looked to be on the brink of disaster over the last 25 years have found the artistic vision and the will to turn themselves around. Once again, one example must suffice – but there are many other bright sparks to be found. The Mercury Theatre, Colchester is one example at the beginning of this century, whose renaissance led Lyn Gardner to pronounce that, "the time has come to stop writing the obituary of regional theatre". It was "not renowned as a hotbed of theatrical innovation," but it was the place where "the greatest miracle has taken place". Two years previously the theatre was "teetering on the brink of closure and hardly seemed worth saving". While it was still not out of the woods, its fortunes had been turned round by Dee Evans and Greg Floy, ditching *Shirley Valentine* in favour of the classics. They also reinstated the actor rather than the marketing manager at the heart of the theatre working with an 18 strong seasonal ensemble. Recognition of its new lease of life brought with it money, including the Arts Council's first ever recovery funding to the tune of £350,000. Gardner continues:

> Underlying all this is a belief in the role of the artist in society. One of the desperate things about regional theatre in recent years is that it has crushed the artistic vision out of those involved. For many, meeting performance targets, balancing the books and justifying the subsidy have become a raison d' être rather than a by-product of a thriving theatre. Evans firmly believes that we need regional theatres such as the Mercury because they contribute to the desire, articulated by the philosopher RG Collingwood, "that most people want a better life". If that means making money by doing some canny co-productions with commercial managements, so be it, but it also means putting the theatre at the heart of the community."[41]

It was, as Gardner points out, a "lesson in how the survival of regional theatre is about not just money but also the will and the vision to reinvent yourself."[42]

Notes

[1] William Rees-Mogg quoted in Nicholas de Jongh & Donald Wintersgill, "Gowrie Grant Cut Staggers Arts and Gallery Chief", *Guardian*, December 18, 1984; Dominic Cavendish, "Drama in Crisis", *Daily Telegraph*, 15 January 2008
[2] Philip Hensher, "You Can't Run a Regional Theatre From London", *Independent*, September 18, 2007; Richard Brooks & Roger Tredre, "Tragicomic Opera" *Observer*, November 9, 1997; John Davison, *Times*, August 10, 1986; Philip Hedley is quoted in Benedict Nightingale, "Sharp Pains in the Extremities", *Times*, October 9, 1990
[3] Quoted in Paul Taylor "Making a Drama Out of a Crisis", *Independent*, February 23 1995. The Holbeck Hall Hotel had collapsed as a result of a crumbling cliff in Scarborough in June 1993
[4] Hensher, "You Can't Run a Regional Theatre From London", *Independent*, September 18, 2007
[5] Paul Kingsnorth, *Real England: The Battle Against the Bland* (London: Portobello, 2009), 8
[6] Ibid.
[7] Ibid. 6
[8] Michael Billington, "No More Theatres, OK!", *Guardian*, July 9, 1997
[9] Dick Downing, *In Our Neighbourhood: A Regional Theatre and Its Local Community* (York: Joseph Rowntree Foundation, 2001), 69-70

[10] Dan Glaister & Martin Wainwright, "Exit North as Sir Ian Tires of London's Bourgeoisie", *Guardian,* September 24, 1998
[11] Kingsnorth, 9
[12] See Marvin Carlson 2004 and Dan Rebellato 2009. See also Jo Robinson 2007.
[13] Michael Billington, *State of the Nation* (London: Faber and Faber, 2007), 254
[14] For other accounts of this period see: Olivia Turnbull 2008; Robert Hewison: 1995; Andrew Sinclair 1995; Richard Witts 1998; Ian Brown and Rob Brannen 1996; Ian Brown, Rob Brannen and Douglas Brown 2000; Ian Brown 2007.
[15] John Maynard Keynes, "The Arts Council, Its Policies and Hopes", *Listener,* July 12, 1945; reprinted in John Pick, *Vile Jelly: The Birth, Life and Lingering Death of the Arts Council of Great Britain* (Doncaster: Brynmill, 1991), 105-8
[16] Quoted in Robert Hutchison, *The Politics of the Arts Council* (London: Sinclair Browne, 1982), 119. The original offices were based in Newcastle, Leeds, Nottingham, Cambridge, London and Middlesex, Reading, Bristol, Cardiff, Birmingham, Manchester, Edinburgh plus Kent, Surrey, Sussex (all based at London headquarters)
[17] South West Arts: 1956; Northern Arts: 1961; Lincolnshire and Humberside: 1964; North West Arts: 1966; Greater London Arts: 1968; Merseyside Arts: 1968; Southern Arts: 1968; Yorkshire Arts: 1969; East Midland Arts: 1969; Eastern Arts: 1971; West Midland Arts; 1971; South East Arts: 1973.
[18] Rowell and Jackson, *The Repertory Movement: a History of Regional Theatre in Britain* (Cambridge: Cambridge University Press, 1984), 114
[19] John Myerscough, *The Economic Importance of the Arts in Britain* (London: Policy Studies Institute, 1988), 6 & 12. The other surveys were published separately by the Policy Studies Institute
[20] David Hewson, Arts Campaign Goes Public, *The Times,* September 13, 1985; Leslie Geddes-Brown, "The offer the government can't refuse", *The Times,* September 15 1985; David Hewson, "Arts Council to fight for 50% increase in government grants", *The Times,* September 18, 1985
[21] "Arts and Business Awards" supplement in *Guardian,* 2007. The supplement also notes that on top of business investment, 2005/6 had seen private investment totalling £529.5 million and trust and foundation investment of £113.7 million. ABSA became Arts and Business in 1999 and in January 2008, ACE announced that its grant was to be cut by a third to £4 million.
[22] Malcolm Pithers: "Political Play Costs Theatre £3000", *Guardian,* February 13, 1986
[23] British Actors' Equity Association, *The Theatre Commission: A Report on Subsidised Theatre in the UK* (London: British Actors' Equity Association, 1996), 13; Turnbull, 91
[24] Sinclair, 183
[25] David Lister, "Thatcherite Model Still in the Red", *Independent,* October 23, 1990
[26] ACGB: *Partnership: Making Arts Money Work Harder,* (London: ACGB, 1986), 3. Housing the Arts ran from 1966-1988 providing money for restoring and rebuilding theatres.

[27] Ibid., 18
[28] For this and other criticisms of Myerscough see Hewison 277-278.
[29] Dominic Shellard: *Economic Impact Study of UK Theatre* (London: ACE, 2004); Dominic Shellard & Bill McDonnell, *Social Impact Study of UK Theatre* (London: ACR, 2006).
[30] Jim Hiley, "Business Treads the Boards", *Times*, October 20, 1990
[31] British Actors' Equity Association, *The Theatre Commission,* 3. Members of the Theatre Commission included David Edgar, Richard Eyre, Miriam Karlin, Brian Rix and Braham Murray.
[32] Hansard 29 October 2002 vol 391 cc229-37WH
[33] The others to receive no funding were Croydon Warehouse, York Theatre Royal, Chester Gateway and the Palace Theatre, Westcliff-on-Sea
[34] *This is Worcestershire,* January 29, 2003
[35] Terry Grimley, "Dying Swan Takes Its Final Bow", *Birmingham Post*, January 6, 2003
[36] Michael Billington, "Red Skies Over the Severn"*, Guardian,* October 29, 2001
[37] This still left The Courtyard, which was also a producing theatre specialising in large cast shows that mixed amateurs and professionals, with an annual budget that was some £50,000 less than The Swan. See Terry Grimley, "Winners and Losers", *Birmingham Post*, March 9, 2001
[38] Ibid.
[39] Turnbull, 9
[40] Kate Kellaway, "The Dramatic Revival of Britain's Regional Theatres", *Observer,* November 15, 2009
[41] Lyn Gardner, "You Can't Market Rubbish", *Guardian,* September 27, 2000
[42] Ibid

Chapter One

From "Rep" to "Regional"—
Some Reflections on the State
of Regional Theatre in the 1980s

Anthony Jackson

In the book which George Rowell and I published in 1984 (but wrote in 1983), we aimed to do a number of things: to tell the story of the repertory movement, and to celebrate and interrogate the contribution of "rep" to British cultural life over 80 or so years.[1] We were also writing at a time of "retrenchment" which gave our discussion a certain edge – the future was not looking particularly rosy. Over the next few pages, I want to re-visit (and remind the reader) of one particular period in the history of regional theatre, not as a history lesson but rather to see if it will help us to get a purchase on those things about regional theatre (or "rep") that seem to have been constant and those that have fluctuated. The shift in the terminology used to describe this theatre - from "rep" to "regional" - was one of the markers of the change evident in the early eighties, and this will provide a peg on which to hang some of the discussion. In the process some questions will emerge – ones that we raised in 1984, but which still, in my view, have relevance today even if the material circumstances have changed.

First, just how long ago was 1984? Among the events that occurred that year that serve to characterise and to locate the period were the following. The Thatcher government had been in power for five years and had already embarked on a second term having won a landslide victory in the 1983 election. Inflation had fallen to 4.6% from a high of 20% only a few years earlier – due largely to the monetarist policies that were zealously implemented during Thatcher's early years in power. Whole tranches of the public sector were being privatised, including in 1984 one of the great public sector icons, British Telecom. The cost in industrial jobs especially in the public sector was, in the post-war era, unprecedented, and 1984 saw the beginning of the year-long national miners' strike called in protest at the planned closure of pits across the country. It was also the year of President Gorbachev's first visit to the UK; the eviction of the peace protesters from Greenham Common; and the IRA bombing of the Grand Hotel during the Conservative Party annual conference in Brighton. If that were not enough, York Minster was hit by lightning; Andrew Lloyd Webber's *Starlight Express* opened at London's Apollo Victoria; Band Aid recorded "Do they know it's Christmas?" for famine relief in Ethiopia; and Winston Smith finally came to love Big Brother. Of particular note too was the arrival of the (remarkably cheap) Amstrad PCW home computer: academics began to discard the typewriter, but it came too late for writing *The Repertory Movement*. And finally, of course the Arts Council launched *The Glory of the Garden* – its "strategy for a decade" for the arts in England.

The coincidence of the publication of *The Repertory Movement* and (several months later) *The Glory of the Garden* offers a useful starting point for assessing the state of regional theatre in the early 1980s. Sir William Rees Mogg, the then-chairman of the Arts Council, signalled on the first page of his preface to the report exactly where the most urgent priority of the Council lay: in redressing the imbalance between London and the regions. Indeed, de-centralisation of the theatre – from its obsessively London-oriented focus – and the closely-related if complex notion of "repertory programming", with all the ideas and practices that that term seems to embody, such as subsidised ticket prices, the promotion of new plays, the raising of standards, and the relationship of theatre to its community, are the two key themes that characterised the repertory movement throughout its history. The themes are symbiotically linked and I will return to them in more detail later. They likewise formed the backbone of our 1984 study, which offered a history of the regional repertory movement spanning the period from the late 19th century stock companies to "the present"; and culminated with a snapshot of six "representative" companies in the early 1980s: namely, the Glasgow Citizens, the Liverpool Everyman, the Nottingham Playhouse, the Royal Exchange, Manchester, the Salisbury Playhouse, and the Victoria Theatre, Stoke-on-Trent.

We had seen the post-war development of rep as happening over three broad overlapping phases. First – from 1958 through to the mid-1970s – was the period of undeniable optimism as the gradual re-building of Britain after the war began to take shape, and as the new Arts Council subsidies began to make a difference: allowing companies to escape from the tyranny of "weekly rep", increase the period available for rehearsal and set (or keep) ticket prices at affordable rates. A sense of expansiveness and a renewed belief in the idea of "rep" and of what it might encompass was, before long, accompanied by an extraordinary building and refurbishment programme to provide new and updated theatre spaces - from the Belgrade, Coventry (1958), the first purpose-built repertory theatre to be constructed in the post-war period, to the Royal Exchange, Manchester, and the National Theatre (both opening in 1976). Much of the innovative repertoire programming and, more critically, of the more adventurous new writing was now emanating from leading reps such as the Nottingham Playhouse under the direction of Richard Eyre, who gathered around him some of the most significant talents of the day: Howard Brenton, David Hare and Trevor Griffiths to mention but a few. Under Giles Havergal's leadership the Glasgow Citizens' Theatre began to demonstrate that British theatre could achieve the kind of imaginative and inventive reinterpretation of the classics more commonly associated with the European mainland. And during Peter Cheeseman's remarkable and enduring tenure at the Victoria Theatre, Stoke-on-Trent, the idea of what a genuinely "community theatre" might look like was being redefined, largely though not exclusively through the series of ground-breaking documentary plays dealing with topical and locally-relevant issues (such as the steel industry, its history and its threatened future, or the development of the railways) but which also made for entertaining theatre in their own right.[2]

Beginning later but running concurrently with phase one, from the mid-1960s through to the late-1970s, was a period of experiment and remarkable energy, marked by the establishment of the Liverpool Everyman, and later the Contact Theatre in Manchester and the Young Vic, London, as "alternative" reps– appealing to specific rather than catholic audiences, and especially to young people. These theatres were, in spirit and personnel alike, youthful, experimental, provocative, and motivated by a belief in the inspirational and, in many cases, the educational potential of live theatre. In response, many of the larger theatres began to build studio theatres to complement the main house, dedicated to riskier new plays or plays for children. At the same time outreach work was being developed for schools and youth centres: Theatre in Education began at this time, initially at the Belgrade, Coventry, but spreading quickly to other regional theatres such as the Leeds Playhouse, Bolton Octagon and Nottingham Playhouse. There was too an increase in the number of small, independent alternative theatre companies which in turn challenged and subsequently fed the mainstream reps. As we noted in 1984, "For three decades after the end of the Second World War, the notions of theatre as a civic institution, as a cultural focus for the community, as an expression of local identity and pride, became accepted – as the increasing scale of public funding and municipal theatre building demonstrated."[3]

During the mid-1970s, however, a third phase came to predominate, triggered largely by a faltering economy and a loss of faith in some of the expansive ideas of the 1960s. In 1975, as inflation peaked at 25%, the disadvantages of the prestigious, new large buildings began to make themselves felt – the costs of keeping theatres open, let alone mounting the adventurous and often large-cast productions of earlier years, became prohibitive. While there were exceptions, the creative energy and the initiative for new and exciting developments seemed increasingly to be centred either in (what we called then) the Fringe or in the hugely subsidized national companies. So, while the regional rep network had become by the late 1970s the main provider of theatre in Great Britain, by the early 1980s the sense was clearly one of a dwindling momentum. The crisis in arts funding was hitting building-based companies especially severely. This was then a period of retrenchment: withdrawals of grant-aid began and some theatres closed (Chesterfield, Crewe, Canterbury); some larger theatres shut down their outreach teams and reduced, or terminated, the work done in their studio theatres. Funding levels in real terms fell, and arguments intensified about not just the level of funding but the ideologies that underpinned the decisions made and the criteria being applied; and the pre-eminence of London came increasingly to be questioned now that the National Theatre and Royal Shakespeare Company between them attracted nearly 50% of the whole ACGB Drama allocation (in 1970 it had been 30%).

In his study of British theatre since the second world war, Dominic Shellard, writing some 15 years later, recapitulates these phases but argues that worse was yet to come.[4] He proposed two further phases: one commencing in 1984 in which the trend we had identified in phase three became more marked – the tightening of the grip of market forces upon the organisation and funding of the arts; and, in the 1990s, a fifth phase characterised by the effect on the arts of new funding from the National Lottery – as a result of which, the new money that began to come through was hedged around with conditions: it was short term and it required competitive bidding. I am not sure that "phase 4" was really anything other than an intensification of our third phase, but the advent of National Lottery funding, together with the push to get theatres to seek sponsorship from business, was undoubtedly significant in its impact. The additional pressures upon theatre administration (coping with a constant stream of funding applications, and having to market "product" in a far more aggressive and time-consuming manner) were considerable.

All these developments combined to shape repertory theatre in Britain as it approached the millennium: in terms of its buildings, its staffing, its programming, and, more importantly, the evolution of artistic policy as aspiration had to be tempered with unremitting economic, social and political imperatives. Underpinning the changing policies and fortunes faced by regional theatres in this period was a recurring debate about what exactly repertory theatre was or should be. At a time of financial constraint, declining audiences and the temptation to play safe and produce only small-cast plays, what exactly were the ideals and rationale that could be said to sustain regional theatre – if any? First, then, just what was meant by the term that defined the movement which itself played such a major role in the shaping of British theatre in the 20th century: "Repertory"?

Repertoire and repertory

Matthew Arnold, in a famous essay published in 1879, bemoaned the state of British theatre in comparison with the standards and range of plays offered by such European companies as the Comédie Française, and called for a sea change. The theatre was "irresistible": "The people will have a theatre; then make it a good one. ... Organise the theatre!" he challenged.[5] By "organise", he meant that the theatre needed something that could not be achieved by market forces alone, by the lowest common denominator, by the long run and by what was understood to be popular. A key element from the very beginning of repertory – at Manchester's Gaiety Theatre, at Glasgow's Repertory Theatre and at the Birmingham Rep – was the establishment of a repertory system of presenting plays - whether that be "true rep" or "short run". By "true rep" was meant the repertoire system favoured on the European mainland in which a programme of plays is offered in constant rotation through the year, allowing audiences to see two or three different plays in the course of any one week (the system employed by the National Theatre, the RSC and a handful of regional theatres); by "short run" was meant the practice of running each play in sequence for two, three or perhaps four weeks before replacing it by the next play in the season – the system employed by most regional theatres now. The latter has the economic advantage of giving a cash-strapped director casting flexibility. He or she can cast play by play and is not committed to keeping all actors on the books for a whole season. Whichever the system employed, it marked out the repertory theatre – in the early 1900s and in the early 2000s just as much – as clearly distinct from the mainstream commercial practice of the West End, and of many touring houses in the major cities, in which the "long run" is the aspiration and the measure of success. By contrast, repertory theatres could more effectively offer a variety of plays and maintain a degree of freshness that the long run generally could not. Closely tied in with the repertory system, then, were the objectives of the provision of a high quality and varied repertoire of plays, including the promotion of new drama and dramatists; the improvement of standards of acting and staging; the securing of civic or state patronage; and the forging of the vital links that must exist between a theatre and its community (however that community might be defined).

Although ideas and practices have varied enormously since the beginnings of the "modern" rep movement in early 1900s (from "true rep" programming to the short run; from permanent ensemble companies to play-specific casting; from "mainstream" rep to "alternative"), what animated the movement throughout its history was the ideal of offering a genuinely varied and balanced fare of plays and related artistic events each season that would command the interest and nourish the imagination of the community it served – fare that would include good plays of all types, new and classic, serious and comic. Theatre was seen as a cultural service rather than a commercial enterprise and to be justified in the same terms as one would a library, art gallery or swimming pool.[6] How different theatres chose to interpret that service was another matter and would be governed by the diversity of circumstances within which they operated – and indeed the vitality of rep has been demonstrated time and again in that very diversity and individuality of artistic policy. In the post-war period, the range of work at our six representative regional theatres, from the Royal Exchange to the Liverpool Everyman, from the Glasgow Citizens to the Salisbury Playhouse, crossed almost the entire spectrum of theatre activity in Britain at the time, as did the variety of their repertoires, artistic philosophies and policies, their architecture and their audiences.

De-centralisation

Decentralisation of theatre from its persistent London-centredness was equally part of the original ambition of repertory pioneers such as Annie Horniman and Barry Jackson.[7] The theatres they founded, in Manchester and Birmingham, and (under Waring) in Glasgow, were assertively a regional rather than a London phenomenon; and, for the rest of the century, their geographical location and local base have been part of their raison d'être and their development as "independent centres of growth",[8] providing range, richness, vitality. In the post-war period, one of the most demonstrable ways in which the post-war push to re-vitalise theatre in the regions was manifested was in bricks and mortar. An integral component in the post-war reconstruction and renewal of the country's cultural infrastructure was the extraordinary theatre building programme, intermittent and localised though it was. By 1980 the number of new theatres built since the second world war throughout the country totalled 40, of which 34 were in the regions (including major new conversions such as Manchester's Royal Exchange). Many were built in part as monuments to civic pride with large investments by local authorities – but others, such as the Liverpool Everyman, were built to be explicitly non-monumental, having a more experimental, "alternative" character to them and aimed at bringing in new, younger audiences, or at providing performance spaces that could accommodate more adventurous types of plays and styles of playing. The Victoria Theatre in Stoke, an old cinema converted into Britain's first theatre-in-the-round; and the Glasgow Citizens, an old-fashioned theatre stripped of its gilt and gloss and its picture-frame stage in order to create a venue for surprising and enormously inventive re-interpretations of the classics are other notable examples.

We wondered then if the prestige theatres built in the expansive days of the sixties and seventies would prove manageable still in the cost-cutting eighties – and indeed the question continues to haunt us in the still-precarious present, exacerbated yet further by the worries over carbon footprints and the promise of ever-rising energy costs. But the question is not one exclusively to do with cost. The original artistic director of the Royal Exchange, Michael Elliott, when explaining the rationale behind the construction of the in-the-round theatre within a much larger hall, talked about his conviction that theatre buildings should have obsolescence built in to them – who knows what kinds of buildings, actor/audience relationships or styles of plays will be needed in 20 years time?

In fact, the Royal Exchange's first temporary theatre in the exchange building, 1973-6, proved to be an exciting space in its own right; and again, after an IRA bomb exploded close by in 1996 and forced a move to temporary accommodation in Upper Campfield Market, many found the very transience of the space exhilarating. As Michael Billington put it in *The Guardian*, recalling that 1996 challenge to find quickly an alternative space while the theatre was rebuilt, "there was an extraordinary buzz and intimacy about its ephemeral replacement".[9] Likewise there was, he argued, a similar quality of rough-and-ready excitement about the "temporary" Young Vic in London too. Stephen Joseph, the great pioneer of theatre-in-the-round in Britain and founder of the Vic in Stoke, passionately believed in theatres that were adaptable and responsive: his creation of the first theatre-in-the-round rep at Stoke proved immensely flexible, the performers were close to their audience, the cost of sets was reduced to a minimum, and the corresponding incentive to be innovative created rich artistic dividends, which Peter Cheeseman, Joseph's successor, was quick to exploit. While most of the large purpose-built theatres from phase one have endured and many have continued to thrive (if sometimes intermittently), many have undergone adaptation, renovation and renewal, while others have struggled to fill their auditoria on a regular basis. They have faced a challenge from yet another quarter too: some of the most exciting theatre of recent years has become more site-specific, taking place mainly outside conventional theatre buildings, for example in outdoor parks and "found" spaces such as warehouses, or transforming regular theatre interiors by creating thrusts, promenade performance areas or "installations". Some of the more monumental theatres have sometimes, by comparison, looked rather marooned in the contemporary landscape. The West Yorkshire Playhouse in Leeds, for example, built in 1990, perched on a rise overlooking an inner ring road, looks imposing and provides a richly varied programme of plays but, in its airport-style spaciousness and surrounded by car-parks, perhaps lacks the direct, umbilical connection with its immediate communities that other theatre spaces have achieved.

One of the most notable symptoms of change since the late 1970s has been the gradual shift in the terminology used to refer to theatre in the regions from "repertory" to "regional". While some major regional theatres still (and proudly) keep the word "Rep" in their title – the Birmingham Rep being the outstanding example – it was becoming clear by the early 1980s that "regional" was increasingly gaining favour as the term most theatre directors, trustees and funders preferred. This was a trend confirmed during the 1990s (Shellard's fifth phase) as commercial imperatives came to predominate and the ability and indeed the willingness of theatre directors to mount regular, home-produced seasons of plays diminished. Hosting touring productions and developing collaborative projects with other regional theatres (or touring companies) was becoming increasingly prevalent – an emerging trend identified in 1984 although the future scale of it had been difficult to predict. "Rep" was an affectionate nickname for a theatre system that had for decades fought to raise the flag for locally-produced and locally-responsive theatre – of and for its area. But as the 1970s gave way to the 1980s, there had developed, for many, an association of "rep" with "old-fashioned", even of "second-rate", not surprisingly as theatres endeavoured to re-position themselves in a rapidly-changing world in which they had to assert their contemporaneity, their ability to speak today's language and their readiness to meet the challenges of a society in which fashion, celebrity and new, digital media were providing a widening range of entertainment options, particularly for the young. The gradual switch of terms merely reflected what had been taking place ever since the creation of the "alternative reps": a change of mind-set, the ending of one kind of campaign, one cluster of beliefs about what to value in theatre for the contemporary age. The new emphasis was now not so much on the value of subsidised theatre in the regions *per se*, but on the debilitating inequality of the allocation of public funding between London and the regions.

The Glory of the Garden was the Arts Council's most serious attempt yet to address the London-centredness of the arts and the needs of the regions. Rees Mogg acknowledged that the original aim of the Arts Council, as articulated by J M Keynes – "to decentralise and disperse the dramatic and musical and artistic life of this country" – had "not been adequately realised".[10] After 40 years it was time to de-centralise, despite the obstacles, and the report argued for a radical shift in the balance of funding away from London to the regions. But it was severely and angrily criticised by many in the arts world for failing to show how it could be done when government funds were being kept at or below the rate of inflation, other than by cutting funds altogether to a substantial number of existing arts organisations. Beneath all the arguments about policy was the pivotal and highly contentious question of subsidy for the arts from the public purse – was it really justified and if it was on what scale, and what degree of accountability was it reasonable for the state to expect? And this was the report's Achilles' heel. In 1984, still recovering from a period of high inflation, the Thatcher government's policy was that the theatre should learn to love the market economy, run theatres as business enterprises, reduce reliance on public subsidy, seek commercial sponsorship and increase the proportion of income from box office. Interestingly, Rees Mogg was, as he declared in his preface to *Glory*, keen to acknowledge the fine ideals of the original movers and shakers at the Arts Council and admitted that, whilst a monetarist in things economic, he was a Keynesian in respect of promotion of the arts.[11] The State did have a role, not just to support and respond, but also to intervene. Intervention was, in his judgment, now a necessity - in part because of the continued dominance of London and in part, with an ironic twist that Rees Mogg appeared not to notice, because of the very monetarist policies, and genuflection to market forces, that had led to the constricted funding available from the Treasury in the present. As the financial straitjacket tightened and priorities had to be re-thought, it is tempting to conclude that it was the real-term reductions in grant-aid that led to the new policies rather than idealism about de-centralisation. What comes through the 'strategy' document quite unambiguously is its readiness to accept that the government was unlikely to provide any serious new money. In the event, several companies were closed, including three repertory theatres judged to be in decline, and no real increases in subsidy were received by any except two theatre companies: those in Sheffield and Leicester.[12] *Glory* marks a critical point in the evolution of the relationship between government, the Arts Council and the arts.

Writing the year before the publication of *Glory*, we worried then that many of the gains made in the previous two decades, for example widening access through ticket subsidy, were in serious danger. In a world in which the notions of multi-culturalism and community identities have become the subject of heated debate, does the regional theatre have a part to play in making connections with all its potential communities? If it does, just how does it go beyond making its programmes more accessible to all sections of society through better marketing and targeted ticket subsidy, and develop what Clare Venables once called 'the conversation you are trying to have' with those audiences,[13] especially when the chasing of sponsorship too often gets in the way of that conversation?

Theatre and community

The notion of a 'conversation with your audience' moreover begs the further question of just who that audience is, or could be. The relationship of regional theatre to its community, or communities, was, in some ways, the most challenging of all the aspects of regional theatre provision – and is still now, perhaps even more than then.

John Elsom, in his 1971 survey of British theatre, had asked what exactly was meant by the oft-quoted claim that 'theatre should serve the community.'[14] Debates about the most important or useful functions for the regional theatre were often heated, and the questions we identified in 1984 are still ones that require answers now. Indeed, the parallels with government-led policy initiatives in the late 1990s to promote 'social inclusion', significantly re-calibrated by the McMaster Report in 2008,[15] are striking. Should it provide a 'social service'? Should it have a social mission (political, educational), responding to perceived needs and government policy rather than apparent wants? Should it be the venue for an artistic experience quite distinct from the criteria or obligations associated with other social services or public utilities – allowing the director full artistic freedom? Should it try to be all things to all men, women, adults/children, dominant/minority cultures? Or should the artistic director trust to his/her own personal vision of what theatre should be, ploughing new furrows, and hope to be able to take audiences on a journey towards it? If the theatre does indeed have an obligation to 'serve the community', then how does it most effectively find out what communities are out there and, more critically, how does it appeal to one without deterring another? The latter question has been addressed energetically by some theatres in recent years, but avoided by others.

Questions, paradoxes and contradictions abound. It may often be that the director who ploughs his or her own furrow may produce the very programme that surprises and delights its regular audience or that attracts new audiences to the theatre for the first time. And of course what may seem to be a winning formula one year may prove a disaster the next. In 1984, we had noted the range and diversity of practice at a representative number of reps, but also recognised that not all theatres were as adventurous. The very notion of 'serving the community', of providing something for everyone, had led many directors into formula programming – the predictable pattern of plays that looked remarkably similar to programmes found up and down the country, dictated all too often by the tastes of the predominantly white middle class audiences that tended to patronise the theatre but justified by their apparent success in attracting regular loyal audiences. The choice of plays that might go into that programme may look very different now compared with 1984 (there is less Shaw, Priestley, Rattigan and Ayckbourn) - but do theatres still get locked into that vicious circle in which regular audiences determine choice of plays and that choice of plays deters new, younger audiences from coming? Even drama students in higher education need some persuading to go to see plays at the major reps in their area, while happily creating their own drama and attending each others'.

We noted in 1984 that "While the received opinion had for decades been that the regional theatre was a means of improving understanding of and access to the cultural heritage for everyone, an increasingly voluble (if minority) body of opinion argued that, organised as it was, this theatre was bound to be only an extension of the "establishment"... [and enmeshed] in 'a form of cultural imperialism, imparting the values of the dominant middle-class ideology to those who came to listen ... [so] 'enshrining the status quo".[16] In Bourdieu's terms, the cultural institution of theatre was likely to appeal primarily to those from relatively privileged backgrounds who already possessed the cultural capital to appreciate what was on offer.[17] There is an important if precarious path that any cultural institution has to negotiate, between "reaching out" and "serving the community" on the one hand, and exploiting, confidently and daringly, the unique resource and opportunities that the building itself can offer. Institutional theatre is always likely to play a key role in the cultural life of the region in which it finds itself. As I have argued elsewhere, the theatre's institutional set-up does by definition allow it to pay attention to well organised, carefully planned programmes of plays and events, and "its ability to cater for large audiences, its relative permanence and ability to look to the medium if not the longer term, and its visibility in the community, means that it can at its best be a powerhouse for balanced, well-crafted, high definition theatre".[18] At its worst of course it can constrain, play safe, commodify, centralise, exclude and constitute a drain on cultural resources that might better be deployed elsewhere.

The achievements of regional theatre over the past 40 years have been indisputable. Indeed, in 1984 we argued that "Regional rep has shown signs of finding what, in a video age, it can do that television cannot", and pointed to the example of theatres such as the Victoria Stoke, and the Glasgow Citizens. As we put it then, Repertory had over the years undoubtedly contributed to British theatre's sense of itself. It had

> provided the basic network of the nation's theatre, without which it would be wholly London-based and deprived of much of that new talent in writing, acting and direction which found its opportunity in the regions. Repertory has provided the decentralised nurturing of artistic strength and individuality and the focus for local cultural growth which has given British theatre the vitality and variety for which it has become so internationally renowned.[19]

But we also concluded that we had probably seen, not just the end of a further phase of the repertory movement, but, in many respects, the end of the "repertory movement" per se. It had become less and less easy to speak of a unified movement, driven by campaigning zeal, to establish regional theatre as the backbone of national theatre provision. To a large extent that had been accomplished. The priorities in the mid-1980s were different – as they are still in the early 2000s: they were about buttressing and defending the achievements and the resources from damaging erosion and, just as critically, about re-defining their functions in the light of changing social and cultural needs. But as we put it then, "the end of a movement does not matter; the end of movement does".[20] Moreover, if the term "repertory movement" no longer seemed completely appropriate to describe the "range, comprehensiveness and apparently established order of the present British regional theatre system", it nevertheless did still have some value, we believed then and I believe now, as a timely reminder of "the "alternative" roots and pioneering ideals at the beginning of the century from which that present system grew".[21] They are roots and ideals with which the regional theatre needs to retain its connection. However, we also warned that "The broadening of and greater responsiveness to theatre audiences is possibly one of the most pressing items now on the agenda for regional theatres."[22] I suspect it still is.

Notes

[1] George Rowell and Anthony Jackson, *The Repertory Movement: a history of regional theatre in Britain* (Cambridge: Cambridge University Press, 1984).
[2] *Fight for Shelton Bar* (1974) documented the attempt to keep the local steelworks operational, *The Knotty* (1966) examined the history of the local railway line.
[3] Rowell & Jackson, 186
[4] Dominic Shellard, *British Theatre Since the War* (London & Newhaven: Yale University Press, 1999)
[5] Arnold, Matthew, "The French Play in London", in *The Nineteenth Century* (August 1879), 243.
[6] See Rowell & Jackson, 181-5.
[7] See Anthony Jackson, "The Repertory Theatre Movement in England, 1960-1990", in *Englisches Theater der Gegenwart: geschichte(n) und strukturen* (Tubingen: Gunter Narr Verlag, 1993)
[8] Michael Elliott, interview with author, March 1982, quoted in Rowell & Jackson, 189
[9] *Guardian* 21 June 2006
[10] *The Glory of the Garden: the development of the arts in England – a strategy for a decade*, iv
[11] Ibid., 1
[12] Jackson 1993, 110
[13] Venables, qtd in Jackson 1993, 111.
[14] John Elsom, *The Theatre outside London* (London: Routledge, 1971), 10.
[15] See Brian McMaster, *Supporting Excellence in the Arts: from Measurement to Judgement* (London: ACE, 2008). This significant report, which influenced subsequent Arts Council policy, argued for the prioritising of "excellence" in arts provision, but sought to redefine excellence not in elitist terms but rather as life-changing experiences through the arts available to all.
[16] Rowell & Jackson, 187
[17] Pierre Bourdieu, *Distinction: A Social Critique of the Judgment of Taste.* (Harvard: Harvard University Press, 1987).

[18] Anthony Jackson, *Theatre, Education and the Making of Meanings* (Manchester: Manchester University Press, 2007), 266.
[19] Rowell & Jackson, 190
[20] Ibid. 191
[21] Ibid. 191
[22] Ibid. 187.

CHAPTER TWO

"GUARDING AGAINST THE GUARDIANS":
CULTURAL DEMOCRACY AND ACGB/RAA
RELATIONS IN THE *GLORY* YEARS, 1984-94

IAN BROWN

An important theme of *The Glory of the Garden* was the need to develop better provision for the arts in the regions vis-à-vis London, devolving authority to the (then) Regional Arts Associations. This chapter sets this process in the context of underlying attitudes. It examines the history of the theatre decisions outlined in the *Glory* report. It considers some Platonic "noble lie(s)" to which many participants in the funding system seemed to subscribe, including without doubt at times the current author. This chapter recognises that it is of the essence of the British arts funding systems that sincerely held values may come into conflict, although less regularly than is often supposed. It argues that, when they do, individuals will, according to professional conscience, believe themselves to be defending their artform, community, national or regional priorities. As will be seen, these conflicts can sometimes lead to what may be seen as bad faith. They often, however, involve perfectly honourable collisions (or happy coincidences) of sets of values and priorities that are unavoidable in a pluralist democracy.[1] The chapter considers why and how *Glory* was developed and implemented. It also addresses the nature of and principles behind *post-Glory* negotiations between theatre companies, ACGB, local authorities and RAAs. Throughout, it assesses and illustrates the relations between the Arts Council of Great Britain (ACGB) and Regional Arts Associations (RAAs) between the 1984 *Glory* report and the 1994 delegation of the majority of arts organisations to the (by then) Regional Arts Boards (RABs).

One means of grasping both ACGB and RAA actions lies in Plato's *The Republic*. There he proposes guardians (sometimes called philosopher-kings) leading the ideal state and being told a "noble lie".

> The noble lie will inform them that they are better than those they serve and it is, therefore, their responsibility to guard and protect those lesser than themselves. We will instill [sic] in them a distaste for power or privilege, they will rule because they believe it right, not because they desire it.[2]

The danger critics like Juvenal saw, in his sixth Satire, was that the guardian elite could very easily become self-serving and self-justifying. "Quis custodiet ipsos custodes?" ("Who will guard, or guard against, the guardians?"). Such conceptions, however, of a "higher" morality, imbued with the ideology of ruling groups, as socially beneficial are found in, for example, Matthew Arnold's *Culture and Anarchy* (1869). There he argues the positive impact of his definition of culture in doing away with classes and creating an atmosphere of "sweetness and light" in which all may live. His conception of culture as a force for sweetness and light, asserting order in society and with underlying moral power, influenced the Bloomsbury Group. Group members were also particularly affected by G. E Moore's arguments in his *Principia Ethica* (1903) that the "pleasures of human intercourse and the enjoyment of beautiful objects [...] form the rational ultimate end of social progress".[3] Arnoldian values and Moore's relating of the enjoyment of "beautiful objects" and "social progress" underlay the 1945 foundation of the Arts Council of Great Britain out of the wartime Council for the Encouragement of Music and the Arts by, *inter alia*, key members and associates of the Bloomsbury Group. ACGB's roots lie in Arnoldian and Bloomsbury values not only in its founding personnel,[4] but in its formative rhetoric (as its Royal Charter's dual emphases–developing and improving knowledge, understanding and practice of the arts; and increasing their public accessibility–demonstrate[5]). In the post-war years, such values were widely promoted as a good.[6] And they underlay Harold Wilson's appointment of the first Minister for the Arts, Jennie Lee, in 1964.

In fact, of course, these values contain an inherent tension between what the Charter calls "development and improvement", sometimes summarised as "excellence", and what is considered "accessibility", often related to wider social or community benefit. Many of the conflictual issues discussed in this chapter arise at least in part from this inherent conflict. It has been argued – most recently by Olivia Turnbull[7] – that the Bloomsbury version of metropolitan excellence was the prime priority of ACGB for the first twenty years of its formation. Her case is surely strong, although it would be unfair to over-generalise. The work, for example, of the Drama Department in that period, however constrained by funds, was often focused on developing regional provision, not least because in it earliest years it was directly responsible for providing touring companies, such as the one it managed in the Midlands. On however limited a platform at that time, there were genuine attempts to create and support high quality arts and make them available regionally, to fulfil both potentially conflicting aims of the Charter. Nonetheless, Turnbull suggests a direct conflict between the founding principles of ACGB embodied by Keynes and the Labour initiatives linked with Lee and a conflict between both and popular audiences:

> The 1965 Labour Party's *A Policy for the Arts* set the main agendas as participation, access and community provision, on which increased subvention, particularly from non-statutory bodies such as local authorities, was subsequently based. [...] If Keynes' civilizing mission and Lee's socializing mission have on occasion proved incompatible, they have also been constantly at odds with the demands of the popular audience.[8]

Potential conflict between "civilising" and "socialising" and popularity is a matter for another debate. But as is clear from the discussion so far, whatever potential contradictions Turnbull describes – the occasional incompatibility of Keynes and Lee – they sought, both from their philosophical roots and in their practice, to harmonise the conflict between excellence and access. This is particularly so with Lee who never rejected the earlier work of the ACGB, even as she extended the emphasis on access in Labour policy during her term of office, which lasted till the end of the Harold Wilson's first period as Prime Minister in 1970. And from her input, based on ultimately Arnoldian principles, arose the injection of substantial additional funds into the Arts Council's work over much of the next decade and a half, until 1979 saw the election of Margaret Thatcher's government. Although in the 1970s some years saw less than inflationary increases as the oil crises of the period took effect, there were also years like 1973-74. Then the grant-in-aid (£14,090,619 in 1972-73) was increased by over £3 million to £17,138,000, an increase of 21.6% against a going inflation rate of 14.3%.[9]

Given such long-term thinking and the development of a cross-party, generally consensual, ethos of arts provision, it is not surprising that the arrival of Thatcherite attitudes in public life came as – to excuse a pun – a culture shock. It was also a financial shock. From 1979 and through the 1980s and beyond, these attitudes imbued the predominant publicly-avowed vision of the role of government funding. This vision's basis, seen by many as benighted, was monetarist. Genista McIntosh quotes Adrian Ellis as defining monetarism as "where the Darwinian operation of the market simultaneously encourages efficiency and punishes inefficiency".[10] The primary governance slogan emerged as "Economy, Efficiency and

Effectiveness" and the assumption seemed to be that government spending had had none of these qualities. In her first few months as Prime Minister, Margaret Thatcher announced cuts in public funding of one per cent. The cultural and financial shock of Thatcherism's inception underlay the thinking behind the development of 1984 *The Glory of the Garden* report.

The "Christmas Cuts" of 1980 were an important influence in this development. Forty-one arts companies, including eighteen theatre companies, were told their grants would be withdrawn with effect from April 1981. This was not in itself the act of a Thatcherite organisation, and in the end several survived, finding other funding sources, a number being taken under the wings of Regional Arts Associations. In fact, the Arts Council's operation, as this chapter will discuss later, is in no sense monolithic in a way that could adequately be described by a simple all-encompassing term like "Thatcherite". Indeed, its Chairman at the time of the cuts was Kenneth Robinson, a senior Labour politician. But, like any public body, the Arts Council was faced with finding ways of coping with reduced funding. After decades of development and, generally, grant increase, robust and reasonably developed systems for dealing with cut back did not really exist. Meantime, lists of funded companies had grown in a rather serendipitous way; some were on relatively small grants, as little in some cases as a few hundreds of pounds a year; the development process that grew out of Lee's bounty was generally aimed at nurturing and very little at weeding. Arguably too, some of the companies cut–for example, Crewe Rep, which this author regularly then attended–were of poor artistic quality. Yet systematic ways of coping with such funding withdrawals did not exist: the reason for the cutting of Crewe Rep was, for example, given as low levels of local funding, when in truth an argument based on quality would have been much more widely seen as defensible.

The timing, of course, was hardly helpful in terms of public perceptions. Undoubtedly the Council members and officers responsible genuinely cared for the artforms they worked with, but notifications, – effectively of immediate funding withdrawal – were distributed on the eve of Christmas, sometimes by courier, to organisations in various artforms, without explanation of what general principles might underlie individual cases. In fact, the schedule of decision making processes, including the sequencing of government budget decisions and Arts Council Panel and Council meetings meant that the choice was either to make an announcement as quickly as possible or delay until the new year.[11] In other words, the pressure of the funding cycle brought the conclusion of the decision-making process hard up against Christmas. The act of sending out the notifications on Christmas Eve was actually, though deeply ironically, intended as a kindly act to give as much notice as possible to companies. Many saw this as a shambles, both in the sense of ungainly awkwardness and, in the literal sense, "slaughter-house" or "place of carnage or wholesale slaughter".[12] The conception of public service and service of the arts embodied in ACGB members and officers' consensual values and self-perceptions had contained Plato's "noble lie": they often personally had "a distaste for power or privilege, [but] they will rule because they believe it right, not because they desire it." Now, ACGB's good-hearted consensual Platonic guardians had become butchers.

Clearly, what happened resulted from flaws in the system of assessment and decision-making. While a system did exist of advisers, supplementing the work of officers and advisory panel members, reporting on the performance quality of ACGB-funded companies, there was no clear feedback system to companies or artists. An informal process existed within departments, but in light of the prevailing expansionist mood of ACGB, more or less since its foundation, its emphasis was on mentoring and development. Andrew Welch, during the late 1980s General Manager of Plymouth Theatre Royal, in the 1970s managed smaller ACGB-funded repertory theatres. He considered it was always then possible to telephone the ACGB Drama Department and receive both sympathetic hearing and avuncular advice, but that that ethos had gone by the late 1980s.[13] The reasons it might have gone are almost certainly linked to a changed funding regime and the kind of policy changes this chapter discusses, but the existence of a 1970s mentoring ethos such as Welch identifies was certainly widely perceived. In fact, Drama officers and panel members continued in the 1980s and 1990s to support and mentor theatre, but the Christmas Cuts had changed perceptions and the frame in which ACGB officers worked. Of course, before the cuts, hard decisions had emerged from time to time and companies had felt aggrieved, but it was possible then for ACGB to seem to act, and to be seen as acting, as a guardian of theatre. This perception at that time had reinforced the "noble lie" of ACGB dispassion and supportiveness.

Such perceptions carried for some officers and Council members the "guardian role's" danger: they would believe "that they are better than those they serve". This could lead in certain, though far from all, cases to logrolling of agendas within the Arts Council itself, particularly at director level. Examples of this way of thinking are to be found in *Giving it away*,[14] the memoirs of Charles Osborne, Literature Director of the Arts Council from 1971 until 1986. These reveal a director for whom internal Arts Council politics and related loyalties were of key importance and who felt a paternalistic, even patronising, relationship to the artists his department funded. In fact, such patronising attitudes led to Osborne and his then Chairman Melvyn Bragg being perceived as not standing up for the needs of literature during the *Glory* process so that the literature budget was severely cut. The cut was not substantially replaced, despite an above average rise of 31% in 1988-89, until the late 1989 budget process. Then their successors, Alastair Niven and P. D. James, successfully made a case for a 28.5% increase for 1990-91 that all other artform Chairs and Directors recognised and to which they allowed free passage.[15] Such intermittent internal Council and officer attitudes, embodying their "noble lie", were widely perceived by arts networks, often through feedback from departmental officers and advisory panels' members. One persistent rumour, just pre-*Glory,* for example, was that, at one ACGB artform panel budget-setting meeting, when the artform director presented a proposed budget, a senior Finance officer had it withdrawn, tabling what was called a later version, which was approved. The allegation, widely believed then, was that the ways that budget differed from the artform director's included larger increases for specific organisations in which the Finance officer had a regionally-focused mentoring (though, it must be emphasised, not a personal financial) interest. It is no part of the purpose here to comment on such allegations, nor to impugn the integrity of former senior officers, but it is undoubtedly the case that such stories then circulated freely in the arts community and, wrongly or rightly, were believed. Belief in idiosyncratic logrolling and the absence of clearly-understood procedures for funding increase or withdrawal contributed to the shock and dismay the Christmas Cuts caused. William Rees-Mogg, on becoming Chair in 1982, arrived with a sense that systems must be tightened. This is not to suggest he arrived as a Thatcherite simply intending to cut arts funding. His record suggests a more complex man, an intellectual, no simple ideologue, but rather someone believing in rational, systematic thought. Rees-Mogg formed the defensible view that what was needed before any further major funding decisions were made was a review of ACGB's portfolio against clear criteria, including the balance of provision between London and the regions. Hence a Council retreat to Ilkley and, thence, in 1984 *The Glory of the Garden.*[16]

This recognised an imbalance between London and regional provision, unduly unfavourable to the regions. It recognised Regional Arts Associations as potential major partners, rather than relatively minor regional funders. (These acted across all of England, except Buckinghamshire, as, in effect, regional arts councils working with smaller companies and local communities.) It argued that a number of companies with a fundamentally regional remit might be better funded and sustained through RAAs. It sought to challenge local authorities to increase their arts funding. None of this was in itself dishonourable. But there was an absence of adequate preliminary analysis even as the report also sought to "rationalise" arts provision. It proposed, for example, cutting such "redundant" companies as the Tricycle Theatre, Kilburn, the Horseshoe Theatre, Basingstoke and the Gateway Theatre, Chester. In the event, none of these companies was cut–and it is not easy, given the track record of such companies then, to see why they would have been considered for cutting. In fact, of ten building-based companies proposed in the report for withdrawal of support, only five actually had funding withdrawn and, of five touring companies, two, M6 and Temba, retained funding.

As some proposals for cuts were problematic and, in the end, thwarted, so were some candidates for what was then called "devolution" to RAAs. The definition of a company with regional remit rather than a national role and scope, while intended in principle as a rational criterion, could be problematic. At both ends of the scale, definitions might be straightforward, but in the middle they were genuinely unclear. While no one argued for the retention of the Duke's Playhouse, Lancaster, by ACGB or the devolution of Manchester Royal Exchange, Bolton Octagon was initially proposed for devolution and then, after some coming and going, retained in the ACGB portfolio. The distinctions between its role and that of, say Chester Gateway, which was devolved, might well be seen as fine. Considerations of "regional remit" versus "national role" could even mean that devolution worked in reverse: responsibility for the Nuffield Theatre, Southampton, set up with Southern Arts support, was, in effect, unilaterally annexed by ACGB because of its scale and role. Problems of definition of regional/national roles might lead to departmental infighting. The Palace Theatre, Watford, was a prime devolution candidate given its role in the Eastern Arts area – or so its then Artistic Director, Michael Attenborough thought –and it was included in the *Glory* devolution list alongside its regional compeers: the Mercury, Colchester, and Palace, Southend. Yet, it was not devolved. Ruth Mackenzie, its departmental officer, informed the author on his appointment to ACGB in 1986 that lobbying within the department retained Watford in ACGB's portfolio when logic would have devolved it.

Rumours of such decision-making processes, partly in the shaping, but also in limiting the implementation, of *Glory* abounded. In short, *Glory* was seen as a well-meaning attempt to make sense of difficult decisions and rationalise provision, but ultimately inconsistent, subject to interested interference and , so, unpopular. This was in spite of the fact that part of the *Glory* agenda, largely positively achieved, was to bring in additional new money for the arts. This it did usually by using new funds made available to the Arts Council as a result of *Glory* to challenge additional new money from local authorities. Despite this financial incentive, the *Glory* report became a ghost of what it might have been as a result of the agenda making and politicking that went into its creation and then its thwarting. There was substantial resistance to it by the Drama Panel, half of whose members finally resigned in early 1985, in protest at the handling and implementation of *The Glory of the Garden* (among them, Mike Alfreds, Brian Cox, Pamela Howard, Nick Kent, Guy Slater and Olwen Wymark). In the autumn of 1985, a meeting of theatre directors at the Riverside Studios declared no confidence in the Drama Director, Dickon Reed: he was obliged to go.

The noble lie was exposed, in so far as it had been concealed. Close observers had been aware of the hidden processes behind Arts Council decision-making before. Now, however, this was widely thought to involve logrolling and, sometimes, small group interests and clique-driven agendas. Rees-Mogg desired greater rationalisation and better accountability, not only in an economic or even Thatcherite sense–and not only of arts organisations, but of ACGB systems themselves. And even if his *Glory* ambitions were somewhat thwarted, one development under his chairmanship intended to meet that aspiration was the Arts Council company appraisal scheme successfully introduced in 1987. In all artforms, teams of independent assessors and officers visited companies to review financial need, artistic performance and management practice. They then made recommendations for a company's future, seeking to establish appropriate funding levels in agreement, as appropriate, with RAAs and local authorities. The local authority input, of course, was always a key factor in the support of regional theatre. Some discussion since the 1980s of art policy and provision has seemed to suggest that right-wing councils were less likely to support the arts and left-wing more. In fact, the truth is that in almost every case across England local funding of the arts was a matter of the local culture. Changes of party in power tended not to lead to significant differences in local government support for the arts: Bristol, whether led by Tory or Labour, for example, was always inclined to stint, while Birmingham whether ruled by Labour or Tory tended to be supportive. Local culture of support was far more important in dealing with local councils than the party in power. A converse problem, though, could arise with companies perceived as having a national role like the Royal Court in regard to new play writing developments. Local authorities might consider that such companies, of which there were in fact few, including the National Theatre and the RSC, should not reasonably seek local funding to fulfil a national role.

Anthony Everitt, Deputy Secretary-General since 1985, developed the appraisal system to answer Rees-Mogg's, possibly Thatcherite, concern that the arts might be poorly managed. The system also arose, however, from Rees-Mogg's and Everitt's desire to find a more reasoned and transparent way of assessing companies rather than leave the absence of system that led to the Christmas Cuts. They sought to achieve more objective advice on appropriate funding levels – or whether funding should be available to specific companies at all. In fact, appraisals showed, repeatedly, how efficiently and well companies were managed, often achieving remarkable creative results under difficult funding constraints. They also provided a means of adjusting funding levels in a publicly accountable way agreed by co-funders, most spectacularly in theatre perhaps in the cases of the Royal Court in 1989 and the RSC in 1990. Appraisals enabled the Royal Court to regain its funding level before *Glory* had reduced it and the RSC to resolve its chronic late-1980s funding crises. No theatre company report ever found less money needed, though one in 1993 found that money previously awarded was not being used for its intended purposes and recommended a return to earlier funding levels. Many reports offered best practice advice to artists, managers and boards. This is hardly surprising given the calibre of team members who included, to take some random names, Genista McIntosh, Richard Eyre, Yvonne Brewster, Clare Venables, Jatinder Verma, Ruth Mackenzie, Bill Wilkinson, Frank Dunlop, Giles Havergal, Stephen Barry, Joan Knight and Michael Attenborough. As the present author has noted:

> By this means, it was possible to reward good artistic work and sound management and, indeed, to demonstrate–as objectively as could be achieved–that, far from the arts being a drain on the country, they were well-run and generally achieving very good results–and doing so in Thatcherite terms. What began as a quasi-Thatcherite strategy, became the opposite, proving that the arts, and theatre in particular, were generally well managed, productive and deserving of more support.[17]

This perhaps unanticipated result – the use of the appraisal system to undermine any Thatcherite agenda for theatre that might conceivably be intended at the highest Arts Council levels – highlights a key element in this chapter's analysis: that it is inaccurate and inappropriate to identify a single Arts Council agenda, especially in the period 1984-94. From the start of ACGB's history, there have always been debates, conflicts and even hi-jackings on the road to decisions. Such debate did not disappear, even if the decision processes were beginning to be based on attempts at more objective assessment of quality and need: elsewhere I have described, for example, the ACGB Drama Department and Panel's subversion in the period 1986-94, counteracting and undermining any anti-theatre Thatcherite agenda.[18]

In 1986, following a post-Reed interregnum under Jean Bullwinkle as Acting Drama Director, I was appointed ACGB Drama Director, having spent nearly a year as Secretary to Sir Kenneth Cork's Inquiry into Professional Theatre in England and its report *Theatre IS for All*.[19] This included many recommendations, some implemented, some not, and a request for additional funding of roughly £12 million, of which only £1.5 million, focused on touring, was forthcoming. The Cork Report's implications and claim for additional funding can, however, be seen to underlie the later success of the 2000 Boyden Report in bringing English theatre an additional £25 million. Key among those implications was the Cork vision of an interactive and interdependent theatre ecology in England. Until the mid-1980s, there had been a tendency, rooted in oppositional thinking of the early 1970s and perhaps earlier, to see competing categories in theatre. The national companies were everyone's enemy, seen as leaching money from regional theatre. Radical touring companies opposed building-based companies they saw as mostly bastions of bourgeois tradition, despite their intermittent infiltration by artists like Peter Cheeseman from 1962 (when the Victoria Theatre in Stoke opened), Richard Eyre at Nottingham Playhouse (1973-78) or Philip Hedley at the Theatre Royal Stratford East (from 1979). When, researching for Cork, I took evidence from Jatinder Verma, Artistic Director of Tara Arts, he informed me as part of that evidence "The National Theatre is not my national theatre". Meanwhile, it was possible to hear an older generation of artistic directors describe outreach and work with young people as "social work, not theatre". What *Theatre IS for All*, swiftly endorsed by the theatre community, demonstrated was that these divisions were not simply counterproductive. They actually denied the ways in which English theatre had evolved and was interdependently operating. Striking evidence of the changes Cork facilitated is that, within five years of the report, Verma's Tara Arts was performing on the stage of the National Theatre he had so recently disowned.

The genesis of the RAA movement, meantime, was resistance to perceived centralisation and metropolitanisation of the arts. By 1980, the RAAs to which *Glory* proposed substantial devolution, including six of the seven reprieved drama companies referred to earlier, had developed from the first, South West Arts. That was formed when the Arts Council, which for most of its first decade had worked through regional offices as well as its London headquarters, decided to close the last of its regional offices, that in the South West, in 1956. From its conception, then, the arts association movement suspected and resented ACGB whose action in closing its regional arms was perceived as cavalier, insensitive to local needs and local democracy. As the movement developed from the mid-1950s, it reached across England to form twelve associations covering everywhere except, as already noted, Buckinghamshire. Following the foundation of North West Arts in 1961 with significant local authority input, local authorities often dominated their executive committees. This happened, even though by the late 1970s the Arts Council provided well over 70% of the funding of all RAAs – and sometimes much more – while local authorities provided, alongside some private donations, the balance. RAAs often focused on local and regional arts activity, had budgets very much smaller than anything managed by ACGB and were supposed to be consulted on matters affecting their regions by Arts Council artform and policy departments, but often were not. When the present author was a member of the North West Arts Association (NWAA) Drama Panel at the time of the Christmas Cuts, it was made quite clear to NWAA panel members by senior NWAA officers, like Director Raph Gonley, that those officers felt cuts had been made precipitately without adequate consultation. This was particularly galling to the RAA directors because attempts had been made in the late 1970s to create a better, more communicative, more positive, relationship between ACGB and the RAAs. In 1977 an internal working party had produced a working document, *Towards Decentralisation*, while in 1980 a working party of ACGB and RAA representatives produced a report, *Towards a New Relationship*. Supposed to mark a new consultative and co-operative way forward, this emerged, ironically, earlier in the year of the Christmas Cuts.

The RAAs had come as a body, partly because of their genesis and developmental history and partly because of what they saw as ACGB's arrogant and clique-driven metropolitan highhandedness, to distrust it. Many RAA directors, officers and committee members felt themselves outside what they saw as an undemocratic London-focused ACGB system. They had their own noble lie. This was that they were the repository of local cultural democracy, enshrined in their movement since the centralising Arts Council had closed its regional offices, so cutting the "people" off from "their" arts, or at least from being able directly to bring their influence to bear on their development. For the RAAs, virtue and democratic accountability resided in this worldview. This was seen to be particularly so since the RAAs had substantial local authority elected member representation (even if this was appointed to RAAs by closed-door caucus), while the Arts Council was seen as appointed behind closed doors by ministers in London. Indeed, the secrecy surrounding appointment of Council and advisory panel members was hardly being exaggerated by RAAs. That secrecy was ingrained in ACGB thinking at least until the 1995 Nolan recommendations, which led to public advertisement of places on the boards and committees of quangos like the Arts Council and the introduction of more publicly accessible appointment systems.

Earlier attempts at opening up appointments had been limited and relatively short-lived. In 1986, for example, the present author and his Drama Panel Chairman, Brian Rix, introduced an appointment system for Drama Panel members involving some public accountability. Nationally representative bodies like Equity, the Theatrical Management Association and the Standing Advisory Committee on Local Authorities and the Theatre were each invited to nominate a number of potential panel members. These would then be considered together in order to produce a panel balanced by gender, age and regional origin. There was some resistance at senior levels to this idea, it being argued that panel members should be individually appointed on grounds of expertise and not representing organisations. Certainly, this position was understandable, but it had left, in effect, the appointment of influential ACGB panel members to senior Council officers' whim. In fact, the national theatre organisations nominated, as expected, potential members of indisputable expertise to serve in an individual capacity. The Drama system meant that, while there was still some pre-selection, it was undertaken by representative national bodies, while the sole role for senior Arts Council officers was, using these lists of nominations, to provide a balanced panel. This system worked very well for eight years, but after Rix resigned in 1993 and an interim period under an Acting Chair Paul Allen, the new Chair Thelma Holt, a radical in her youth, reverted in 1994 to a system of appointing by cronyism. She soon, for example, changed a more or less equal balance of men and women on the panel to a substantial male domination. In brief, there was a strong case that the RAAs' perception of centralising, fundamentally unrepresentative and artistically conservative systems dominating ACGB was not unfounded. It was against this background of relationships and attitudes that the *Glory* proposal to develop the importance of the RAAs and delegate many companies to them emerged.

The decision to enhance the RAAs' role in ACGB's work, in particular its policy development contained in the 1984 *Glory of the Garden*, then, had behind it such initiatives as the 1977 *Towards Decentralisation* and the 1980 *Towards a New Relationship*, however compromised by the 1980 Christmas Cuts. Its implementation proceeded with some energy. It was led by Luke Rittner, Secretary-General from 1983, and even more by Everitt, his Deputy after 1985, previously Director of East Midlands Arts and from 1990 Rittner's successor. ACGB organisational changes were instituted intending to facilitate reaching out to RAAs, where a previously existing Regional Department had perhaps not been seen, however unfairly, as effective enough. These included the 1986 appointment of Jane Taylor as director with specific responsibility for regional liaison. A series of roundtable meetings between ACGB and RAA directors was launched, one of the earlier ones being held at Leeds Castle in September 1986 (these democratising meetings tended to be held in rather grand venues) to discuss matters of common interest. Rittner was especially concerned that Arts Council directors should be seen to act in a positive manner, seeking to accommodate RAA ambitions. On their side, the RAA directors, supported by Christopher Gordon, Secretary to the Council of RAAs, having been earlier bruised by their perception of ACGB's centralist arrogance, were determined to consolidate their newly-enhanced role. In brief, the RAAs tended to see themselves as engaged in a long campaign to wrest policy and funding control from the metropolitan centre, and to define this campaign as being for cultural democracy. From time to time, this made for fraught meetings, but Rittner had a very clear line to which, by and large, ACGB directors held. This was that it was beholden on ACGB to work co-operatively with RAAs and, however provoked, ACGB personnel were not to react.

Part of the developing RAA "noble lie" represented ACGB as highhanded (and it had certainly been so intermittently), while RAAs were in contact with arts and community grassroots. It is, however, debatable how far this was so and whether RAAs were actually, rather than being in touch with their communities, beholden to local authority members and local arts cliques. In short, the entire ACGB and RAA system, taken as a whole, could be seen to be beholden to different versions of noble lies and responding to influence-peddling by interest groups, whether local, regional or national. Certainly, RAAs in general took lines they perceived as anti-elitist. This led to moments when ACGB directors had to bite their tongues. At a Liverpool roundtable meeting in 1987, for example, Peter Booth, then Director of Merseyside Arts, declared that he was not "answerable" to artists. Perhaps Booth intended to convey a conception that artists should work with, and be at the service of, their communities whose priorities should come first, but what emerged was a philistine, bureaucratic, even Stalinist, statement. There is more than one way to define and develop cultural democracy, but, within some RAAs, the definitions employed could actually slight the role of artists and creative organisations.

Differences in emphasis between ACGB artform departments with their national concern for overall artforms and regional directors with their concern for the arts in their region could, and did, lead to conflict. Examples may be found in different parts of England and illustrate the pressures that RAA directors often appeared under. One relates to parity negotiations with Liverpool local authorities. These negotiations were a process that took place across theatre in England, following *Glory* and the 1986 Cork Report, seeking to achieve broadly equal and equitable contributions from ACGB and local authorities towards a jointly-agreed level of support for those regional theatres that both ACGB and local authorities were responsible for funding.[20] These negotiations were based not only on parity of local and national funding but the matching of the total of both by the income of companies (though reduced box office matches were always anticipated for new writing or young people's companies). The proposal that in general companies might find 50% of their income through box-office, ancillary income – such as catering and bars – and fundraising can be seen in the light that as far back as 1970 such theatre companies were earning 75% of their income through box office income.[21] The parity negotiations for theatre were part of my responsibility as Drama Director and I found myself driven in those negotiations by my experience as Secretary to the Cork Inquiry. During that research it had become clear that many regional theatres needed additional funding. Further it was clear that, if local authorities could be persuaded to pay a fairer share of appropriate funding, not only would regional theatres overall be in a better position, but central funds might then be released to support another area of theatre in crisis: touring and innovative project companies. These concerns may have contributed to my own "noble lie", but I was determined that no ACGB-funded building-based theatre would close under my watch except as necessary for short-term purposes of regrouping, and none did. I was also determined to find means for supporting better the innovative small-scale companies that provided a seedbed for future talent. The parity process was successful in both finding additional funds for regional theatre and allowing some central funds to be used to reverse an alarming drop in the number of touring and experimental companies to which Cork had drawn attention.

These negotiations were often challenging. In the late 1980s, for example, ACGB was funding the Playhouse and the Everyman Theatres in Liverpool at the level of nine pounds for every local authority pound.

Outside Merseyside, this was widely recognised as an unsustainable imbalance and unfair in relation to the funding of other theatres jointly supported by ACGB and local authorities. Peter Booth took the view that to reduce the level of ACGB funding in Merseyside was unacceptable, even when the reasons were explained. In part, his argument was that Liverpool was rate-capped and a poor community by many measures, arguing therefore that parity negotiation was unfair. In fact, of course, the arts element for any local authority at the time was so relatively small that it did not even appear as a percentage in budgets, but rather was contained within "other" or "miscellaneous" categories. The sums requested for parity, while large for the theatres involved and indeed the ACGB Drama budget, were, even in hard times, minuscule within local authority budgets. Of course local authorities at both officer and member level often see a key part of their role as maximising central funding input to their area, whether directly from government or from non-governmental bodies. A converse of this is that they will almost always seek to provide as little from their own funds as they think appropriate within the terms of their historic patterns of support – or, to put it crudely, what they believe they can get away with – to attract that central funding. A crucial moment in this process of clarifying ACGB's position had arisen in the budget setting for 1987-88. Bristol local authorities, as noted already, had historically stinted the Bristol Old Vic and been quite intransigent in negotiations over a period of years. Given the need to manage tight funds, the impulse of *Glory* and Cork and, to be honest, the need to show ACGB was now entirely serious in negotiating the funding of theatres jointly supported with local authorities, it reduced its allocation to Bristol Old Vic by £70,000 to £423,500. This decision – strongly backed by Rix, Drama Panel Chair, who also proposed and saw through a one-year grant standstill of the national companies to release funds for such innovative companies as Tara Arts – created a stir not only in Bristol, but also throughout the country. ACGB was seen actually to follow through in such hard circumstances and other local authorities paid close attention.

The plea from poverty was often made in parity negotiations by local authorities at this time. Yet, in fact such a negotiating position did not prevent cash-strapped authorities in, say, Sheffield, meeting their share of theatre funding. In Liverpool in 1987-88, local authorities, despite cries of poverty, found £100,000 to reduce the inequitable ratio of ACGB to local funding from 9:1 to 5:1 at a stroke. For the next year, 1988-89, there was a further tussle during which at one point the city claimed to be about to offer additional funding that ACGB on scrutiny begged leave to doubt represented quite the new money claimed. ACGB then announced a proposed reduction of 5% phased in halves over two years in its funding of the Liverpool theatres. At this point the local authority talked of being "stabbed in the back". In truth part of the problem at this point was that ACGB had historically taken apparently firm stances about local authority funding and then backed down, so that many local authorities had got used to taking it not entirely seriously in such nerve-wracking negotiations. Meantime, theatres were left frustrated by lack of rigour or progress. ACGB's "treachery" now was that, when it said that in certain circumstances it would do something, it then, if those circumstances arose, went ahead and did it. Before, in some negotiations a deaf ear could usefully be turned to ACGB requests for additional local theatre funding. Now when it said something it was seen to mean it. Any hard decisions that ACGB might wish to make were announced in advance and any "wounds" it might inflict were to the front.

In fact, after its bluster was ignored and bluff called, Liverpool did provide an additional sum in 1988-89 of £200,000 towards its theatre's needs on condition ACGB suspended its proposed 5% reduction and in that year ACGB funding was reduced by less than 2%.[22] By this time the Playhouse was in financial difficulties not fundamentally because of public funding issues, but because after some years of its box office income meeting budgeted targets, it collapsed. The irony was that, as the public funding package came together, the theatre's contribution to the income mix collapsed for reasons of, it appeared, artistic choice. This led to the Playhouse for a time (in the end five years) entering an arrangement with Bill Kenwright Limited after detailed negotiations led by Iain Reid, Director of Arts Co-ordination, and myself and carried through by Paul Barnard, Assistant Drama Director. This sustained the theatre through an arrangement the funding partners sought to honour. In the end, however, whatever the funding package agreed, no funder could remedy extended programming failure that caused box office problems.

Peter Booth, like some other RAA directors, tended to adopt the local authority position and at the time was closely liaising professionally with Keith Hackett, a Merseyside arts consultant but also a Liverpool councillor, Chair of the City's Finance and Strategy Committee from 1987 to 1990. Booth appeared to foster a rumour that ACGB really wanted to close down one of the Liverpool theatres, a position ACGB never adopted, preferring always to fund both theatres to produce, but seeking an equitable relationship with local authorities. More than once he visited Rittner attempting to subvert negotiations between ACGB and local authorities, which were in themselves, while difficult, courteous. Both Rittner and the Council under Rees-Mogg's chairmanship staunchly supported the parity (of contributions) position derived from *Glory* and Cork and Booth's efforts failed. He was, however, seen by local artists as grandstanding. John Stalker, the Playhouse's General Manager, freely reported that, when Booth had telephoned before one London trip to reassure him he was about to take the train to save "your funding", he, tired of attitudinising and obfuscation, had told Booth, "Fuck off". Overplayed anti-centralist agendas could cost RAAs credibility.

Such behaviour, was not, of course, replicated by every RAA or the position would have been intolerable. An example of the positive way in which the parity negotiations and related links with RAAs and local authorities could, and mostly did, work was to be found in the period 1986-87 at the New Victoria Theatre, Newcastle-under-Lyme. The present building had opened after a prolonged period of closure of the old one, while the energies of the production team were naturally taken up in preparing for and moving into the new theatre. When it finally opened, there was an unanticipated, but precipitous, decline in audiences. In short, audiences had drifted away in the interim period and did not seem inclined to return, while the theatre to be filled was now more than twice the size of the old one. Very quickly as this audience crisis became clear, the Chief Executive of Newcastle-under-Lyme, Alan Owen, asked to meet with Everitt, Deputy Secretary-General of ACGB, a meeting I joined. Owen was clearly profoundly committed to the success of the new theatre and the history of its company under Peter Cheeseman. Equally it was clear to him and to us that the present situation was not tenable, nor was the level of local authority (a combination chiefly of Newcastle-under-Lyme, Stoke-on-Trent and Staffordshire Councils) and ACGB funding combined adequate. With the support of Dorothy Wilson, Deputy Director of West Midlands Arts, it was possible to negotiate a restructuring and improvement of the funding of the New Vic. This was related to a consolidation of activity in the new theatre that prevented it from closing, as it might have, within a year of its opening.

This case illustrates an important point. This chapter certainly has to explore the different ways in which tensions and conflicting agendas could be unhelpful. It must, however, also reflect the fact that the far more common condition – in parity negotiations at least – was of a positive, if not always over-friendly, relationship between funding partners and theatre companies with generally helpful results. Naturally the constructive results tended to pass unnoticed, while negotiations that led to conflict drew attention. As has been noted already, it was in the interests of enlightened local authorities to enter such agreements for their theatre because in that way they could bind in for the immediate future what they saw as central government funds to the benefit of their communities. Indeed, Plymouth City Council tried desperately, with some assistance from Peter Boyden as consultant, to persuade ACGB that it should match not only the City's input into the producing role of Plymouth Theatre Royal, but also its input into its touring role. This was despite the fact this was a quite different funding matter, as was reflected by the fact touring in the large scale was not a responsibility of the Drama Department, but the cross-artform Touring Department. Nonetheless, Plymouth was far from alone in seeing the benefit parity agreements could have not just for theatres, but for local authorities and their service to their communities.

Another factor to be considered is that such negotiations did not follow any standard procedure with regard to representation at meetings, and this could be a matter of frustration for individuals. The Staffordshire local authorities as a group, for example, refused point blank to have funding negotiations at which Peter Cheeseman was present. This was because in their view he had been unhelpful – even, in their eyes, unduly truculent – in earlier dealings with them. It is not possible for me, who always found him to have a brusquely affable persona, to comment on the accuracy of their perception; I can only report it. But it is true that they always insisted that ACGB deal with them in the presence of the RAA representative and the absence of Peter, having been briefed by him and his endlessly patient Chair Jim Heron, and then report back results. Elsewhere, theatres were invited in to negotiations after a certain point in preliminary discussions between ACGB and local authorities with RAA representatives present. This was the apparent custom and practice at York. Still other areas, as in Plymouth, negotiated with theatre company representatives present from the start.

Often, the position was confused by the fact that several theatres had senior councillors as Chairs. The redoubtable Councillor Bernard Atha was always highly influential in positive negotiations in Leeds. This could also mean, however, that local political history might have an unpredictable role in negotiations. The Chair of Sheffield Crucible, later Sheffield Theatres, was John Cornwall, not only a councillor who had been senior in the now defunct metropolitan county of South Yorkshire, but a member of the Arts Council itself. For a variety of reasons, he did not take part in direct negotiations, but clearly had a role within council deliberations and even tried, when the going was tough in Sheffield, to use his influence on the Arts Council where he chaired the Touring Committee. When he did this, Cornwall would argue against the Drama Department position, endorsed at policy and implementation levels by the full Arts Council, and wear his local authority hat. He appeared to believe that the kind of horse-trading that might take place between committee chairs in a local authority might work in the Arts Council. Rix and Rees-Mogg, however, were scrupulous in maintaining the integrity of the negotiations.

Generalised discussion in scholarly publication until now has tended to refer to the development and implementation of "parity" as if there was one process across England. It has generally, therefore, failed to take account of such local conditions and conventions. Certainly in some cases, as Clare Venables, Artistic Director in the late 1980s of Sheffield Crucible observed to the present author, theatre managements and artistic directors could feel like pigs in the middle. This sense of disengagement could be reinforced by the governance position that it is Chairs and Boards that funding bodies fund and those have final overall responsibility for funding negotiations. Elsewhere, however, as in Plymouth, both board members and theatre directors were fully involved in negotiations. And in Birmingham the negotiations took place across all artforms between the city's Chief Executive and the ACGB Deputy Secretary-General. While each case contributes to an overall pattern of funding behaviour, each also was individual in its process and so, often, in its results.

Parity negotiation sometimes, like funding negotiations between ACGB and local authorities in all artforms, could create a degree of real confusion between RAAs and ACGB. Background research for the Cork Report, as already noted, had revealed a number of English producing theatres in a serious position, likely to close in a year or two without funding revisions. York Theatre Royal was one, and its position was complicated by the fact that ACGB funding was too high in relation to the higher target local authorities ought in equity to provide. Negotiations towards an agreement to adjust, over a period, ACGB funding, which paradoxically *Glory* has raised, down somewhat and local authority funding up to mutually agreed levels were successful largely through the good offices of Paul Chesmore, the relevant York City Council director. Roger Lancaster of Yorkshire Arts, in whose region similar negotiations were under way in Sheffield, argued that these negotiations were damaging the arts locally. Yet, both the Sheffield and York negotiations actually kept the theatres open, while mutually co-operative parity negotiations allowed West Yorkshire Playhouse to open in 1990. It is no doubt true that, on occasion, ACGB negotiations might upset local arrangements. Lancaster had to intervene at one point when, in order to meet their responsibilities to York Theatre Royal, North Yorkshire Council threatened to reduce funding to Opera North. Negotiations were certainly difficult and, in this case, the RAA's role was to ensure that neither theatre nor opera suffered. Here, ACGB was first to acknowledge Yorkshire Arts' positive role. Still, reaching such agreements often caused RAAs angst, not least because they were often in thrall to local authorities in one way or another, and perhaps because sometimes they shrank from hard negotiation. Chris Bates, Director of South West Arts from 1990, and his predecessor, Martin Rewcastle, for example, both refused point-blank to engage in parity negotiations with local authorities supporting Cheltenham Everyman Theatre, ostensibly reluctant to risk upsetting those local authorities. The result was the Everyman soon closed as a producing theatre and now presents only touring product. Clearly, relationships between the RAAs and ACGB in the years after the *Glory* report were critical. They could even become, at least for a time, negative. One case of this occurred in the early 1990s in the relationships that, until then, had been positive between ACGB Drama Department and Northern Arts. Additional ACGB funding of nearly 20% had been given in 1988-89 to TyneWear Theatre Company, Newcastle-upon-Tyne. Problems, not of the company's making, at the Gulbenkian Theatre, home of the longstanding TyneWear and owned by Newcastle University, had led to its having to leave. It changed its name to Northern Stage Company and the additional funding was intended to support the implementation of a deal negotiated to take up residence in the Tyne Theatre, then owned by an amateur company, which had renovated that building. Issues of programming and management arose, however, between the professional and amateur companies. Attempts to broker an arrangement whereby both might amalgamate collapsed when the amateur company for its own good reasons would not cede control to a new trust. Meanwhile ACGB and Northern Arts could not see how they could directly fund an amateur producing company with funds dedicated to the support of Northern Stage. The attempt to settle Northern Stage in a new home at the Tyne Theatre was seen to have failed by late 1990 and the ACGB Drama Panel duly agreed to withdraw the additional funding it had allocated. As a result of these changes, the level of ACGB support of 1987/88, £379,500, had become by 1989/90 £450,000 and returned (with a further reduction because of other considerations) in 1991/92 to £360,500. Despite the clear connection between the Tyne Theatre move and the additional funding, Peter Stark, director of Northern Arts, argued that the funding should be left with Northern Stage even though the justification for it had gone. His Drama Officer, the late Sheila Harborth reported his view as "Ian Brown isn't getting any money from *my* kitty". Such a personalised view was, if true, fortunately, extreme – and ineffective in this case: Rix, Iain Reid, the new ACGB Chair Peter Palumbo and Secretary-General Everitt stood firmly behind the Drama Department and Panel. Yet, clearly the danger was of over-personalisation and even fractiousness, something some observers thought some RAAs sometimes sought to foment. More, like East Midland Arts under its director John Buston, West Midland Arts under Mick Elliott or North West Arts under various directors, worked with ACGB in funding negotiations, achieving remarkably positive results and managing effective developments at the theatres and other arts organisations in the region. Positively or negatively, what was at stake in the early 1990s was the next stage of the *Glory* devolutionary agenda.

A 1989 report by Richard Wilding on the future of the English arts funding system had, *inter alia*, proposed a radical reduction in the number of RAAs from twelve to, at most, seven. While this was met with resistance by regional interests, the thrust of the report was that there should consequently be greater transfer of funding and assessment responsibility to the regions, with the centre retaining responsibility for national overview and policy co-ordination. Devolution, where theatre companies were entirely in the hands of RAAs, was seen to have disadvantaged companies like Cheltenham, or the Half Moon Theatre, London, which had capital funding problems and was closed entirely in 1990. Delegation, rather than devolution, was now sought, whereby responsibility for arts organisations transferred to RAAs, which would become Regional Arts Boards (reduced in the event to ten), but central co-ordination would remain with ACGB. Part of the RAB agenda in the years until this was implemented in 1994 was to maximise control of companies within their region. This sense of seeking control, when at least one director had declared himself not answerable to artists and another apparently personalised his budgetary powers, alarmed many observers. Everitt, however, worked with ACGB directors and positive RAB directors to calm the developing situation and, by the time delegation came, more inflammatory RAB directors had moved on to other things. The problem of region/centre relationships still, however, had a capacity to be fraught. (It is noteworthy that in 2001, outside this chapter's period, ACGB felt it had to reassume control of the RABs and turn them into a reduced number – more or less in line with Wilding's 1989 recommendation – of regional offices roughly of the kind abolished in 1956). The disquieting element here is that, for years, the attention of the arts funding system was significantly distracted by internal politics and many artists expressed their distress at what they saw as feuding. It is hard to demonstrate with certainty, outside of such cases as the revenue problems of the Cheltenham Everyman or the capital problems of the Half Moon, how individual theatres suffered. Nonetheless, it may well be that, for example, had better relationships been possible in Liverpool in the late 1980s, difficulties both ACGB-funded theatres there faced in the 1990s might have been minimised, if not avoided.

This is not to suggest that theatre was safe only in ACGB hands: many RAAs were supportive of their theatres and at least once in the period ACGB committed a great *faux pas* regarding theatre's welfare. In 1993, facing a government funding reduction, the Council decided to review its portfolio. Every artform panel produced a wish-list for additional funding of up to 25% and its priorities if a budget reduction of up to 25% were enforced. The Drama Panel was uneasy in the face of this request, suspecting a disguised attempt to cut companies, but was persuaded that realpolitik required it to answer the questions asked. In the event, a Council retreat at Woodstock in May, when artform directors were excluded from the decisive session, cut Drama by around £800,000 more than pro-rata with other artforms. A sub-committee led this business, chaired by Christopher Frayling, then Chair of the Visual Arts Panel, and including Mary Allen, then Deputy Secretary-General, and Beverley Anderson. It appeared that Drama, with one of the larger budgets, was to be a target for plunder for the benefit mainly of Visual Arts and Dance, perhaps even, ironically, because it was seen to have negotiated so successfully with local authorities. Meantime, at least one RAB chairman, a Council member, was suspected of misleadingly leaking details of the worst theatre scenario, never likely to eventuate, but creating unrest in his region.

The more detailed story of this is told elsewhere.[23] The gist is that the Chairman, Palumbo, and senior management, having refused to accept the Drama Director's advice on the storm such a move would rouse, quailed before the reality of the rage they inspired, including the resignation of Rix. Within a few weeks, the Drama Director working with Finance officers found an unexpected budgetary source to reinstate Drama's reduction. Palumbo and Everitt agreed its allocation in early July to Drama conditional on this decision's being kept quiet until the Council's November funding meeting. This condition was intended to maintain the theatre campaign, partly in hope of applying pressure to the government for more money and partly to mask a concurrent, and thankfully doomed, attempt to close down one of London's orchestras. It may also have been that Palumbo and Everitt, having seen the chaotic results created by the Frayling sub-committee's raid, did not want other Council members like Frayling to be aware of the windfall, which was recurrent year on year, since that might invite further antagonistic lobbying. In any case, for five more months, theatre suffered unrest and was to some extent destabilised by this financial powerplay. Even the Drama Panel's Acting Chair, Paul Allen, and the other Drama department officers had to be kept uninformed of the financial re-instatement. Conflict outside ACGB reflected unhappy tension inside. ACGB, as has been observed, was not simply monolithic. In fact, when the resolution that allowed the reinstatement of Drama's disproportionate cut was announced at Council in November, Frayling was reported as querying it. This was despite the fact it, of course, did not reverse the Woodstock decision regarding funds re-allocated from Drama to Visual Arts and Dance. He, whose concern for Visual Arts was hardly ignoble, was over-ruled.

This analysis of events before and after *The Glory of the Garden* shows how very often, both within ACGB and RAA/RABs and in their relations with others, two, or even more, sets of "noble lies" very often came into sincere conflict. In these circumstances, personal agendas and fractious relationships could develop that were not beneficial to the arts. This is not to suggest ACGB, *pace* Woodstock, or RABs were not capable of positive internal debate. In 1989, for example, the ACGB Drama Department argued for an additional £70,000 for West Yorkshire Playhouse to lever more local authority money. This was in response to the leader of Leeds City Council, George Mudie, who, inspired by Councillor Bernard Atha, Chair of the Playhouse, had challenged ACGB to find such a sum and so allow the theatre to open properly in 1990 with its smaller theatre fully operative. Community arts focused departments wanted that sum for other projects. After much internal discussion, the preliminary Council budget paper allocated the money away from West Yorkshire, but Rix's late appeal to Rees-Mogg won the day for the theatre. Such legitimate conflicts of priority will always exist in any funding system.

Whatever the errors of Woodstock, ACGB and many RAA/RABs were healthier for committed debate among senior management, departmental officers and expert committee and Council members. And while, before Nolan, those participating in this were often appointed to ACGB and RAA/RABs in mysterious ways, it was out of their debate, and sometimes conflict, any consensual support for the arts emerged. If *Glory* opened up debate by including the regions much more and if that at times created the conflicts of vision and even fractiousness discussed in this chapter, it also sought a more inclusive English arts funding system, with a greater potential for responding to artists more appropriately. Perhaps the "guardians" were always likely to clash. Certainly, where the clashes were amicable–for example in the Midlands, Leeds and Manchester–theatre could benefit through newly open consultations between ACGB and its partners.

Notes

[1] Olivia Turnbull puts this very clearly, although it is to be disputed how "rare" agreement actually was: "[...] the fact that the theatres' main funding bodies have rarely been in agreement, and that their agendas have further been subject to the fluctuation of politics, the economy and internal dissension, has resulted in a situation whereby producing houses have had to expand consistently and adjust their programmes over the years, but have rarely been allowed to scale back their activities, even in times of extreme financial hardship" *Bringing Down the House: The Crisis in Britain's Regional Theatres* (Bristol: Intellect, 2008), 12. In the author's experience, agreement about agendas was far more common than disagreement, allowing such developments in the period under review as the cross-artform consensus between Birmingham and ACGB, the development and opening of the West Yorkshire Playhouse or the flourishing of Nottingham Playhouse under Ruth Mackenzie, even when there was difficulty in finding adequate funding. During my period as Drama Director (1986-94), we sought to be sympathetic to theatres' need from time to time to scale down their activities in the face of financial restrictions and to persuade local authority colleagues to be similarly supportive. Such action at various times helped resolve transient crises at several theatres including those in Newcastle-under-Lyme, York and Newcastle-upon-Tyne.

[2] http://en.wikipedia.org/wiki/Quis_custodiet_ipsos_custodes (accessed July 7, 2007).

[3] Quoted in Margaret Drabble, ed., *The Oxford Companion to English Literature* (Oxford: Oxford University Press, 1986), 110.

[4] ACGB grew out of the Pilgrim Trust's foundation of the wartime Committee for the Encouragement of Music and the Arts (CEMA) in December 1939. Its immediate objectives were to help the arts adjust themselves to wartime conditions and to encourage active interest in the arts. Among its first members were Sir Kenneth Clark, then Director of the National Gallery, and William Emrys Williams, Director of the British Institute of Adult Education and originator of its "Art for the People" travelling exhibitions, a later Secretary-General of ACGB (1951-63). In 1940, the "Committee" became a "Council" and, in 1942 John Maynard Keynes succeeded its original Chairman, Lord Macmillan, Chairman of the Pilgrim Trust. In 1945, CEMA became the Arts Council of Great Britain, still under Keynes's chairmanship.

[5] Some form of these words has run through the Royal Charters of all versions of the UK Arts Councils since 1945. See, for example, their appearance in the current Royal Charter of the Arts Council of Wales at http://www.artswales.org.uk/publications/Royal_Charter.pdf (accessed July 17, 2007).

[6] Further discussion of the impact of such values can be found in Robert Hewison, *Culture and Consensus: England, Art and Politics since 1940* (London: Methuen, rev. ed. 1997).

[7] Turnbull.

[8] Ibid. 11.

[9] This inflation rate is cited in Turnbull 61, although at this point of her argument she suggests that the increase "was not enough to keep up with a hefty inflation rate", when clearly it more than exceeds it – by over 50%.

[10] Genista McIntosh, Annual Marjorie Frances Lecture, Goldsmith's College, University of London, 14 November 2001, cited by Vera Gottlieb, "1979 and after," in *The Cambridge History of British Theatre, Vol. 3: Since 1895*, ed. Baz Kershaw (Cambridge: Cambridge University Press, 2004), 419.

[11] Telephone conversation with John Faulkner, Drama Director ACGB at the time, 16 July 2009.

[12] Definitions taken from *The Shorter Oxford English Dictionary* (Oxford: Oxford University Press, 1983), 1964.

[13] Private conversation with the author, June 1989.

[14] Charles Osborne, *Giving it away: the memoirs of an uncivil servant* (London: Secker & Warburg, 1986).

[15] After Niven was appointed in 1987, he had made an initial case with Acting Chair Robert Woof for 1988/89: Literature funding for the later 1980s went: 1987/88 £489,008; 1988/89 £640,993; 1989/90 £625,644; 1990/91 £804,034.

[16] This paragraph and the next two repeat material from the present author's "The road through Woodstock: counter-Thatcherite strategies in ACGB's drama development between 1984 and 1994," *Contemporary Theatre Review*, Volume 17(2), 2007, 218-229.

[17] Ibid. 224.

[18] Ibid. 218-229.

[19] Sir Kenneth Cork et al., *Theatre IS for All: The Report of the Inquiry into Professional Theatre in England under the Chairmanship of Sir Kenneth Cork* (London: Arts Council of Great Britain, 1986).

[20] The impact of these negotiations is discussed, *inter alia*, in two linked articles: Ian Brown and Rob Brannen "When Theatre was for All: the Cork Report, after Ten Years", *New Theatre Quarterly*, Vol. XII no. 48 (1996), 367-83, and Ian Brown, Rob Brannen and Douglas Brown "The English Arts Council Franchise System and political theatre", *New Theatre Quarterly*, Vol. XVI No 64 (2000), 379-87.

[21] Turnbull, 63.

[22] Turnbull, 175-6.

[23] Ian Brown, 2007, 218-229.

Chapter Three

The Gang of Forty:
A Response to *The Glory of the Garden*

Glen Walford

Below is the response written by the Liverpool Everyman to *The Glory of the Garden* in 1984. Weeks and weeks and weeks of application and work went in to it even though we never quite knew what *Glory of the Garden* was about. We knew it was supposed to be about the future, the glorious future, and we also knew that a lot of theatres were going to be cut and that it was a bid for survival. I had heard strong rumours that either the Everyman or the Playhouse were going to go to the wall and therefore I did consider it a massive fight, and, of course, when you get going on it, you go for the vision. So I went for the massive vision, assuming there was limitless cash and thought about where the Everyman could really go in a big, big way. The musical director Paddy Cunneen, the associate director Han Duijvendak and the administrator Nick Stanley were all involved with it and we spent a tremendous amount of time on it. The thrust of it was that we were going to create a gang of forty. This was around the time when the gang of four were running The Playhouse and I thought, let's go better than that, because they soon collapsed and if it was going to work it had to be bigger and better. And we got more and more wild and wonderful. We started with visions, with streams of consciousness – let's do this, let's do the other. We had a great time and played wild music while putting all this stuff together. Then, you go through the extraordinary and consuming task of crystallising and editing it all down and having to cost it. In the end we came up with what amounted to a 40-page document of visions for the future.

Having looked at it again recently, there's not a thing I would do differently now. That might be incredibly depressing. It might mean that I haven't moved forward at all in my thinking or imagination. Or that I am stuck in a rut of the 1980s which was a prime time – not though necessarily a prime time for total enjoyment because it was as pursued by demons, the utter soul destroying, crunching, vile side of running a theatre (alongside the joys and humanities of it all). But the things that come through in this paper are the things I always wanted to do in theatre, are the reasons that I was in theatre in the first place. And I suppose that is the three Ms – mystery, magic and mayhem, and the Everyman was, of course, the classic place to indulge all three. Without those, all you get is the politics and the incredible daily grind. It was one of the reasons I was employed at the Everyman in the first place and I wasn't at all sure that I wanted to come because I knew very well what Liverpool was like. You love it and then you hate it. You get these surges of immense joy and then you hate it and you hate the fact that the theatre is old and you've got no money. So, we came up with our big vision.

What happened to our response was absolutely nothing. It went into a pile of the rejected and forgotten and never discussed. So it is an unhealed wound. But it is also a reminder about not letting these things go – and a reminder, coming back to it, that the things you do matter.

A Response to *The Glory of the Garden*

The Arts Council wants to encourage and respond to local initiative in helping create new institutions or strengthening old ones.[1]

The Everyman Theatre responds to the stimulating spirit of *The Glory of the Garden* by providing a vision capable of transforming the performing arts, both regional and national.

1: Introduction

Merseyside needs its arts. Its already strong and committed audience (2.3 million a year) need high quality product they can call their own as well as being allowed to sniff occasionally at what large and prestigious companies occasionally deign to bring. A thriving Merseyside arts industry will serve to provide perspective and entertainment for a depressed area. By expanding its present base, it will provide a better and more comprehensive service. Pitching its standards to a level of national importance will broaden parochial chauvinism into an identity worthy of this great port. It will also appeal to audiences that have so far been left out in the cold. And it will be a force for economic rehabilitation of the area, boosting trade, attracting attention and visitors from all over Britain and abroad.

To realise this vision we request public subsidy to establish a "Gang of Forty" which is an ensemble company containing diverse and unusual talents plus the necessary technical and administrative support staff. The establishment of this company will inspire the creation of a unique arts-based industry welding together the talent already present in Hope Street.

2: Current Situation

2.1: The Arts on Merseyside

The sources of Merseyside wealth have been and still are being gutted – the great port, the shipbuilding industries and more...but there is a flame which flickers, flares and illuminates – creativity. The theatres have discovered and nurtured actors, writers, and musicians of the most exceptional quality. But this pioneering success has provided scant returns for Merseyside. Lack of investment in the area means the brightest flames blaze their way southwards or abroad where the money, resources and opportunities exist. Our proposals for a highly trained ensemble of artists will provide a base from which the arts can flourish.

In spite of the continuing desolation on Merseyside, the assumption from outside the area continues that obstacles strengthen the will and if only Merseyside people would 'get on their bikes' their problems would be solved. Far too many Liverpudlians now have to steal a bike before they are able to get on it. But the Everyman has 'got on its bike' and continued to remount it for twenty years. It was founded with energy, talent and vision and has continued to provide for its audiences in an unparalleled way. It is hardly possible to generalise about an audience's needs. Each of the existing organisations in Merseyside plays its own part in arts provision. Two things, however, do apply in general: firstly, the more run-down your city and environment is, the more you demand from your theatre. Audiences need to be able to fully trust that a night at the theatre will be a worthwhile experience and that they will not be reminded of the neglect of investment by seeing shows inhabited by few actors and with imaginative but poorly equipped sets. Secondly, the young on Merseyside have lost all economic function. This makes high quality entertainment product and drama-related activities essential for them, as it can help to restore a belief in the worth of the individual. An arts strategy for Merseyside will have to take both these notions as its starting point.

The funding situation is complicated. Merseyside County Council has a policy of integrated and co-operative arts provision. The Metropolitan District Councils since 1974 have tended to concentrate on priorities which only marginally include arts provision. The local authorities' statements on their financial positions are well known. Commercial sponsorship is not a new idea. The Walker Arts Gallery was founded by a brewer and even the relatively tiny Everyman obtained considerable private sums to re-build its auditorium. But the erosion of the wealth base has had predictable results.

2.2: The Everyman Theatre

The Everyman Theatre has always played a pioneering role within the arts in Merseyside. The theatre opened in the early sixties when young visionaries poured blood and sweat into the project in the belief that such commitment would be rewarded with imaginative investment. But in spite of its contributions to the performing arts on a national level, the reward has been the expectation that the wondrous achievements of the 'holy poverty' sixties would continue into the pragmatic eighties and presumably onwards to the end of the century.

Throughout the years the welcoming atmosphere, the thrill of the space, the sheer vibrancy of design and performers have led to a strong loyalty from Merseyside audiences. But in the 1980s small and impoverished shows, no matter how imaginative they may be, are not seductive to the potentially enormous audience of the region. During the seventies and continuing into the eighties, there is no doubt the most popular fare for Merseyside is that which celebrates itself. The city loves its own inimitable street language and style and genuine Liverpool actors uttering 'wet nelly' or 'blind scouse' in a show is enough to be rewarded with grunts of approval or roars of laughter. A gross, broad, funny show which accurately captures the local rhythms can be expected to do well, even if the message it contains is minimal or nothing other than self-celebratory and its vision limited to the common-place.

The success of Willy Russell and Alan Bleasdale in using the Liverpool rhythms but elevating them to poetic levels and imbuing them with the best politics i.e. those which deal with people on the deepest level are the greatest accolade to 'local theatre'. The bulk and warmth of local audience response to such truly grassroots fare provides the natural temptation for an impoverished theatre to boost its box office and its local popularity by continuing the well-loved traditions.

While recognising the craving need here for the Liverpudlian spirit to bastion itself against outside neglect, the Everyman has begun to take the first steps towards creating a more universal, aspiring, challenging kind of theatre, offering a bold mixture of many different art forms to challenge and stretch the imaginations of the audience. The response has been encouraging and integrally linked with a policy of low prices which start at £1, has produced an increase in earned income in 83/4 of 67%. But the experiment can proceed no further without more outside investment to support the existing self-help.

For the last six months, the Everyman has managed to persuade nationally known designers and lighting designers to present their work at the theatre for absurdly low fees. The result has been stunning environmental theatre productions, designed and lit with total flair. To complement this, a small company of nine actors possessing an extraordinary mixture of talents stayed together and developed and presented their talent.

This seemingly lavish fare has opened a whole new vista of interest for the audience which must be developed and enriched. The tab for these theatrical feasts has been picked up by the staff, company and guest "specialists", interested and stimulated by our aims, to the extent that they have 'subsidised' the theatre by contributing far beyond the call of duty. Such altruistic exhaustion can only exist for a short time without financial back-up and our brave new world has temporarily halted. But the excitement and energy released have generated our vision for the future.

Parallel with the theatrical explosions in the main house has been an almost unhandleable deluge of young people eager to belong to, express themselves in and perform in the Youth Theatre. Although severely financially stretched, the Everyman has decided to retain responsibility towards the young people of Merseyside. The insecurity of these young people needs to be supported by a secure set of people on the Everyman Youth Theatre staff. Due to a Manpower Services Commission scheme which intrinsically leads to a high staff turnover, this security is lacking. With an 'open door' policy, rare in many Youth Theatres, our Youth Theatre is firmly committed to the principles of social and personal development through the medium of drama, going hand in hand with theatre of quality and excellence.

The doors of the Everyman remain open to all sorts and conditions of men and women; the evidence can be seen day and night from the foyer and bar, the bistro below, to the annexe next door bulging with arts and social activities of all kinds. It is time for such a wealth of need to be offered the treasures which hard cash wealth can provide.

3: The Way Forward

It is our conviction that the Everyman can only keep playing its stimulating role for its regional and national audiences in the decade to come if it shakes off its 'holy poverty' label. Only then can the talented people who are already here be persuaded to stay, develop, inspire and be inspired by the nourishing of a totally original ensemble company where all the different art forms are able to be tended to and to inter-react, based in a unique area where resources can back up and market the work.

The roots are here; Merseyside's unique creative talent, the Everyman with its wonderful performance space and Hope Street, with its amalgam of people and arts-related enterprises. If irrigated promptly and adequately, these roots can grow into a permanent cultural Garden Festival. If not, these roots will wither away forever, leaving an already deprived area even more desolate.

Our proposals consist of the following:
1. The constitution of a 40-strong resident company ('The Gang of Forty') plus the necessary support staff
2. A regionally integrated plan for Youth and Education
3. Training for all personnel including engaging of artistic experts leading to animation of the entire region
4. Wider availability of our resources to provide the performing arts in all forms to the community in the region
5. An outline for co-operation with other organisations in the region.

3.1: The 'Gang of Forty' and Support Staff

3.1; Objectives: From the very beginnings the Everyman has been famous for its honest, brave, spontaneous 'house style'. The opportunities for development given by long-term contracts not only built an audience's trust in whatever product was offered but made the actors themselves into nationally and internationally known 'names' (Barbara Dickson, Julie Walters, Jonathan Pryce, Anthony Sher). In the 1980s, although the house style is still the prime offering, the audience loyalty is less consistent, partly due to the fact that financial limitations mean that actors have to be put on short-term contracts. We are still finding and nurturing talent, but the financial lures of television or the prestige of the larger companies can snatch this talent before either the performer or the audience receives the benefit.

An ensemble company which can be a driving force in the performing arts, both regionally and nationally and can act as a home for the regions mature and young talent will have to realise the following premises:
1. In order to develop an artistic identity with a recognisable house-style capable of producing 'total theatre' to a high standard, the company needs to be large, stable and long-term.

2. The various art forms which combine to produce this style of theatre must be taken from the broadest range and then developed within the organisation.
3. Such broad-based theatrical style within a multi-racial society inevitably and profitably incorporates many cultural backgrounds.
4. Such a wide selection of talent must be made available to the community, both to widen the artist's perceptions and to increase the accessibility of the arts.

3.1.2: Composition

A core of the kind of actor for which the Everyman is noted; experienced in various forms of theatre and skilled in traditional theatre craft plus special skills (musical, physical, comedy…..). Fearless, flexible and spontaneous in dealing with a true cross-section audience.

- Plus: *Trainee actors*: Young Merseyside talent which would benefit from being part of a varied and multi-talented ensemble; actors straight from Drama school who will benefit from the confidence giving of a large ensemble. This will be specially beneficial to actors whose roots are in the north and older Merseyside talent – the notorious Scouse 'misfit' who finds some outlet in the pubs and clubs of the city but who needs to develop professional skills so as to use this charisma to effect.
- Plus: *Actors from different cultural backgrounds* and actors who because of physical or other disadvantages usually find it hard to obtain work. They will be incorporated not as a gesture to integrated casting but because of the riches they have to offer, and the benefits that can be offered to them.
- Plus: *Actors with wider interests in the profession*:

There is a forceful minority of actors with wider interests. This ensemble company can make full use of them by incorporating and extending their talents.

Actor/directors can be trained in the ensemble and then help to meet the continuing demand throughout the community for professional direction.

Actor/writers will be nurtured not only to contribute to the originality of certain productions, but also to be of great value in the evaluation of scripts which are continually sent to the Everyman and in many writer's workshops.

Actor/teachers would work closely with the Youth and Education Scheme, principally on the Theatre in Education plan outlined in 3.2.2.

where their talents are appropriate they would contribute to the main housework.

Actor/musicians, actor/dancers, actor/administrators and *actor/technicians* will all contribute to the ensemble and will be available on loan.

- Plus: a limited number of 'guest' actors need to be allowed for: some actors have talents to offer or fit extraordinarily well a specific part or a specific production might be unable to join the company for a long time. Being able to take some actors in for short periods will also inject the permanent company with new ideas and new personality. [2]

It is an essential component of the style which we pursue, that it relies on, will create and attract support staff. One of the strengths of the Everyman has always been that it is a complete artistic family. In expanding to fulfil the true potential of the scheme it is essential that every member of the staff retains their absorption in and over-all sense of responsibility for the artistic standards.

3.1.3: Programme of Work

The 'Gang of Forty' would undertake in a typical year:
1. *10 main stage projects*: Productions which will give true expression to the energy, vision and many talents within the company. Everyman-based productions, for instance *Tosca* or *The Elephant Man* would embrace wide-ranging splendours of grand opera and epic-style performance embellished by many additional talents developed by the company. The result would be an all-embracing and original theatrical experience which is accessible and inspiring to our genuine cross-section audience. The programming would draw on both classics and new work.
2. *20 small-scale projects*: A wide range of productions and events, some of which will take place in the Everyman, some in Hope Street and many further afield. The possibilities of, and demand for, such projects in Merseyside are endless but a breakdown would include Foyer platform-type performances, late night cabaret on the main stage, studio seasons at Unity Theatre and tours to outer districts or special interest groups. It must be possible to take the sort of risks which the nurturing of new writing and new performance arts demands. The projects would make the Everyman, Hope Street and Merseyside a thriving centre for the performing arts all day, every day. The basic features, as with the

main stage projects will be talent, innovation, quality and accessibility.
3. *Large scale external projects*: Occasional celebratory events (a traditional firework display can be enhanced considerably by incorporating a theme, involving performers to play out this theme, inter-relating with imaginatively conceived pyrotechnics) in co-operation with both the Youth and Education base and local agencies to tie in with special occasions on Merseyside.

3.2: Youth and Education

In acknowledgement of the enormous need for provision in this area, we propose a separate autonomous base set up in Hope Street but integrally linked with the Everyman. This Youth and Education base will provide the focus for several smaller organisations whose strength is often in their independence. It will concern itself with four main areas of activity.

3.2: Youth Theatre

With improved facilities and increased staff the Youth Theatre will be able to give its 300 members more individual attention in developing their skills, energy and enthusiasm for theatre arts. The Youth and Education base will need to incorporate a small performing venue for the demonstration of the immense potential talent among its members.

3.2.2: Theatre in Education

The Youth and Education base with the 'Gang of Forty' would work closely with Merseyside Young People's Theatre, Merseyside Arts and the Local Education Authorities to ensure the possible provision of performing arts in schools. The Everyman's contribution would principally be in secondment of actors, staff and skills.

3.2.3: Playdays and Workshops

From a Youth and Education base, the expertise can be provided to create a comprehensive programme of workshops and playdays based around the Everyman and Playhouse productions. Actors from the 'Gang of Forty' will prepare with Youth and Education workers a workshop session which prepares for or follows up a visit to the theatre by school parties etc.

3.2.4: Special Projects

Various types of special projects will be mounted from the Youth and Education base which make a contribution to different areas of the community and respond to special events and occasions. As examples: actors and drama workers would contribute to character development of children in special schools who, at the moment, hardly receive any cultural stimulation, and the resources of the entire organisation – both Professional and Youth - would combine in large scale celebratory events.

3.3: Training

We believe that being creative in the arts requires continual training. The enormous use of the London Actors' Centre by those able to travel to it indicates actors' desire and need to develop and explore their talents. The great desire to be a spear-carrier or, at best, Fortinbras, in one of the two National Companies must reflect a hunger to belong to a company providing expertise to develop talent.

The success of Merseyside Arts' artist-in-residence projects in many disciplines proves the demand from the community to acquire and develop artistic skills.

Training within and around the 'Gang of Forty' will happen in four separate but interdependent ways.

1. Outside experts of national and international repute (Dario Fo for farce, Arlene Phillips for dance, Yehudi Menuhin for music) would be brought in to work with the 'Gang of Forty' and other professional organisations. They would also be available to Merseyside Arts for various schemes.
2. The members of the 'Gang of Forty' and staff would train and be trained by other professional arts organisations in the region. The possibilities are legion but might include construction in the Playhouse workshops, music for MYPT actors, movement from Spiral, marketing from Unity Theatre, Box Office in the Empire.
3. The members of 'Gang of Forty' will train each other e.g. the musicians will learn acrobatics, the dancers to play the saxophone, the Southerners to speak proper Scouse. This is vital to develop an integrated house-style dependent on multi-talented performers.
4. The 'Gang of Forty' and staff will train others in the community. The range of skills on offer will be so broad that they will have an impact in all areas of Merseyside life. The main thrust of this work will be through the Youth and Education base, but might also

include open workshops for performance skills, technical workshops for local amateur groups or administration for the launching of a new Community arts project.

All training would be integrated as closely as possible with the Playhouse and we note the idea for a 'Northern Regional Training Centre'.

3.4: Wider Availability of Resources

There are two major ways in which the new Everyman will make its resources available to the wider Merseyside Community.

We will implement a 'borrowing' system which will make talent and expertise readily available for the Youth and Education base, the Playhouse, MYPT and Merseyside Arts. Under this scheme actors from the 'Gang of Forty' can be borrowed for periods of the year by any of these organisations to participate in specific projects, be it production or community arts. Outside experts, brought in to the Everyman to train the 'Gang of Forty' (see 3.3) can also be borrowed to take community classes, to run open workshops or to train actors from other companies in the region.

The programme of work includes a number of smaller scale productions which can be toured throughout the region. Some of these will be specifically aimed at providing the Unity Theatre with part of its 'Studio Season' programme; others will be designed to tour small venues in more arts-deprived parts of the region under Merseyside Arts' 'Night Out' scheme.

3.5: Areas of Co-Operation

The future must lie in an integrated service in all the arts. Merseyside has an unparalleled provision of museums, art galleries, orchestra and theatres, with the rare advantage of its own Regional Arts Association. In this service, it is the producing theatres who under-achieve due to under-funding, although every effort is made to co-operate to bring down costs and spread available funds more effectively.

The Everyman co-operates closely with all arts organisations in the region, through combined marketing schemes, sharing of equipment, provision of premises and the exchange of ideas and talent. The proposals outlined above will enable us to fill many of the perceived gaps and co-operate fully to produce the best possible service.

The Everyman's closest partners will always be Merseyside Arts and its clients and the Playhouse. The Playhouse has indicated its desire to work in complementary but totally different areas, its willingness to participate in the training scheme, its desire to use members of the 'Gang of Forty' and its enthusiasm for having a strong and stable partner.

Merseyside Arts has indicated its total support for the vision, most particularly for the resources which will be made available for its own ambitions to develop innate creativity on Merseyside. The Everyman's closest links with Merseyside Arts' clients are MYPT, Spiral Contemporary Dance and Unity Theatre. The Youth and Education Scheme, and most particularly Theatre in Education, would be a co-operative venture with MYPT, who are\at present based in the Everyman Annexe. Spiral Dance are also based in our Annexe and although the links between theatre and dance are under explored, the benefits for training and development of the house-style have already become apparent. Unity Theatre is 200 yards along Hope Street and plays a vital role as a receiving house for small-scale tours, both national and regional and including MYPT, Spiral and our Youth Theatre. The possibilities of an expansion of this role, combined with presenting 'Studio Seasons' from the 'Gang of Forty' and other small performance events produced within the new Everyman would be of great benefit for all concerned.

A strengthened Everyman can become the cornerstone of an entertainment and creative industry on a national scale, based in Hope Street and drawing artistic inspiration from its colourful array of people. It will be instrumental in welding together the various subsidised and commercial arts and entertainment ventures already based in and around Hope Street (e.g. the Everyman Theatre and Youth Theatre, Everyman Bistro, MYPT, Quintet North, Spiral Dance, Art College and Graphic School, Philharmonic Hall and Orchestra, Philharmonic Dining Rooms, Unity Theatre, Chaucer's Lunchtime Theatre, Chauffeurs Nightclub, The Unemployed Resource Centre, John Mills Graphics and Photography etc) and in augmenting these with:

Sound and video studio
Production company and agency
Publishing house
Music and cabaret venue
Studio/exhibition space for fine artists, designers, textile workers and crafts people

This will establish a unique co-operation between subsidised and commercial arts and entertainment producers, to the benefit of both. Time, facility and staff share schemes will attract – and keep – both private investment and creative talent of the highest order. The sound and video studios would enable the Everyman to use the talents within the 'Gang of Forty' to play a full and profitable part in the provision of product for the rapidly expanding markets of television (both cable and conventional) and commercial radio. Such product might be advertisements, video cassettes of set text work or the re-working of main stage plays. The Everyman auditorium has often been used as a venue for live broadcasts and would complement any such studio provision.

The availability of sound and video facilities will give performers and technicians scope and opportunities to develop their professional skills and give the theatre access to sound and video product of high quality for use in productions at economic rates. A production company will offer resident playwrights, directors and performers the means to exploit their product in a systematic way. Joint record releases both in the classical and popular repertoire become a possibility. The theatre's production departments can use and cater for costume, scenery, sound and lighting hire and sale outlets. Tours can be mounted and properly marketed. Young talent of every kind can be discovered, nurtured, trained and put in front of audiences on the scale required.

As potential exporter of actors, playwrights, poets, pop-stars, scriptwriters, top-class technicians, directors and arts entrepreneurs Merseyside has no equal. There is a growing demand for arts and entertainments product. Property and premises are relatively cheap. If one industry stands out more than any other as being ripe for development it is this.

At present, creative talent has to move South to find investment and expertise to develop and exploit its product. In many cases this goes accompanied with losing the mere essence of its creativity, its Merseyside identity, and as a consequence it doesn't always realise its full potential. Both artistically and economically this is wasteful – for Merseyside and for Britain.

The Everyman's geographical and social position means that an injection of public money could provide the cornerstone of the first mixed economy arts centre in England and the crucial link in the best integrated regional arts provision in the land.

4: Conclusion

We present a strategy that uses the talent of Merseyside to enrich the region both culturally and economically. Indeed it is based on the premise that the two are inextricably linked. The objective is to become a centre of high quality work, capable of attracting tourists, able to export from strength, ready to take its proper place in a truly integrated provision of the Arts in the Region. By opening avenues for co-operation between subsidised and commercial arts enterprises the new Everyman could become part of a permanent International Cultural festival.

The strategy depends on expanding the already considerable Merseyside audience, making the arts accessible to all. The Youth and Education base outlined will be a central factor in these efforts as will the wider availability to the region of the 'Gang of Forty'.

Our proposals have already inspired genuine enthusiasm and support locally for their vision and innovation. Imaginative investment now will allow the dream to become reality.

> The purpose of the programme is to enable the major, existing building-based repertory companies within those areas to achieve two broad objectives: to sustain the highest artistic standards of theatrical performance and to bear a much greater responsibility than they have in the recent past for enriching the theatrical experience of the wider community in the whole of their regions.[3]

Notes

[1] ACGB: *Glory of the Garden*; preface.
[2] The appendix includes a breakdown of the 'Gang of Forty' as follows: sixteen 'core' actors; six trainee actors six actors from different cultural background; six actors with wider interests; four guest actors.
[3] ACGB: *Glory of the Garden*: paragraph 50: 22.

CHAPTER FOUR

DEVOLVE AND/OR DIE: THE VEXED RELATIONSHIP BETWEEN THE CENTRE AND THE REGIONS, 1980-2006

ROS MERKIN

The story of regional theatre can never be wholly divided from the story of the Arts Council. This chapter seeks to explore that relationship and the history of the Arts Council's regional policies through an analysis of some key reports issued by the council which aimed to change, refine and develop the relationship between the centre and the regions. What follows then is a sense of 25 years of fumbled change which begins to show a complex web of relationships not only between the regions and the centre but also involving the government – both local and national.

The Glory of the Garden (1984)

As Jackson and Brown have already described, *The Glory of the Garden* is seen as the landmark report and for Olivia Turnbull it marked "the first significant step in the move towards an increasingly heavy emphasis on accountability in the Arts Council".[1] But its main emphasis was on devolution, more equitable funding between London and the regions and finding more local money. It aimed to be the largest single programme of devolution in the history of the Arts Council, the reassertion of its original idea. In his introduction to *Glory*, Rees-Mogg argues that Keynes' first aim, "to decentralise and disperse the dramatic and musical life of the country" had not been adequately realised and no theatre company "based entirely in the regions enjoys an Arts Council subsidy equal to one-tenth that given to the two national companies…Most receive less than a fiftieth."[2] To rectify this, *Glory* set out a development scheme focusing on thirteen strategic areas to ensure much of the country was covered, in which, for drama, the focus was on the existing building-based repertory companies.[3] These were to be encouraged to expand their work and to "bear a much greater responsibility...for enriching the theatrical experience of the wider community in the whole of their regions."[4] This might include, for example, extending seasons of studio work (with an emphasis on new writing), providing facilities for touring companies, touring some of their own work and providing a focus for the provision of TIE and Young People's Theatre. They were also to be encouraged to house and support small-scale independent companies.

To facilitate this, the Regional Arts Associations (RAAs) were to be given increased budgets and increased responsibility, including the devolution of clients to their direct control. At this juncture, the RAAs already directly funded some 150 organisations, giving out over 6000 grants annually. From 1985/6, their portfolio was to be expanded.[5] Of course, such developments would take funding and the Arts Council estimated that the complete programme in the 13 areas would cost a maximum of £6.5 million. One way of raising the money was issuing "challenges" to local communities to match its funding".[6] Another was the encouragement of greater support from business and industries. The third way was by making cuts or, as *Glory* preferred to call it, reductions. The building based companies to lose their subsidy (and named in *Glory*) included five in the London area (in Bromley, Croydon and Hornchurch, plus the King's Head and the Tricycle) plus the Horseshoe in Basingstoke, Chester Gateway, the Yvonne Arnaud Theatre in Guildford, the White Rose in Harrogate and the Connaught Theatre in Worthing.[7] The total saving was claimed to be £1,404,000 which included a withdrawal of £376,000 from building based companies in the regions.

Inevitably, *Glory* re-emphasised and exacerbated a bi-polar split in the funding landscape; London was set against the regions and for all its arguments about devolution and assertions that it did not believe that London people "always know best", *Glory* was also keen to ensure that London remained a place to visit and wonder at. "Of course" mused Rees-Mogg, "London will always be favoured" and he was concerned about the difficulties of dispersing "a metropolitan quality of art."[8] In actual fact, the fractures created were far more numerous as responses to its publication showed, although before looking at these it is worth pausing a moment to assess why the Council had felt the need to develop its strategy for a decade.

Why *Glory*?

Glory, despite Andrew Sinclair's claim that Richard Pulford, then deputy Secretary-General, had written most of it overnight, did not come out of thin air. As Ian Brown notes in this volume, it had its roots in events throughout the 1970s when the major task facing the Arts Council was to manage generally increasing funding creatively. Then, in 1979, Margaret Thatcher was elected and everything changed. A 1% cut was ordered (taking effect more or less straight away) across all government spending, with the exceptions of defence and education. The Arts Council's rather knee-jerk reaction to this (having no clear strategies in place for enforcing or deciding about cuts given the previous years of plenty) led to the Christmas of 1980, the council's own St Valentine's Day massacre, when 18 theatre companies were informed on Christmas Eve that their grants would be withdrawn with effect from April 1981.[9] The huge impact of the announcement (the insensitivity of the way it was announced notwithstanding) is well described by Sinclair; "[f]or thirty-five years, the Council had hardly dropped a client. The withdrawal of support from the Carl Rosa Company at the end of the nineteen-fifties, and later from Phoenix Opera, had stirred up a storm of protest."[10] Now, it fell to Richard Hoggart to announce the cuts and "police then had to guard the doors of 105 Piccadilly to keep out protestors carrying banners with slogans HANGMAN HOGGART and HANG HOGGART HIGH."[11] In the event, only three of the 41 companies did go to the wall but the Arts Council had been warned. It would have to learn to pass on cuts.

William Rees-Mogg arrived the following year as Chairman of the Arts Council with a mission to strengthen the systems and with the "defensible view that what was needed was a review of the companies being funded against clear criteria" and a clear balance of provision between London and the regions.[12] Hence a Council retreat to Ilkley, which, according to Sinclair, they treated as seriously as the Roundheads had treated Marston Moor "determined to fight back against the forces of the Queen's government". From there was issued what became known as the Ilkley letter. Sent to 250 leading clients, it asked what would happen if their subsidy were withdrawn or massively reduced (or, indeed, increased) and also used horticultural metaphors to highlight the key problem the Council had to address with some urgency:

> The arts, like seeds, need to grow if they are to blossom. Some of the seeds we have nurtured over the years are now bursting to grow but are held back by lack of space and nourishment. This strategy will help the Council to

thin out the seed-bed and to give more room for them to develop, and for new seeds to be planted.[13]

The council had to deal, not just with the threat of cuts and then real cuts from the Government but in the light of this, to find ways to manoeuvre. From its inception, the Arts Council had steadily been increasing its list of revenue clients, from 30 in 1950 to more than 80 by 1984. At the same time, the scope of the council's work had expanded so it found itself trying to fund an ever-increasing number of clients. This left them trying to spread resources more and more thinly and in a time when it was becoming increasingly clear that more money was not going to be forthcoming from the government, cutting clients and looking for other sources of funding were the only routes to enabling the development of new companies and new work. The acceptability of these strategies to the arts community was paramount. Hence the need for *Glory*.

Glory Before *Glory*

Glory was not, however, the first attempt to reassess the relationship between the Council and the RAAs. In 1980, the Council and the RAAs had produced *Towards a New Relationship* (swiftly followed in 1983 by *A New Relationship)*, a joint paper which outlined the "many and deep-seated" limitations of the relationship between the two and which outlined many of the concerns and problems which both informed *Glory* and which were to rumble on for the next thirty years. Key amongst these was the lack of any real structure in their relationship and the question of decentralisation of both money and responsibility. The latter had been on the agenda from the mid-1960s and whilst there had been some moves towards joint assessment of clients in the regions, movement had been very slow and there was some concern about how committed the ACGB really were to the notion of devolution, despite repeated reaffirmation.[14] Now, the working party set up to examine the problems suggested a tripartite system of funding – those clearly of national significance, those clearly of greatest significance at a regional level and those of strategic national significance. The latter (which included Bolton Octagon, Chester Gateway and Oldham Coliseum but not Crewe or the Duke's at Lancaster in the north-west) would be jointly assessed.[15]

RAAs were also very concerned, not for the first time, about their representation on the council itself which was seen as being "disproportionately low" and some attempts were made to distinguish between the differing roles that each body might take on. At this juncture one of the key suggestions was for RAAs to be "characterised as covering the 'public service' element of arts funding (closer perhaps, to the philosophy of social service or recreation provision)" and there was already concern about what the role of the ACGB might be if it gave away all (or too much) of its grant giving activities, especially in a time of little real growth:

> The Council doubts whether any national arts agency can maintain an authoritative advisory function unless it also has direct financial responsibility for a significant volume of activity on the ground, including an ability to stimulate and sustain experimental work and other new developments.[16]

Nor was it just the Arts Council and the RAAs who were concerned about the relationship between London and the regions. In 1982, in response to *The Public and Private Funding of the Arts,* a report by the House of Commons Select Committee on Education, Science and the Arts which had expressed concerns about "the considerable inequalities of provision across the country. Robert Hutchinson, who worked as a senior research and information officer at the Council, was asked to produce a working paper to provide a more accurate picture of the division of Arts Council spending between the regions of England. *A Hard Fact to Swallow* made depressing reading, finding that subsidy per head was ten times as large for Londoners as it was for those in East Anglia and three and a half times more than in Merseyside, the second most favoured region.[17] Whilst the national companies were receiving 38% of Arts Council expenditure, the National Theatre was producing eight times as many performances in London as outside and a rough North/South divide suggested 151p per head subsidy for the south and 73p per head subsidy for the Midlands and the North. "England", Hutchinson concluded "is two nations in reaping the benefits of arts subsidy."[18] What was already clear, before Ilkley and *Glory* was the need for "much stronger formal links" between the regions and the centre.[19]

Given the way the RAAs had emerged (as outlined in the Introduction), it was not surprising that some sorting out of relationships and responsibilities needed to take place, the real surprise is that it had taken anyone so long to get round to doing anything.

Organising the Regions

The RAAs were fiercely autonomous, independent and individual organisations, as *Towards a New Relationship* was at pains to point out, varying in their composition, functions and procedures as well as in the scale of the operations. They were doing what they perceived the Arts Council could not, as their pamphlet *England's Regional Arts Associations* (1983) made clear, seeking to distinguish "a role, an area of work and responsibility, and an approach to the arts which is uniquely regional in character."[20] Represented nationally firstly through the Standing Conference of Regional Arts Associations (SCoRAA) and later through the Council of Regional Arts Associations (CoRAA), by the early 1980s associations had a turnover in excess of £13 million and provided some 6000 subsidies.[21]

Financially, they received most support from the Arts Council but overall they were considered to be more closely affiliated to the local authorities in their region, with whom they worked more closely. Several of these had been instrumental in establishing the associations, with North East Arts in 1961 leading the way. In many ways, the Council were happy for them to develop those affiliations; they saw it as a way of expanding audiences (at one time suggesting that the role of the RAAs should be to promote the arts in their regions) and most importantly of trying to increase overall arts spending in the country. The latter desire though was somewhat disappointed by the 1974 reorganisation of local government when a firm brake was placed on spending and from 1976, the RAAs income from local authorities was never more than 30%.

The RAAs perceived themselves to be neither regional branches of the Arts Council nor solely local authority associations, but sat, somewhat uncomfortably, between the two. On the one hand, they were financially dependent for approaching 80% of their income on the Arts Council:

> that is to say, central agencies which are funded by government but whose policies and operation are not subject to direct political control; on the other hand, the Associations are constitutionally dependent on the goodwill and active support of a consensus among the elected local authorities in each region, whose work is obviously subject to political considerations.[22]

In reality, relationships were far more confused (and confusing) than suggested by this, as *Towards a New Relationship* was at pains to point out. The RAA system involved a number of distinct partnerships with the ACGB (and other central funding agencies) and with local authorities; from the viewpoint of the recipients of subsidy it was even more confusing as there are also partnerships between ACGB and RAAs, between ACGB and Local Authorities, between the RAAs and Local Authorities or indeed between all three bodies.[23]

All of this, without the RAA Councils and management committees which brought together local authorities, commercial and regional interests, or the RAAs' role in persuading local authorities to fund work independently of the RAA or the fact that the RAAs had a strange double relationship with local authorities, working sometimes as funding partners and sometimes having to go cap in hand to them for revenue funding. The potential for confusion and mistrust was enormous.

Despite the Council's having a Chief Regional Advisor for a short period (for the five years between 1973 and 1978), relationships between the Council and the RAAs was always, at best, a little suspicious, or as Rittner was to put it later "spiced with creative tension verging on rivalry."[24] On the side of the Arts Council, there was quite often a metropolitan sneer to the provinces. William Emrys Williams, Secretary General of the Council in 1962, was "quite clearly" concerned there was a risk of standards being lowered if RAAs were allowed to be involved in local programming. Ten years later, Lord Goodman, then Chair of the Council, was moved to state in a House of Lords debate that:

> when we hear the matter presented on the footing that they are probably able to speak for the regions my answer is, 'Yes, but in some things and some things only.' We are concerned with the Arts. This business about amateur theatricals, the crafts and the like is something about which one needs to be very sceptical indeed.[25]

Little wonder then that Lord Feversham, the first chairman of SCoRAA, told a conference in 1974 that during the five years he had been involved with regional arts, he had been constantly baffled by "the expression of mystification which comes into the eyes of Arts Council mandarins" at the mention of RAAs and that every visit to the London headquarters had left him feeling that "one is some kind of orange three-headed Martian with antennae sprouting from the forehead who has just landed by flying saucer in Green Park."[26] Such attitudes were also flamed on the pages of the newspapers summed up by Sebastian Faulk's later proclamation that there was a tacit recognition that "many of the regional arts boards could not administer a village fete, let alone the life of a major orchestra."[27] On the other hand, the RAAs regarded the Arts Council with growing suspicion and a growing sense of wanting to protect their own power base. As Wilding was to point out in 1989, RAAs were quick to resent all symptoms, both real and imagined, of metropolitan highhandness" and they often complained that the Arts Council treated them as just another client.[28] Overall, the problems were compounded by the lack of structure between the two sets of organisations, the haphazard nature of the RAAs development, inadequate communication and ill-defined roles. Little wonder that *Glory* sought to rectify this.

Ramifications of *Glory*

Given such a great sense of inequality, it might have been expected that *Glory* would have been welcomed with open arms but responses were, inevitably, mixed. In government, Labour saw it as mere "lip service"; the Liberals as "well-intentioned but farcical."[29] Michael Bogdanov was less reserved in his response, seeing it as "a muddled hotchpotch of ill-conceived, illogical, arithmetically untenable, ideologically unsound, reactionary, unreasoned rubbish."[30] It was cautiously welcomed by CoRAA:

> Of course we see the danger signs. The strategy does appear to propagate the overriding importance of a metropolitan culture. The virtual silence on areas of work already devolved (community arts, arts centres) suggests a lack of interest. The money available to the regional arts associations for development is very little when spread over twelve regions. The power retained will ensure that the centre is still all pervading. Why pick holes in a colander?[31]

In the RAAs and amongst the local councils responses were also mixed. Many did welcome the move in general terms but with reservations. The City of Manchester was moved to write an angry six page response stating that it could not "discern the logic" in why the Bolton Octagon and Duke's Playhouse had been earmarked for devolution rather than the Contact, Royal Exchange and Oldham Coliseum and offering detailed figures to suggest that out of the £5.5 million earmarked for *Glory* developments, £3.1 million was actually coming from the regions. These were concerns reflected by Raphael Gonley, chair of North West Arts (NWA), when he wrote to Rittner about the withdrawal of funding to both Chester Gateway and M6. In the end, Chester Gateway was reprieved (in part because the demise of Crewe Lyceum as a victim of the Christmas cuts in 1980 would have left Cheshire without a repertory theatre), albeit, with slightly reduced funding, but this did little to assuage concerns. In the ensuing months, letters flew backwards and forwards between NWA and the Council, outlining increasing concerns over staffing in the regions to deal with devolved clients and responsibility for theatre's debts and indeed quite which companies were to be devolved – Bolton Octagon, in the end kept on for the time being by the Council, found its name on, then off, then on the list.[32]

Amidst a surfeit of horticultural jokes, responses were also mixed in the press. Vivian Nixson argued that the appointment of new design consultants was not going to help the Arts Council

> reassure the arts establishment that the new strategy will harm not one hair of their precious metropolitan heads, whilst convincing the rest of us (regional arts associations, local authorities, community and ethnic minority arts groups, arts centres, and thousands of underpaid actors and dancers) that it represents 'a genuine and major act of administrative decentralisation,' which will financially benefit us (and thus the public in our regions).[33]

Battle lines between London and the regions were drawn up early on, mostly precipitated by the lack of money to implement any new developments. Although, the Council were able to announce in the July that £500,000 had been 'found' to reprieve 20% of the organisations from which it had withdrawn support (ERPTs 'saved' in this instance included the Gateway Theatre in Chester and the White Rose Theatre in Harrogate), yet things quickly soured.[34] By December 1984, the arts world was reacting angrily to the news that the annual grant increase amounted to only 3% - a rise to £103 million plus an additional £2 million to implement *Glory*.[35] William Rees-Mogg was warning that many of the Council's clients "would find their existence jeopardised" while Peter Hall hailed the news as "a tragic day for the subsidised British theatre", believing that if the 3% increase was given across the board (in reality 2% below inflation) then it would "kill off many theatres that are already pressed beyond endurance".[36] Rittner tried to keep the regions happy by stating that the emphasis would be on theatres outside London and as much momentum as possible would be kept to maintain the regional strategy – a statement which must have rung hollow to those regional theatres (Nottingham Playhouse and Sheffield Crucible included) who were to discover in early 1985 that they would receive the same grant in 1985-6 as they had received in the previous year and to the inhabitants of the West Midlands who were to receive development money equivalent to 2.5p per person.[37]

But trying to keep the regions happy in the face of a shrinking pot meant trouble continued brewing, especially in London and by March 1985, the Council were faced with "one of the most serious revolts in its 40-year history."[38] A press conference, attended by almost every subsidised theatre in London and headed by the National Theatre, paraded their complete lack of confidence in the Council. Speaker after speaker suggested that the Glory of the Garden could not be transformed into a paradise of flowering theatres in regional places without budgetary increases and a press statement announced that 10 London theatres had decided, subject to the approval of their boards, to pool and share out the differing increases given them by the Council for 1985-86.

More significantly for the Council, almost half of the drama advisory panel resigned in protest at their decision to continue with its regional development strategy despite lack of funds. They were concerned about the relationship of the Council to the government but were also angry over the withdrawal of separate funding for new writing, which theatres had been allocated since 1980 and which was now to be subsumed into the whole budget.[39] William Rees-Mogg was held responsible for seeding the Garden without sufficient money to carry through the plans but he responded robustly by perceiving the revolt to be "a great agitation to see that London does not lose a penny of its immense arts overfunding in relation to the rest of England. I regard that as an attempt to maintain an unjust state of affairs. The interests of London must not always be put first."[40]

He continued his attack a week later expressing anger over criticism of the Council's decision to make:

> a tiny shift, at most a 3 per cent shift' from metropolitan to regional arts. It was an inevitable shift from the rich to the poor, from rich audiences to poor audiences, from institutions funded in millions to institutions funded in tens of thousands. He sympathised with the National Theatre, 'housed in that great concrete dreadnought on the South Bank,' but he sympathised far more with the Everyman Theatre in Liverpool, 'on the edge of the worst area of social suffering and deprivation in England.' The National received £6.7 million from the Arts Council, the Everyman, even after money for developments would receive less than £250,000.[41]

The Arts Council *Annual Report* of 1985-86 reaffirmed its commitment to *Glory* and outlined increased funding for RAAs which it claimed in the majority of cases had doubled their money and trumpeted that the first year's implementation of the Glory strategy "demonstrated a genuine shift of resources away from London and towards the regions".[42] Yet the following year, triumph was a little more tempered with Rittner arguing that it needed to be seen as a strategy for a decade with a promise to review the strategy at a two day meeting and plan for the future.[43] And by 1987-88, the tone was still flatter; whilst much had been achieved there was still a long way to go and there was disappointment that the gap between London and the rest of country "is still as wide as ever".[44]

Trying, maybe, to encourage and rally support, the Arts Council published their own assessment of *Glory* in 1988, *Glory Reflected: A Progress Report on The Glory of the Garden* but from the outset they had to state that "*The Glory of the Garden,* as a detailed programme, is a thing of the past".[45] However, what was most important was the fact that "the underlying purposes of which these policies were the practical expression" (decentralising and dispersing the artistic life of the nation and encouraging 'challenge funding') had "lodged themselves permanently in the Council's mind". *Glory* had been "a statement of intent…that would be more just to the regions…"[46]

So, *Glory* was to be read as a statement of intent, a statement of principle, not a concrete, deliverable strategy. The commitment was backed up by an assessment of the achievements so far and the report is certainly strewn with figures claiming that things had changed. London's share of the overall allocation was deemed to have fallen from 48% of the Council's total grant-in-aid to 40.5% "representing a percentage shift, adjusted for inflation, of more than 10%" and money to the RAAs had increased in leaps and bounds. Figures suggest that the budget for Lincolnshire and Humberside had increased by 77%, that to Southern Arts by 65% and that to East Midlands Arts by 54%. At the same time nearly £2 million had been spent on regional theatres with the Leicester Haymarket and the Sheffield Crucible being the notable beneficiaries (two of the strategic areas with very new producing theatres at the time)[47] with promises that greater changes were about to happen in the eastern seaboard and the southwest. Overall, the Council was happy to report that it had built on partnerships with RAAs and local authorities to expand the base of arts funding and that out of their original list of 45 clients to be devolved, all but two (Tara Arts and Bolton Octagon) had been taken on by RAAs.[48] Even as late as 1989, the Council was still trying to argue that *Glory* was a success. Another glossy pamphlet, this time entitled *More Than Meets the Eye*, claimed that in real terms in 1987-88 10.5% less cash was given to London while 21% more was given to the arts outside London and announcing its intention to widen and deepen the policy.[49] But despite the late good news, the "resolve had evaporated" and *Glory* "withered away courtesy of civil-service cynicism and Council dithering" and certainly by the time the ACGB published *Glory Reflected* it had been supplanted by the Cork Report, *Theatre IS for All.*[50]

Did *Glory* Make a Difference?

Before burying it completely it is worth pausing a moment to assess if anything had been achieved. There is of course much cynicism in hindsight; Richard Witts argues that Rees-Mogg's "money tree failed to bear much fruit" seeing it as ambitious but "altogether Disneyland."[51] John Pick is even more scathing about the "mighty language hiding midget action" and concerned that it was always less about the details of proposals and more about being the harbinger "of a new politicisation of the Council". It was, he argues, "a propaganda leaflet" which dressed up the actions of the Council in a new tough language. He continued: "At the time the brutalism of this new Arts Council language was excused as "talking to the government in the only language it understands" but it soon became apparent that the men at the top of the restructured bureaucracy could think and express themselves in no other way." Rather than being a plan for devolution, *Glory* marked the beginning of a new era which was to be dominated by the business of assessment (there are fourteen criteria in *Glory*).[52]

In real terms, some things did change. Although the Nuffield Theatre in Southampton was retrieved from its RAA as a result of *Glory*, others, primarily those not in strategic areas or cities identified by *Glory* as the priority, were devolved. In the first wave of 1984-1985, fourteen building based companies found themselves moved including the Connaught Theatre in Worthing, Derby Playhouse, Farnham Repertory Theatre, Scarborough and the Duke's Playhouse in Lancaster. In the second wave, the following year, they were joined by a further 8 including the Cheltenham Everyman, Colchester Mercury and the Palace Theatre in Southend.[53] After that, things rather ground to a halt. Of the companies earmarked to lose funding, de Jongh suggests that 20% were saved by the Arts Council (although unsure they would retain funding at the same level as previously) and two others were 'safeguarded' (M6 and The Horseshoe Theatre Basingstoke) by RAAs and local councils.[54] In the end, though, it is worth asking if it made any fundamental difference to the number of clients of the Arts Council, did it leave any space to develop new clients and new work? When *Glory* was published the Arts Council had 156 revenue clients. The proposal was to reduce this to 94 and "most of that was done" but new clients were added and by 1989 there was once again regular support for 140 clients. Money going to the RAAs did increase; in 1984-85 £12million or 15% of the Arts Council's expenditure went to the regions and by 1987-1988 this had gone up to £28million or 28% although a little under half of the Arts Council's money was still being spent in

London. Although Richard Wilding, a civil servant, could later argue, "It is…not true to say that *The Glory of the Garden* policy was a failure; without it, the present imbalance would be substantially larger than it is", something had clearly not worked.[55]

One thing that had not worked was the abolition of Metropolitan County Councils, a county layer of local administration, following the Conservatives publication of *Streamlining the Cities* in 1983. As all of these were Labour-controlled, it was widely believed that abolition was a cynical move by the government to remove what it perceived to be a layer of opposition. There had indeed been a series of high profile clashes between the councils and government (notably with the Greater London Council) about spending and policy. *Glory* recognised that this was a concern (it had been a promise in the Conservatives election manifesto for 1983), noting public anxiety about the future of the Metropolitan Counties but seemingly dismissing the implications by stating: "the arts represent less than one hundredth of those Councils' expenditure; an observer might well have supposed recently that the arts were their only function."[56] Fears of the implications for the arts of abolition were very real as *The Arts in Crisis,* a publication by Tyne and Wear County Council, which railed against the "irrational and thoughtless" intentions, made plain:

> The biggest crisis for years is facing the arts. The Government with its threatened abolition of the GLC and the six Metropolitan County Councils, including Tyne and Wear, has – at a stroke – put the funding of theatres and numerous artistic organisations in jeopardy…fears that the North East could become a cultural desert are very real. Tyne and Wear County Council alone pumps around £3 million into the arts every year.[57]

It goes on to outline how the Theatre Royal had received £1.23 million from the county since 1974 and the Tynewear Theatre Company (based at the Playhouse) had received £351,200 since its formation five years previously. Also in jeopardy was the funding (to the tune of £54,000 in 1983) to support the RSC's annual performances in the city. The inclusion of theatres like the Theatre Royal shows an often overlooked implication of abolition; not in receipt of Arts Council funding, it would now be faced with no money, trying, alongside the subsidised theatres, to persuade the districts to produce money or looking to the Arts Council, adding to the queue of clients at the door.[58]

The sheer amount of arts funding lost is suggested by Sinclair's assertion that abolition would remove some £34 million from arts subsidy and by a former RAA director's assessment of them:

They basically had a lot of money and nothing to do, so naturally they got involved with the arts. Just as the GLC had developed its South Bank Centre, so the others had to have showcases...something which could offer cultural kudos.[59]

In the event, the Government did come up with some money to cover the loss; £25 million in 1987-1988; £21 million in 1987-88 and £20 million in 1988-89. However, as Leslie Geddes-Brown argued, if the Council decided to divide the shortfall equally, none of those bodies that would lose out "can expect to get more than 60%-65% of their old metropolitan grants." Peter Hall reckoned that he would be short by about £400,000 stating, "if all the money from the GLC had gone, we'd have been dying. As it is, the minister has allowed us to go on being invalids."[60]

Given the shortfall, the Arts Council were looking to district councils to step in which created as many problems as it solved. In Liverpool, for example, the five councils argued about who should pay more and which council benefited most from the existence of the arts institutions in their backyard. Alongside this they, like many other councils, simply did not have the money as they were facing the prospect of rate-capping, an attempt by the government to limit the level of rates a local council could charge. The Tories had long believed that local councils had been setting high rates in order to bolster their income and were determined, by direct government intervention, to curb what they saw as irresponsible and excessive rises. This would lead to cuts in councils' income and in 15 local councils, notably the Militant-led Liverpool, councils refused to set budgets. All these additional problems threw a spanner in the works of devolution and also start to highlight one of the key problems faced by ERPT throughout this period: the pros and cons of involving the local authorities (discussed below). What is clear however is that, in Robert Hutchinson's words, "*Glory* was sunk by the abolition of the GLC and metropolitan councils."[61]

Theatre IS for All (1986)

Whatever the pros and cons of *Glory* by 1986 it was indeed effectively dead in the water. The independent inquiry commonly known as *The Cork Report* had been published in September 1986 stating unequivocally that:

> the proposed shift of funding from London to the regions has not yet led to the envisaged spread of benefit in the regions. On the contrary, non-*Glory of the Garden* companies are in fact marginally worse off in real terms than they were before.[62]

In fact, only two theatres had received sums of money approaching the levels envisaged (Leicester and Sheffield) and the combined income of the National and RSC had actually increased from 30% of the total budget in 1970-71 to 48% in 1985-86. At the same time, the total for building based theatres had fallen from 62% to 39%.[63] This legacy of *Glory* did make "dismal reading" and those who ran theatre buildings might have been even more concerned to hear Cork's response to a map showing all the theatres in England drawn up at the start of his investigation: "Too many theatres!"[64] In the end, the number of theatres was not Cork's only concern and he issued stark warnings about the state of the theatre's health both generally (theatre in England has reached a critical point "which must not be allowed to become a crisis") and in relation to the regions in particular.[65] Here it was argued that unless the gap between the national companies (alongside television and film) and the regions was addressed now, regional and touring theatres were in danger of collapse – by turn endangering the survival of the national companies. Dismal reading indeed.

Whilst the report focused on a holistic and integrated approach to the country's theatres, Cork did reserve some space specifically to deal with the problems of the regions. Despite the clear lack of progress, he recommended further devolution of all regional companies to the RAAs (with the exception of a few national companies in the regions) which had a new maturity and authority thanks to the 1984 devolution and the major contribution they had made in helping replace funding abolition. But his most innovative suggestion came early on in the report with the suggestion of the establishment of a small number of theatres (six in the first instance, including one touring company) to be designated as major regional companies which could balance, challenge and stimulate the RSC and the National Theatre whilst also ensuring that "all English people" were in reach of "the best of world drama". This drew on French models of theatre, the Maisons de Culture, where companies such as Roger Planchon's Théâtre National Populaire acted as national stages and ensembles in the regions and were successful not just in producing work of international standard but also in attracting talent out of the capital. The report provides detailed outlines of what these companies, to be nominated on a three year rolling franchise, might be expected to do including co-productions, international touring, providing homes for London companies on tour and, above all, taking risks in their repertoire, but is also at pains to point out that these should in no way be seen to "challenge the national companies". They would not be funded on the same levels and their productions would not be as lavish.[66]

These suggestions were never acted on in any formalised way, although in practice it could be argued that major companies have evolved in the regions including Manchester Royal Exchange and Bristol Old Vic, as they were already doing in 1970, when the *Theatre Today* report identified a number of regional theatres as "major theatres". What Cork's suggestion did do was point to a potential two-tier system outside London that was to be further deepened by the next major report, *The Wilding Report*.

Supporting the Arts (1989)

The last review of the decade was once again trumpeted as "the most far-reaching inquiry into arts funding since 1946."[67] But it was different in one major way to those that preceded it. Wilding's *Supporting the Arts: A Review of the Structure of Arts Funding* came at the behest of the government, in particular, the Arts Minister Richard Luce, and the Arts Council chose not to provide evidence. This meant it had a different impetus but many of the concerns and (to some degree) recommendations were very familiar and served to show just how little had changed since *Glory*. Commissioned in December 1988 and delivered in 1989, Wilding's report was to go through several changes and several arts ministers before aspects were finally introduced in 1994.

The key remit of the review was:
- Accountability of RAAs in their spending of public money
- Lack of coherence between national and regional funding bodies in the formulation and delivery of policy
- Unwieldy structures and processes
- Administration costs.[68]

Once again, a key problem was the relationship between the Arts Council and the RAAs, although there is also far greater concern about how local authorities fitted into the picture. He pointed out, for example, that local authorities had the dominant voice on the RAAs and the tone and style of the RAAs had a "distinctly local government flavour".[69]

So far from being a problem solved, the problem continued. From this account, little real headway had been made in terms of devolution; the Arts Council favoured it in principle but was unwilling to let major clients go for fearing of losing the power that accompanied funding and overall the real net effect of devolution since *Glory* had been somewhat random. In Yorkshire, for example, Harrogate and Scarborough were devolved but York Theatre Royal was still funded by the Arts Council. In the Eastern

Region, the Palace Theatre, Westcliff and the Mercury in Colchester had been devolved but the Palace Theatre, Watford and the Wolsey in Ipswich were still centrally funded. "It is hard to find a rational basis for the difference," stated Wilding, and, more than that, such lack of rationality was, "an obstacle to progress at the regional level".[70] One of his challenges was to find a more organised way for devolution to progress.

Wilding also sought to find ways to mend the relationship between the Arts Council and the RAAs which were still rife with "mutual resentment and suspicion", one RAA director comparing being in the regions to being a boy "in short trousers waiting to be allowed to grow up".[71] All the debates, conferences and working parties that had taken up so much time and money over the last decade had not solved the problems and he identified the lack of clarity over roles and duplication of work as (still) being the problems. Wilding is also at pains to point out the levels of success of the RAAs notably in terms of the increased involvement and funding of the arts by the local authorities:

> Over the last 20 years, the present system has achieved one signal success. The local authorities, recently in circumstances of great financial difficulty, have steadily broadened and developed their support for the arts.[72]

This may, he admitted, have happened without the help and encouragement of the Council and RAAs but development would not have been so widespread or so rapid. But here too issues were confused; it is too simplistic to argue that at least some of the problems could have been solved by suggesting the RAAs worked with local authorities while the Council stood back from this, for at times (and Wilding cites as one example the case of the possible move of Sadler's Wells to Birmingham) the Council needed to be the one to negotiate them. In any case, part of the Council's concern was that there was too much local authority say (and by implication power) already in the RAAs. Prising the two apart in terms of distinct roles and functions was going to be a tough job and was to involve much to-ing and fro-ing about the number of local authority members to be allowed on the newly formed Regional Arts Boards by the Arts Council.[73] Nor was it just on the level of relationships with local authorities where the water was very muddy. The two were so intertwined and co-dependent, it would be impossible to unpick them. They would, in Wilding's words, just have to learn to get along better.

Although Wilding does say confusion, whilst being "grievous to the tidy mind", could prevent "undesirable uniformity", he did set about tidying things up, trying to find a structure which would allow the two sides to work together harmoniously, quite often to the annoyance of the

RAAs. Peter Booth of Merseyside Arts, for example, argued that administrative tidiness was in danger of eliminating the real strengths of the RAAs.[74] The first specific proposal was a redefinition of the role of the Arts Council into a body with a wide brief to act as an advocate for the arts and a forum to increase subsidy, support and perceptions of the arts. In essence, a campaigning and policy making national body no longer responsible for funding apart from the major national companies. The RAAs were to be reformed as Regional Arts Boards (RABs), an attempt to tidy up and unify their organisation, and be reduced in number from 12 to 7 (Wilding's preferred figure although he offered a number of alternatives and there was to be as much to-ing and fro-ing on this number as there was about local authority involvement and who selected the Chairs of the Boards in the months and years to come).

With the Arts Council primarily out of the picture in terms of funding, Wilding decided on a three tier system which seemed to favour neither side (indeed much of his role in the report was seemingly to try and placate both sides) arguing that what was needed was not "the systematic subordination of one perspective to the other, but appropriate ways of bringing two views together".[75] Major companies and clients plus touring companies that spent more than 50% of their time outside the region plus any that were not geographically located (plus – to add more potential confusion – a small list of "leaders" in artistic innovation to be overseen by the director personally) were to be assessed and funded by the Arts Council with the RAAs as part of the team. Major arts bodies not included in what was called the first tier and including all building based companies (other than those in the first tier) were to be funded and assessed by the RAA but with the Arts Council approval being sought for key decisions. Everyone else was in the third tier with the RAAs alone taking responsibility.[76]

Such vague phraseology as 'major' and 'leaders' and the division of funding into tiers was bound to cause upset and indeed it did. While Tony Banks awarded Luce five out of ten for the structural changes, the ninety-two organisations down for devolution "howled with anguish".[77] A senior arts officer writing to Ian Brown, the then Drama Officer, in June 1990 suggests, "The theatres are demonstrating considerable resistance to devolution, particularly the "big ten".[78] Braham Murray, at Manchester Royal Exchange, expressed the views of many: "It will be relegation, not devolution".[79] To the RAAs, it should have been "milk and honey" and many did welcome it, David Cargill of Eastern Arts Association likening the future of subsidy in Britain to the collapse of the Soviet Union and "the end of central control for good and all".[80] Others were less enthusiastic.

Nor was the Arts Council, in danger of being turned into "little more than an advertising agency", that keen on Wilding. Indeed, the first casualty was the secretary-general, Luke Rittner, resigning because he "fundamentally disagreed with the course".[81]

Such concern was understandable. Unfortunately for all concerned, the first announcements of more devolution came at the same time as yet another funding crisis. 30 out of 32 theatres were running at a deficit; the drama committee was threatening that everyone would have to "think the unthinkable" and floating emergency plans that included closing regional theatres for 6 months of the year and closing studio theatres for good. At Bristol Old Vic, Jonathan Miller resigned as artistic director, six months before he was due to leave, when two productions were cancelled for financial reasons. It was not a good time to become less visible, less national.[82]

In many ways the theatres and the Council did not need to be overly worried. No-one was in a hurry to implement Wilding's changes. It was, as Luce was at pains to point out, a consultative document and the Arts Council itself held a two-day meeting at Leeds Castle near Maidstone to form their response while the proposal was also subject to a three-month consultation process. Failure was in part due to changes of Arts Ministers, three in one year, each with different approaches and agendas.

In September 1990, Luce was replaced by David Mellor, at heart far more of a centralist than Luce. Within four days he had announced that the Arts Council would retain responsibility for four times as many organisations as had been forecast, 81 in all with 120 going to the regions. Membership of the boards would now be halved to about twelve, to be selected by consultation between the Arts Minister and the Arts Council. And nothing would happen in terms of devolution until he had "cleaned up" the Regional Arts Boards.[83] Tim Renton took over in November of the same year, saying he was "by instinct a devolver and delegator, not a centralist".[84] Three weeks later, he was telling the Arts Council that he had torn up the list of 92 companies due for delegation, calling for a new list the following April and extending the timetable for setting up the Boards. From then on, the number of companies to be devolved careered between 23 and 60 (31 had appealed against the original devolution plans). Even Peter Brooke was admitting there was no consensus on the way forward and Simon Mundy, director of the National Campaign for the Arts, described the sense of disenchantment that had shrouded the arts world as "things that should have changed have stayed the same" and "things that should have stayed the same degenerated."[85]

But to ascribe the failure of Wilding to changes of Ministers alone would be to miss the underlying point. The story is also riven with tensions between Whitehall and Westminster and which of the two the Arts Council felt most comfortable building alliances with. At the time the Wilding Report was commissioned the National Audit Office was investigating the Arts Council and four RAAs to see if the Exchequer was getting value for money. The fact of Wilding's existence (and some sense that the Arts Council was getting its own house in order) managed to hold off the enquiry for a while and in the end the National Audit Office findings were held back until May 1990 by the request of Luce, to allow Wilding's changes to be aired first. But there were also tensions in cosying up to Westminster who saw devolution as vote catching and therefore to be encouraged, as Sinclair points out:

> At the crude value of arts funding which Jennie Lee had demanded from Lord Goodman of 'how many votes?', the ballot boxes would be heavier for every pound spent and every decision made in the regions rather than in London. There was a harvest of Xs on paper to be reaped from nationwide urban renewal rather than a dearth from continuing metropolitan control.[86]

For the Arts Council to get into bed with Westminster, meant losing power. It was caught in a cleft stick of its own making.

But, much like *Glory*, money and particularly caps on local authority spending, this time in the form of the poll-tax, derailed much of Wilding, which all but left parity funding (the replacement for *Glory's* challenge funding) wrecked, as Joan Bakewell pointed out:

> Local authority funding for the arts has for some four years now attracted parity funding from the Arts Council. All goes well as long as local sums of money are increasing. But when local grants fall, the entire obligation to parity funding shudders. Companies that lose local authority grants could, for no other reason, lose their Arts Council grant, too. The poll tax is not only driving local authority arts funding into a corner with a gun to its head, it's also putting a noose around its neck.[87]

This double bind cost Derby Playhouse up to £134,000 a year as Derbyshire abolished £450,000 of arts funding and left Bristol Old Vic existing on month-to-month handouts from a city council who were talking of reducing or even ending their support. Overall, councils were looking at cutting 9.5% of their spending. The Arts Council introduced enhancement funding to try and stave off disaster but in the end this became a disastrously divisive scheme:

It cannot really be seen as fair to give Bristol Old Vic no extra money, the Bolton Octagon 7% and yet 32% to Hampstead Theatre. For those companies already devolved, the Regional Arts Associations have only 8% to pass on, some of which is bound to be sliced off the top. Their straw looks decidedly short.[88]

In the end, 31 theatres were devolved and ten Boards were decided on – Yorkshire and Humberside was to be taken over by Yorkshire and Eastern while Merseyside was to merge with North West Arts. Given the history of tensions between Manchester and Liverpool, this was greeted by howls of outrage from Merseyside who insisted on merger not absorption, tried to get the office to be in a city other than Manchester and eventually won the right to maintain a Liverpool office. The process took until 1994 to complete. It was, as Anthony Everitt, who had overseen some of the process, "five years of fumbled changes".[89]

Despite the change from associations to boards, the whole Wilding venture fizzled out ignominiously and the concerns of the theatres over finding themselves devolved might have been right. In February 1994, Michael Billington was writing about the plight of the 82 year-old Palace Theatre, Westcliff, yet another regional theatre facing a "desperate future". It had learnt that week that its grant from the Eastern Arts Board for 1994-95 was to be £45,000, a reduction from the late eighties high of £107,000. Chris Dunham, the theatre's director, told him the consequences would be summer closure, higher prices, and fewer productions with fewer actors. Billington concluded: "The blunt fact is that the Palace was better off when it was funded directly by the Arts Council: devolution to a regional arts board, as many theatres are discovering, is a potential recipe for disaster."[90]

Halfway There: The State of Play in the Regions

Following these first three attempts at altering the balance between the centre and the regions is an opportune moment to stop and take stock. What was the reality of life in regional theatre in the 1990s? Had all these reports made anything better? The years following the botched implementation of Wilding were indeed hard years. 1993 saw the first actual cash cut in the grant. At the same time, local authorities were pressurising RABs to take on a greater share of funding as a result of rate capping. After seven years on the Arts Council, Brian Rix resigned reflecting the feelings of many about the Arts Council's attitude to, and relationship with, the government. Threatened with a £5 million cut "we rush like lemmings to the water's edge, devising fatuous so-called policies and strategies and visions and corporate plans which are merely feeble attempts to cover up the fact that we have been defecated on from a great height."[91]

Rix was nearly joined by another ten members of the drama board who threatened to resign. At a meeting in Woodstock in May 1993, the Arts Council asked panel members to come up with a list of clients who would lose money if there was to be a 25% cut. People thought it was a paper exercise; the Arts Council thought otherwise; and threatened to implement the cuts. If they had been implemented, regional theatres known to be at risk included The Belgrade, Coventry, Theatre Royal, Plymouth, Bristol Old Vic, Bolton Octagon, Oldham Coliseum and local London venues including the Lyric, Hammersmith, the Palace Theatre, Watford and Greenwich. Of those under threat, the Lyric had just appointed Neil Bartlett as Artistic Director and Andrew Hay had been at the helm of Bristol for little more than a year. The threats of closure seemed a little random thought Benedict Nightingale:

> Why are these theatres threatened? That's anybody's guess. Not popular enough? Plymouth plays to 432,000 people a year, in the subsidised sector a figure bettered only by the National and RSC. Not bold enough? *La Bête* and the *Morte D'Arthur*, both at the Lyric, broke theatrical conventions galore. Weak when it comes to educational, youth and multi-cultural work, all areas on which the council now places special emphasis? Here, Coventry and Plymouth are among the nation's leaders."[92]

In the end, the Council decided for cuts across the board, but this didn't mean everything in the garden was now rosy. Even before reductions took effect many theatres were already suffering "a lingering death by a thousand cuts".[93] The state of play at the New Victoria Theatre, Staffordshire was not untypical. Ticket sales were down by £100,000 over the year and local government subsidy was down by £80,000. In November 1993, Artistic Director, Peter Cheeseman was forced to cut one fifth of the theatre's staff and, at a time when he believed it was crucial to increase and broaden the service the theatre gave to the local community, he had to cut their education programme and visiting companies, as well as cast sizes.[94] There were implications as well for new writing, as John Stalker at Birmingham Rep noted:

> A few years ago we would have commissioned 12 new plays a year. Now it's only six and we can't afford a literary manager. That means there are 50% fewer opportunities for writers. Where are the new Willy Russells and Alan Ayckbourns going to come from without the support of companies like ours?[95]

The National Campaign for the Arts found that the number of in-house productions at Sheffield Crucible had declined by 37.5% in seven years and at West Yorkshire by 30% while cast sizes had declined at Derby Playhouse by some 42%, leading to concern that the uniqueness of regional theatre, which lay in its ability to "provide drama of relevance to its setting" thus "rooting the theatre in its community" was at risk.[96] West Yorkshire was looking to co-productions to breathe new life into troubled times. Jude Kelly argued it was a way of stretching resources and:

> if what you produce is good, why shouldn't it be seen elsewhere? It's a way of extending subsidy. People are always saying that the RSC and the National Theatre should do more touring. But why not the Glasgow Citizens and the Manchester Royal Exchange? The regional theatres are national theatres.[97]

Whilst this may have been a solution for some of the larger theatres, others, like Lawrence Till at Bolton Octagon saw them as a potential betrayal of the audience:

> Like all regional venues, this theatre is funded by three main sources: the Regional Arts Board, ticket sales and the local authority. If it is the local people who are paying for this theatre then their needs should come first.[98]

The issue of the repertoire dogged theatres throughout the 90s. Struggling with finances many theatres were forced to curtail new work and cast sizes. At Scarborough, Alan Ayckbourn's new play, *Haunting Julia*, was a three-hander and productions of Willy Russell's one woman show *Shirley Valentine* became almost compulsory.[99] A proliferation of safe choices and small cast plays was accompanied in many theatres by rising ticket prices, always one of the first signs that theatre was under pressure to bridge a funding gap and overall, these increased by some 90% between 1986/7 and 1994/5.[100]

By 1995, Robin Thornber was arguing that it was inevitable that:

> in order to fund some companies to a level that enables them to operate effectively, some companies will either have to have their funding removed altogether or receive funding at a level that may mean that they have to radically change and scale down the way they operate.[101]

Three-quarters of the 45 regional theatres in England were thought to be in deficit, adding up to a £6 million shortfall. These included West Yorkshire Playhouse in Leeds, which had only opened in 1990 and by 1997 was to be in receipt of stabilisation money. According to Cameron Mackintosh, the fabric of British theatre had been "eroded to a point where the system is like a worn sock."[102]

In such tough times, competition between theatres became inevitable. Philip Hedley had already pointed this out in an open letter offering advice to Gowrie as he took over the Chair of the Arts Council in 1993:

> You could stop the whole nonsense of one art form bidding against another, which has produced the resignation of Brian Rix from the drama panel, and of one orchestra bidding against another, which led to the resignations of Evelyn Glennie and Priti Paintal (two more actual arts practitioners you'll note) from the music panel, and of one regional arts board bidding against another, which this week produced the resignation of the very valuable Brian Matcham as director of North West Arts."[103]

But damaging fighting over resources became a feature of the next few years. In 1997, South West Arts Board could boast that they had played a leading role in winning a residency from the RSC, the region beating off "stiff competition" from over 20 cities across the UK. It won the residency because "the Plymouth Theatre Royal has a track record for attracting larger audiences than any other regional theatre company".[104]

The argument about underfunding and lack of innovation rumbled on through the nineties and into the new century. A slightly different approach to devolution was taken in 1994, when the ACGB was abolished and its role transferred to three new national bodies in England, Scotland and Wales raising hopes that this might at least allow some national independence but this did little to help the increasing plight of the regions. In mid-2000, some big names (including Judi Dench, Michael Gambon and Ian McKellen) wrote to the Chancellor Gordon Brown asking for additional funding, convinced that if this was not forthcoming, "we could well face a two-tiered system of quality of theatre provision between London and the regions, which would appear to be directly contrary to the Government's desire of providing access to high quality performances throughout the country." The letter was sanctioned by Equity and asked Mr Brown to use the forthcoming spending review to address the problems of theatre with an extra £25 million. The performers concluded:

> We feel in the context of total Government spending, this would be a small price to provide stability in the theatre sector, and the social, economic, educational and cultural returns which would result...We urge you to meet the challenge of rejuvenating our regional theatres as a key creative industry.[105]

The Boyden Report: *The Roles and Functions of the English Regional Producing Theatres* (2000)

Eventually, one "excellent thing" did happen.[106] For Michael Billington, Peter Boyden was "the real theatrical hero of the Blair years" producing, in 2000, *The Roles and Functions of the English Regional Producing Theatres*.[107] The report, focusing on the 50 ERPT, saw this as a pivotal moment:

> of great potential opportunity and great potential cost for the English theatre. Working together to make the case for additional investment in a re-energised sector, the DCMS, ACE and RABs have the chance to redress 20 years of strategic confusion and funding attrition. If the moment is not seized now it may not come again.[108]

Arguing for the fundamental importance of understanding the mixed nature of the theatre ecology, the report placed the producing theatres within a context of a long-term decline in both subsidy and audience. Many had become as a result "fragile vessels".[109] He found that more than half the ERPTs they surveyed were in the red (including the flagship West Yorkshire Playhouse despite a transfer of *Spend, Spend, Spend* to West End and good audiences), arguing that a failure to take risks for fear of further losses was cramping creativity. The preliminary report claimed that without help, loss-making theatres which had clung on through the Thatcher years had little chance of trading their way out of trouble.[110] In the final report, Boyden turns his fire firstly on the Tories who had given the theatres about as much sympathy as they had local authorities, the national industries and the steel, coal and rail unions.[111] He then turns on Labour for their "sticking plaster" response which had been erratic, uneven and without strategic context – although he sees some prospect that things were looking up. He mounts a compelling case for the role of ERPTs and provides a survey of their state of health in 1999. At its heart it is an argument about the need for a national policy to emanate from ACE to reinvigorate the regional theatres but this could not start from the proposition that the 50 theatres under review "have an inalienable right of preferential access to public funding to produce."[112] A 25-point plan of what the national policy should be working towards emphasised that it could not be drawn from the centre and, throughout, Boyden is keen to emphasise the individuality, the variety, the differences of each of the theatres and their ways of working. He offers an enticingly different snapshot of what a re-energised English regional network might look like in five years time and how it might flourish if the case for more treasury subsidy could be made and won. Here we are back in a world where "attractive, welcoming, unintimidating, comfortable and efficient... exciting, stimulating and clearly theatrical" theatres produced their own work and opened their arms to welcome all.[113] They were creative crucibles, educators, community resources, presenters and catalysts in which:

> Audiences, participants and users will feel part of a dynamic process from the point of engagement with venue and staff. The buzz and excitement will spill out beyond the stage and auditorium and into the wider community.[114]

Inevitably, such excitement came at a cost and whilst Boyden was keen to point out that his role was not to tie the health of the theatres into a defined level of treasury investment, he did outline four possibilities:
- Reduced investment, which would imply that the ERPTs have "had their day"
- Same investment differently applied, which could only possibly work for a smaller number of better resourced theatres or engine houses
- Increased investment: stabilisation of ERPTs, which would mean the writing off of the collective debt
- Increased investment: strategic sectoral enhancement, in which he argued for the increased value of investment.[115]

Two months after Boyden, the Arts Council did publish their first *National Policy for Theatre in England* (July 2000) promising to transform and sustain theatre in England, to instil a new confidence and excitement. They outlined eight priorities; the first two (a better range of high quality work and attracting more people) were to apply to everyone. The other six, including, at number eight, regional distinctiveness, were to apply to all but they did not expect "everyone to give them equal priority or delivery". They also warned that money might not solve all the problems.[116]

But little could dent the enthusiasm and sighs of relief that greeted the announcement of a great windfall in the same month. In an overall boost to the arts budget of £100 million over three years, theatre was to receive an additional £12 million in 2002/3, rising to £25 million in 2003/4 and after. A furious last-minute battle between Gordon Brown and Chris Smith, the then Culture Secretary, did nearly wreck the rescue package. Demands from health, education, transport and the environment (not to mention defence) meant the arts were last in line. Brown was said to be put off by "the strident public demands of Gerry Robinson (ACE chair), for a £300 million increase in its budget over three years." Rumours abounded that the Treasury itself wanted to decide where the money was spent (rather than giving it to the Arts Council to make the choices).[117] But there was concern over theatre closures in the run up to an election, so the money did arrive and the results were instantly visible in the regions when ACE announced the outcome in March 2001. Manchester Royal Exchange saw a rise of 36%, Derby Playhouse of 82%, Salisbury of 100% and the Palace Theatre, Watford of 147%. Other rises were even more spectacular; the Theatre by the Lake, Keswick saw its grant improve by £233,000, an increase of 233% and Oxford Playhouse received an increase of 405%. On one level, all of this largesse could be seen as making up the deficit of ten years (and more) of under-funding, but the sighs of relief were audible, as Benedict Nightingale rather cheekily put it:

> This week the Arts Council solemnly issued a list of quotes from regional theatres that have benefited from increased funding. They're "delighted", "delighted", "delighted", "delighted" and "absolutely delighted"[118]

Others were welcoming but a little more circumspect. For Philip Hedley it was:

> the first time I can remember we are being treated like adults and being left to get on with our jobs. My only worry is that the money may come too late for some who have been clinging on by their fingernails.[119]

And Peter Hall was in even bleaker mood: "It is something but more is needed, and it is too late. I just hope there is a regional theatre left by the time the money comes through."[120] Indeed, it was too late for some theatres. The Wolsey in Ipswich had closed its doors in 1999 with a deficit of £198,000 (to re-open as the New Wolsey in 2001) and the Thorndike in Leatherhead had closed in 1997. Billington summed up the mood in an interview with Bill Alexander, the departing artistic director of the Birmingham Rep; the news of the windfall should have led to some "modest cheer in the regional theatre: if they're not cracking open the champagne, they should at least be toasting the chancellor in mineral water."[121]

The Centre Wins Out

If Boyden did not overtly suggest reorganisation of the Council, it did not mean it had stopped happening and, unquestionably, one of the things that has dogged regional theatres throughout the period is the question of almost constant Arts Council re-organisation in relation to the regions. This did not stop with the setting up of the RABs. In 2001, these found themselves suddenly, in the sort of dawn raid more familiar to the City, abolished, to be replaced by a single integrated organisation with regional offices and regional councils. Given just six weeks to hand over all their staff contracts and assets, the boards were less than happy. As Turnbull points out, by the end of the six weeks, nothing had been handed over, the chief executive of London Arts had resigned and eight of the boards were in open rebellion. As South West Arts Board commented of what had become known in the press as "Gerry's smash and grab", "[i]t would be wrong to under-estimate the offence this has caused".[122] But much of this was tempered by a perception that the boards had become unwieldy bureaucratic machines, a hangover from the days of the Tories. Gerry Robinson tried to assure everyone that "for the first time we have created a system where the voice of the regions will be heard at the top table in London" but even this new organisation did not manage to survive for very long.[123] In 2009, the Arts Council, responding to criticism in *The McIntosh Report* of 2008,[124] declared, "we will truly be one organisation" and turned the regional offices (by then nine) into smaller ones (renamed business units) under the care of four executive directors in four super-regions: London, North, Midlands and East and South-East albeit it with a support centre in Manchester. It will be a "single and joined-up organisation", they declared and one a long way away from Rees-Mogg's British "garden of the arts" with its great beauties throughout.[125] This then puts an end to the story of devolution. The urge to spread and disperse at the heart of *Glory* ends by organisational centralisation. The new chief executive, Alan Davey, claims that he wants to create "a culture that moves away from the false polarities of national versus regional." But the rifts and tensions between the local and the central explored here (and in Ian Brown's chapter) may prove hard to heal.[126]

Notes

[1] Olivia Turnbull, *Bringing Down the House: The Crisis in Britain's Regional Theatres* (Bristol: Intellect, 2008), 87.
[2] *The Glory of the Garden* (London: ACGB,1984), iv.
[3] *Glory* does talk about other drama developments including touring, children and young people's theatre, new writing and Black and Asian drama. See Glory: 21. The strategic areas included 11 cities (Birmingham, Bristol, Leeds, Leicester, Liverpool, London, Manchester, Newcastle, Nottingham, Sheffield and Southampton)

plus Plymouth and Ipswich/Norwich in the east. The last two were included to ensure better geographic coverage.

[4] *The Glory of the Garden*, 16.

[5] The English Regional Producing Theatres to be devolved included the Mercury Theatre, Colchester; Palace Theatre, Southend; Watford Theatre; Derby Playhouse; Northampton Repertory Players; Half Moon Theatre; Oval House; Richmond Fringe (The Orange Tree); Theatre Royal, Stratford East; Bolton Octagon; Duke's Playhouse, Lancaster; Farnham Repertory Company; Thorndike Theatre, Leatherhead; Everyman Theatre, Cheltenham; Swan Theatre, Worcester; Scarborough Theatre Trust.

[6] *The Glory of the Garden*, 11.

[7] In addition the following touring companies were also told their subsidy was to be withdrawn: CAST, M6 Theatre Company, Mikron Theatre Company, 7.84 Theatre Company (England) and Temba.

[8] *The Glory of the Garden*, vi & v.

[9] See Ian Brown: "The Road Through Woodstock: Counter-Thatcherite strategies in ACGB's Drama Development Between 1984 and 1994, *Contemporary Theatre Review* 17:2 (2007), 218-229. Overall, 41 clients were to be axed and the money used to increase grants of 46 others at substantial level whilst remaining 1000 or so remained at standstill level. In the event, only two ERPTs lost their funding, the Lyceum at Crewe and the Marlowe at Canterbury.

[10] Andrew Sinclair, *Arts and Cultures: The History of the Fifty Years of the Arts Council of Great Britain* (London: Sinclair-Stevenson, 1995), 248.

[11] Ibid. 249.

[12] Ian Brown 2007, 220.

[13] Sinclair, 265-6.

[14] The House of Commons Estimate Committee's *Eighth Report, Grant for the Arts* (1967-68) and Lord Redcliffe-Maud's 1976 report *Support for the Arts in England and* Wales (London, Calouste Gulbenkian Foundation, 1976) had both discussed devolution.

[15] *Towards a New Relationship* included an appendix which listed suggestions for clients to be devolved. ERPT to be kept as being of 'national significance' included Leicester, Nottingham, the Royal Exchange in Manchester, Bristol Old Vic, Birmingham Rep and Sheffield Crucible.

[16] *A New Relationship* (London: ACGB, 1980) in Arts Council archives: ACGB/1/6010 (83-84).

[17] Robert Hutchison, *The Politics of the Arts Council* (London: Sinclair Browne, 1982) 31.

[18] Ibid. 32.

[19] Ibid. See also paper by Regional Director: "Assessment of RAA Estimates 84-85" in ACGB/1/6010. In this, he attempts to create 2 divisions of RAAs based not on work or initiative but on size and character of regions. The most limited, in his view, in terms of output and coverage (both geographical and artistic) were Lincolnshire and Humberside and Merseyside, whilst those graded at "A" included Eastern Arts, North West Arts and Northern Arts. Debate had already been

ensuing, since the mid-70s on ways to devolve decision making to the regions and to encourage local councils to spend more on the arts. See Lord Redcliffe-Maud: *Support for the Arts in England and Wales*.
[20] Council of Regional Arts: *England's Regional Arts Associations*, 1983: 1 in ACGB/44/10.
[21] Paper by CoRAA; ACGB/44/10.
[22] *Towards a New Relationship* (London: ACGB, 1980), 4.
[23] Ibid., 8.
[24] *Annual Review* 1988-89, 5.
[25] Quoted in Hutchinson, 125.
[26] Ibid.
[27] Sebastian Faulks, *Independent* 30th September 1990.
[28] Richard Wilding: *Supporting the Arts: A Review of the Structure of Arts Funding* (Arts Council, 1989), Paragraph 2:20.
[29] Leslie Geddes-Brown, "Why the Arts Council is Hedging its Bets", *Guardian*, September 7, 1986.
[30] Quoted in Vivian Nixson, "Waiting for Moggo: The Government's plans for the Arts Council", *Guardian*, July 14, 1984.
[31] Ibid.
[32] Gonley was the Director of NWA. See ACGB/44/5. The City of Manchester response was written on 15th May 1984 and Gonley's on the 1st May 1984.
[33] Vivian Nixson, "Waiting for Moggo: The Government's Plans for the Arts Council", *Guardian*, July 14, 1984.
[34] Nicholas de Jongh, "Theatres Given New Lease of Life as Arts Council Lifts Subsidy Threat", *Guardian*, July 17, 1984. Other companies to be saved included M6 in Rochdale and the Horseshoe Theatre Company in Basingstoke.
[35] By early 1985, this figure had risen to £3 million for the implementation of the first phase of the Glory of the Garden. See Nicholas de Jongh, "2pc Rise for Arts Causes Dismay", *Guardian*, February 2, 1985.
[36] Nicholas de Jongh and Donald Wintersgill, "Gowrie Grant Cut Staggers Arts and Gallery Chief", *Guardian*, December 18, 1984. Overall Arts funding (including Galleries and museums) had increased by 5.3% to £272 million.
[37] Michael Morris, "Arts Cash Switch Fails to Rescue Regions", *Guardian*, February 14, 1985.
[38] Nicholas de Jongh, "Theatre Revolt Over 'Political' Arts Council", *Guardian*, March 1,1985.
39 Ibid and Nicholas de Jongh, "Stage Flight from Arts Council", *Guardian* March 1, 1985. The seven resignations were Olwen Wymark, Mike Alfreds, John Bond, Brian Cox, Pamela Howard, Nicolas Kent and Guy Slater.
[40] Nicholas de Jongh, "Criticism fails to deter Arts Council", *Guardian*, March 2, 1985.
[41] Nicholas de Jongh, "Arts should not pin their faith on subsidies, says Rees-Mogg", *Guardian*, March 9, 1985.
[42] *Annual Report* 1985-86, 14.
[43] *Annual Report* 1986-87, 7.

[44] *Annual Report* 1987-88, 5.
[45] *Glory Reflected A Progress Report on The Glory of the Garden*, (London: ACGB, 1989), 2.
[46] Ibid. 3.
[47] The Haymarket in Leicester was built in 1974 and The Sheffield Crucible (a replacement for the Repertory Theatre) in 1971.
[48] Ibid 4, 8 & 10. The report states that the newly established South West theatre Consortium, which incorporated Plymouth Theatre Royal and the Northcott Theatre, Exeter, was to receive £207,000 in 1989/90, matched pound for pound by local authorities.
[49] Geordie Greig, "Council claims a record crop", *Times* June 4, 1989.
[50] Richard Witts, *Artist Unknown: An Alternative History of the Arts Council* (London: Warner Books, 1998), 136.
[51] Witts, 252 & 253.
[52] John Pick, *Vile Jelly: The Birth, Life and Lingering Death of the Arts Council of Great Britain* (Doncaster: Brynmill, 1991), 82.
[53] Those devolved in 1984-5 were: Horseshoe Theatre, Basingstoke; Chester Gateway; Churchill Theatre, Bromley; Croydon; Derby Playhouse; Farnham Repertory Theatre; Yvonne Arnaud Theatre, Guildford; White Rose Theatre, Harrogate; Hornchurch Theatre; King's Head Theatre; Duke's Playhouse, Lancaster; Thorndike Theatre, Leatherhead; Northampton Repertory Players; Scarborough Theatre; Swan theatre, Worcester; Connaught Theatre, Worthing. In 1985-6 they were joined by Cheltenham Everyman; Colchester Mercury; Half Moon Theatre; Oxford; Oval House; Pioneer; The Orange Tree, Richmond; Palace Theatre, Southend.
[54] Nicholas de Jongh, "Theatres given new lease of life as Arts Council lifts subsidy threat", *Guardian*, July 27, 1984. Those reprieved by the Arts Council were: Chester Gateway, White Rose Theatre, Harrogate, Tricycle Theatre and Temba.
[55] Wilding, Paragraph 2.27 & 4.7.
[56] William Rees-Mogg: Introduction to *Glory of the Garden*: vii. The Arts Council had, however, responded to the proposals with the publication of *The Arts in Metropolitan Areas* (January 1984).
[57] Tyne and Wear County Council: *The Arts in Peril* (January 1984): 1 & 3 in ACGB/44/7.
[58] Other theatres in a similar position were the Sunderland Empire and the Liverpool Empire, both in the end turned down (with Theatre Royal) for money from the Arts Council as they were not producing houses.
[59] Quoted in Witts, 242.
[60] Leslie Geddes-Brown, "How a Hard Sell Blunted the Grants Axe", *Times*, November 17, 1985.
[61] Geordie Greig, "Council Claims a Record Crop", *Times*, June 4 1989.
[62] Sir Kenneth Cork et al., *Theatre IS for All: The Report of the Inquiry into Professional Theatre in England under the Chairmanship of Sir Kenneth Cork* (London: Arts Council of Great Britain, 1986), 11.

[63] Ibid, 17 & 100. These figures deserve a little more detailed analysis to paint the real picture. In part, building based theatres had benefited at the same time from an increase in local authority spending (although according to Cork (110) this had amounted to little more than a 5% increase from 1980-81 whilst Arts Council income had declined by 3%). As Kate Dorney notes, touring had also been one of the beneficiaries during this period and this included work in the regions.
[64] Baz Kershaw (ed.), *The Cambridge History of British theatre, vol. 3: Since 1895* (Cambridge: Cambridge University Press, 2004), 312; Ian Brown and Rob Brannen Ian Brown, Rob Brannen and Douglas Brown 'The English Arts Council Franchise System and political theatre', *New Theatre Quarterly*, Vol. XVI No 64 (2000), 369.
[65] Cork, 4.
[66] Cork, 18-19.
[67] Geordie Greg, "Arts Council Faces Sweeping Changes", *Times,* October 15, 1989.
[68] Wilding, Paragraph 1.3.
[69] Ibid. Paragraph 2.13.
[70] Ibid. Paragraph 2.32. Ian Brown has argued that personalities were one of the key influencing factors in whether or not a theatre was devolved. See his chapter in this volume.
[71] Ibid. Paragraph 2.24.
[72] Ibid. Paragraph 2.17.
[73] Richard Luce, for example, stated that he had decided that local authorities should have substantial representation on the new boards "provided it is less than a majority". See *Hansard* 13th March 1990 vol 169 cc154-70.
[74] Wilding: Paragraph 2.36; for Peter Booth's response see Nicholas de Jongh: "Regional Arts Groups Face Axe", *Guardian,* October 11th, 1989.
[75] Wilding, Paragraph 4.9.
[76] Wilding, paragraph 5.5-5.10.
[77] Sinclair, 332.
[78] ACGB/44/10. For Tony Banks see *Hansard* 13th March 1990 vol 169 cc 154-70
[79] Nicholas de Jongh, "Theatres Angry Over Devolution", *Guardian,* September 29, 1990.
[80] Sinclair, 322.
[81] Sinclair, 318.
[82] See *Times* 27th September 1990; *Independent* 8th October 1990; *Guardian* 4th October 1990. Theatres of special concern were deemed to be Bristol, Sheffield, Plymouth, Derby, Nottingham, Newcastle and Liverpool.
[83] See Sinclair, 332.
[84] *Independent* December 15, 1990.
[85] Simon Mundy, "Forget the Bureaucracy, Find the Money", *Observer,* December 23, 1990. For Peter Brooke see *Times*, December 12, 1992.
[86] Sinclair, 295.
[87] Ibid., 332.

[88] Simon Mundy, "Forget the Bureaucracy, Find the Money", *Observer*, December 23, 1990.
[89] Anthony Everitt: "Minds, Hearts and Balls", *Guardian*, April 18, 1992. The devolved theatres were: Birmingham Repertory Theatre; Coventry Belgrade; Bristol Old Vic; Bush Theatre, London; Contact, Manchester; Crucible, Sheffield; Greenwich, London; Hampstead, London; Jeanette Cochrane, London; Leicester Haymarket; Liverpool Everyman; Liverpool Rep; Lyric Hammersmith, London; Newcastle Playhouse; Northcott, Exeter; Oldham Coliseum; Plymouth Theatre Royal; New Victoria, Stoke; Nottingham Playhouse; Nuffield, Southampton; Bolton Octagon; Polka Theatre, Wimbledon; Manchester Royal Exchange; Salisbury Playhouse; Soho Poly, London; Unicorn Theatre, London; Watford Palace Theatre, London; West Yorkshire Playhouse, Leeds; Wolsey, Ipswich; York Theatre Royal; Young Vic, London. See Robert Hewison: "Darkness at Noon?", *Sunday Times*, September 19, 1993.
[90] Michael Billington, "Noises Off, Heading for the Exit", *Guardian*, February 5th, 1994.
[91] Brian Rix, "One Farce I'm Happy To Quit", *Guardian*, 11th June 1993, 4.
[92] Benedict Nightingale: "Farce likely to end in tears", *The Times*, August 3, 1993.
[93] Lyn Gardner, "The Final Curtain", *Guardian*, November 29, 1993.
[94] Ibid.
[95] Ibid.
[96] National Campaign for the Arts, *Theatre in Crisis* (London: NCA, 1998), 5-7.
[97] Lyn Gardner, All The World's A Stage Direction, *Guardian* November 15, 1995.
[98] Ibid.
[99] Robert Hewison, "In Search of More Local Heroes", *Sunday Times*, July 24, 1994.
[100] National Campaign for the Arts: *Theatre in Crisis*, 4.
[101] James Meikle and Robin Thornber, "Local Theatres Face 'Spiral of Decline'", *Guardian* May 31, 1995.
[102] Cameron Mackintosh, Arts Council Review 1995-96, 12.
[103] Philip Hedley, "Counselling The Arts Man", *Guardian*, December 24, 1993.
[104] *Annual Report* 1996-1997, 55.
[105] David Lister, "Regional Theatre Is In Crisis, Warn Leading Actors", *The Independent*, July 1, 2000.
[106] Michael Billington, *State of the Nation* (LONdon: Faber & Faber, 2007), 375.
[107] Michael Billington, "Tony Blair: British Theatres Accidental Hero", http://www.guardian.co.uk/stage/theatreblog/2007/may/03/tonyblairbritishtheatresac; accessed 11/8/09.
[108] Peter Boyden Associates Ltd, *The Roles and Functions of the English Regional Producing Theatres* (London: Arts Council of England, 2000), 52.
[109] Ibid, 32.
[110] Fiachra Gibbons, "Curtains for debt-laden theatres?" *Guardian* January 28, 2000.
[111] Peter Boyden, 8.
[112] Ibid: 33-34.

[113] Ibid. 40.
[114] Ibid. 40
[115] Ibid. 45-50.
[116] *National Policy for Theatre in England* (2000), 4 & 3.
[117] David Hencke, Policy and Politics: "Cabinet clash over theatre funding" *Guardian* July 13, 2000.
[118] Benedict Nightingale, "Arts Council Funding", *Times* March 17, 2001.
[119] Fiachra Gibbons, "Regional theatres take hope as arts win record sum", *The Guardian* July 26, 2000.
[120] Ibid.
[121] Michael Billington, "I've Run Out of Ideas", *The Guardian,* July 26, 2000.
[122] Turnbull, 214. At the same time the Council dropped the 'of' in its title becoming Arts Council England in 2003.
[123] Fiachra Gibbons, "Arts Council Axes Local Boards", *Guardian,* March 16, 2001.
[124] The report's full title was: *A Review of Arts Council England's RFO Investment Strategy 2007/8* published as an annex to Alan Davey's *A Review of Arts Council England's RFO Investment Strategy: Lessons Leaned* (London: ACE, 2008).
[125] Rees-Mogg, Introduction to *Glory of the Garden*: vii; for detail of the restructuring see: "Arts Council Organisation Review: Briefing Notes" available at http://www.artscouncil.org.uk/news/organisation-review/.
[126] Charlotte Higgins, "Arts Council England will save £6.5m as staff cut by a quarter", *Guardian,* February 26, 2009.

CHAPTER FIVE

TOURING AND THE REGIONAL REPERTOIRE: CHEEK BY JOWL, COMPLICITÉ, KNEEHIGH AND EASTERN ANGLES

KATE DORNEY

This chapter examines the role of subsidised touring product in the ecology of British theatre since 1980. It argues that, increasingly, touring product has become a way of filling gaps in the regional repertoire created by a lack of funds which left some regional producing theatres unable to programme either a full season of in-house work or a diverse repertoire. It also looks at the development of some of today's most high profile companies from small set-ups addressing niche audiences to international, cosmopolitan models, often working in collaboration with the national companies. The chapter ends with three case studies exploring successful touring companies who fit this model: Cheek by Jowl, Complicité and Kneehigh, and one rural touring company, Eastern Angles, who work at a local level. Despite the Arts Council of Great Britain and then England's policies of "raise and spread", it seems that in an age of turbo capitalism, companies with an international touring base are capable of higher levels of achievement against all funding criteria.

Background

Touring theatre has always been key to the Arts Council's vision of widening access to artistic excellence, of providing, in Jennie Lee's words "the best for the most".[1] From the early days of CEMA, when Sybil Thorndike and Lewis Casson toured Welsh mining villages during the second world war to the boom-time of the 1970s when funding was available to companies exploring the politics of class (7:84, C.A.S.T, Foco Novo) and identity (Temba, Gay Sweatshop, Monstrous Regiment) as well inspiring versions of classic works (Prospect, English Shakespeare

Company), through to the present successes of non-building-based companies with an international reach (Forced Entertainment, Complicité, Shared Experience, Kneehigh), touring product has always played an important role in the ecology of theatre. The discernible, and often remarked upon, diachronic view of trends in funding patterns which sees the classical repertoire giving way to explorations of class politics, then giving way to identity politics and then to physical theatre is unhelpful for a nuanced understanding of Arts Council practices and policies. A synchronic approach reveals that these strands of activity have always run concurrently – artform panels, and Drama in particular, tending to encourage new developments as well as supporting existing ones. In this respect, the garden metaphor deployed throughout *The Glory of the Garden* (1984) provides an apt description of the role of Arts Council Drama staff: tending and feeding the saplings and weeding to make space for them in the garden. The motivations behind this "weeding" are not the subject of this discussion, although they have been the subject of many others.[2]

Touring, or non-building based, or alternative, theatre occupies a peculiar place in the mythology of the Arts Council. The most famous victims of its unkind cuts are all touring companies - 7:84, English Shakespeare Company, Monstrous Regiment, Gay Sweatshop, Foco Novo, Temba – yet they are also Arts Council offspring, brought into existence in the first place through the Council's largesse. Richard Eyre and Nicholas Wright's description of the Council in the 1970s is an unusually benign one, blessed with the benefit of hindsight:

> its function, as far as anyone in alternative theatre was concerned, was to be milked, bilked and complained about. Looking back from the 2000s one sees something very different: a haplessly well-meaning organisation, thickly infiltrated with liberal well-wishers, all of whom wanted nothing more than to shower money on interesting young people and take it away from clapped-out old ones.[3]

Touring companies have also provided the national companies and the regions with some of its most vibrant and innovative theatre – and have proved an important source of personnel for them. As a sector, touring has seen an increase in funds and infrastructural support since the dark days of the 1970s and early 80s, and has been the subject of increasing Council scrutiny via dedicated funding streams, specially commissioned reports and recommendations precisely because its inherently flexible nature has increasingly allowed it to cover a number of Council and local authority objectives. *The Glory of the Garden* recommended, among other things, that regional theatres open their studio spaces to touring companies; that national companies tour their productions more widely (at that stage the National Theatre was barely able to tour at all) and that touring should be "strengthened" by focussing more money at fewer clients. In the Annual Report for 1985/86, Secretary General Luke Rittner provides a monetarist spin to the old adage of necessity being the mother of invention noting that one consequence of a dwindling grant from the government has been:

> a marked growth in the number of companies pooling resources for their mutual benefit and to achieve more satisfactory levels of work. In most cases, a larger company has hosted a smaller company's work prior to its touring nationally. Leicester Haymarket are the pacesetters in this field, collaborating with Foco Novo, Paines Plough and two companies funded from the Council's Project Allocation – Bristol Express, as part of a triple partnership with the English Stage Co and Open Hearted Enterprises. Birmingham Rep initiated two co-productions in its Studio with small-scale touring companies, Foco Novo and Monstrous Regiment.[4]

Touring was very much on the Council's mind during this period. As well as the recommendations made in *Glory*, in 1985 they also commissioned two reports specifically on touring provision. A working party was set up to examine large-scale touring while Graham Devlin, artistic director of Major Road (a touring company), was asked to investigate small and middle-scale touring provision and produced a report called *Keeping the Show on the Road: A Report on Touring in England in 1985*.[5] *Theatre is For All* (1986), more commonly known as the *Cork Report*, drew on both these earlier works, explicitly stated the value of small-scale touring companies to the health of British theatre's ecology, and recommended a number of initiatives and funding increases to improve it. Many of them went unregarded, but two of the most successful outcomes of the research done for the report were the initiation of a Great Britain Touring Fund of more than a million pounds and the development of a new franchise system for touring companies. Touring theatre had faced extinction in 1970, and was rescued by the findings of the Theatre Enquiry (conducted by Wiliam Emrys Williams) and published as *The Theatre Today in England and Wales: The Report of the Arts Council Theatre Enquiry 1970*.[6] This established a network of receiving venues for work (a "circuit" of theatres in the regions with a "catchment area of population large enough to provide reasonable audiences") and developed large and middle-scale touring companies such as Prospect, The Actor's Company, the Cambridge Theatre Company and the Oxford Playhouse Company.[7] The report also ushered in a golden age in which eleven companies were adopted as revenue clients and only one had funding withdrawn.[8] Cork was to do the same in the 1980s, giving small- scale touring a funding uplift of 85%, recommending that mime companies such as Complicité were adopted by the Drama Department rather than continuing to be funded through Dance and securing additional funds for touring projects. As regional producing houses waned in the 1980s and 90s, overwhelmed by rising running costs, and buildings no longer fit for purpose, touring companies became a cheaper and more convenient way of getting a quality product to a large number of people – and therefore a cheaper way for the Arts Council to achieve its mission.[9]

The value of touring theatre

The Arts Council came to appreciate the value of touring theatre in the 1980s, not only because of its ability to fulfil the outreach side of its mission by bringing the best to the most, but because of the cost-effective way in which it operated. Prior to this, although the Council had paid lip service to the importance of touring, it was difficult for companies to make ends meet without commercial sponsorship or management deals (although the grid system established in 1976 did allow small-scale companies to tour to small venues, arts centres and non-traditional performance spaces for one or two nights).[10] Touring companies didn't get the benefits of programme or bar sales, they had to share the box office takings with the venue and very few companies based outside London got any local authority subsidy. In addition to this, funding levels for touring fell by 46% in real terms between 1977 and 1986.[11] No wonder then, that many of the companies of the late 1970s had an almost missionary zeal to challenge and explore notions of identity and class or to bring theatre to the masses – being a member of a touring company was not, at this point, the obvious route to a successful or lucrative career and was beset by administrative headaches, so conviction was a necessity. The *Cork Report* noted that application forms for grants for touring companies were so complicated and time consuming to complete that many companies simply did not bother. *Cork* was at pains to stress that touring should be recognised as effective in terms of cost and mission spread, stating that:

> touring is often the only way certain areas of the country can experience large-scale live theatre productions. It makes theatre more accessible to taxpayers throughout the country.[12]

> Touring theatre offers a means of spreading the cost of large-scale work across a number of venues which could not, alone, support such work.[13]

Smallness, accessibility, variety and innovation are the distinguishing features of this sector [...] Companies like Paines Plough, Joint Stock and Shared Experience have developed out of this sector, and the vitality and innovation which their work represents continues to characterise many of these touring companies. They have often been concerned to develop new work of interest to particular communities within the larger community. Such companies have a record of developing new forms and new writing and of presenting live theatre in underprovided areas of the country.[14]

Cork also recognised that touring companies provided a training ground for young practitioners which was an additional way of spreading artistic excellence. Interestingly, it also recommended that all companies involved in national touring should come under the purview of the Drama department rather than the relevant Regional Arts Association, and this is highly significant in terms of the way in which a certain kind of touring product was deployed to fill gaps in the repertoire of regional theatres. As their funding declined and their ability to produce classical work diminished (sometimes because of cast sizes but also because of box office risk), so companies like English Shakespeare and Cheek by Jowl who had time and money to develop high quality high-end product began to take on the role of delivering this element.[15] The Devlin Report suggested that Cheek by Jowl should be one of the companies given a substantial uplift in order to become part of a matrix of four companies given a strategic role to tour large-scale classics throughout the country (alongside Cambridge Theatre Company (CTC), Oxford Playhouse Company (OPC), and Century Theatre). This shaping of the repertoire through strategic funding is one of the clearest examples of the Arts Council as a proactive development agency rather than simply a reactive funding unit. During the evidence gathering for the Devlin report, the OPC had even suggested that given the "inability of many reps to produce Shakespeare to high standard due to financial constraints, this might be a role that OPC and CTC could adopt".[16] This meant the worst of all worlds for the regional producing theatres as the case studies in this book demonstrate: trying to retain their existing audiences on a diet of Ayckbourn, Priestley *et al*, while trying to attract new audiences with more experimental work (whether in terms of subject or style), and all the time worrying about how to fix the roof and improve the toilets. Touring companies could be in and out with a slick, high quality Shakespeare or classic adaptation and build a following in each location they visited. And this is precisely what Cheek by Jowl did.

Cork raised concerns about the lack of variety in repertoire, it identified that very little classical work was being done nationally, and that small-scale touring was producing a high proportion of new writing and adaptations. It also recognised that small-scale touring had seen "the exploration of new and experimental forms of physical and visual, or non-literary theatre" citing the pioneering work of Lumiere and Son, Welfare State and Impact in the 1970s.[17] It is no surprise then, to learn that the companies who see a substantial increase in funding are Paines Plough (new writing) who get a 19% increase in funding in 1988/89 and Cheek by Jowl (classics and Shakespeare), who move from project funding and are awarded £29,500 from touring projects and £30,000 from the Great British Touring Fund in addition to their grant.

Cork also recognised the work of Trickster and Trestle in producing mime which "escaped the hidebound forms of white-face mime and explored a vital theatricality which made use of sound and sound effects, masks, commedia techniques and humour", alongside the British Council's highlighting of mime as "crucially successful in the overseas presentation of British theatre both because of its non-verbal form and its high international quality".[18] This was followed by the adoption of Trestle, David Glass Mime and [Theatre de] Complicité as Drama clients.

Companies who were successful in moving from project funding to touring franchise reflected *Cork's* concern with repertoire. Ian Brown, secretary to the *Cork Report*, and Drama Director from 1986 to1994, notes that the work of new franchise companies and successful older companies:

> tended to reject a state-of-the-nation emphasis on the word for a greater emphasis on physical and visual performance, often accompanied by a return to the classics of classic narrative. Examples of this include Tara Arts' *Tartuffe* (1990) and *Oedipus* (1991), Theatre de Complicité's *A Winter's Tale* (1992), Kaboodle's *King Lear* (1994) and The Bacchae (1995) and Out of Joint's marriage of new writing with a classical repertoire. When Graeae mounted a production of *Ubu* (1991), with its themes of greed and power-grabbing, disabled performers were allowed to give the work their own personal and political angle.[19]

Alongside *Cork*, the Council's organisational review had major implications for touring. In the 1986/87 restructuring, Jack Phipps was made Controller of Touring (he had always been in charge of Touring department, but his previous title was Director) and under his aegis, the department "set out to explore new areas of work in drama touring for large regional theatres through a programme of direct investment in productions from both subsidised and independent sources".[20] Council hoped this would be the first step in the creation of a full-scale management operation as recommended by the 1985 Touring Working Party, but this soon fizzled out. The same year the English Shakespeare Company launched with a national tour of *Henry IV Parts 1 & 2* and *Henry V*, followed by a season at the Old Vic and a visit to Canada, which Luke Rittner (who, after all had been head of the Association of Business Sponsorship of the Arts before taking up the post of Secretary General) approvingly described as "a good example of a funding partnership between the Council's producing theatre, a London theatre and a sponsor [Allied Irish Bank], of a kind which could be seen as a model for the future".[21]

In 1988, the Council endorsed the touring franchise scheme by which all twenty-two middle and small-scale touring companies within the Drama Department were placed on staggered three year franchises. Every three years companies would apply to renew their franchise alongside companies on project funding who had managed to attract project funding three years in a row. This took care of one of the major concerns expressed in *Cork* that many promising companies could not be bothered to apply for project funding because the success rate was low and the application process was onerous. Franchise applications were written in company's own words and had only to set out their plans for the next three years with their estimated funding requirements. The Drama panel then judged the applications on artistic, financial and managerial merit.[22]

International/national/regional/local

In his first report as Chair of the Arts Council in 1989 Peter Palumbo gave a clear indication of his view of the arts as a money-making enterprise. He looked forward to Britain's dominance of the European Union in terms of artistic output (so many more punters, so much greater profit), but was careful to stress that rather than this being a cause of anxiety in terms of dilution of national identity, it was an opportunity to move toward a unified one:

> Whilst it is vital that we recognise the importance of maintaining regional identity and variety, it is equally vital that we work together to frame agreed priorities and objectives for a long-term national cultural policy for the arts, embracing the millennium and beyond, that will give the country as a whole a coherence that it lacks at the present time.[23]

Palumbo's words reflected the fact that, increasingly, the arts were looked upon as a means of assisting in urban regeneration (a theme which has persisted through to the present day), and of being measurable in terms of social as well as economic impact as a result of John Myerscough's pioneering study *The Economic Importance of the Arts in Britain* published by the Policy Studies Institute (PSI) in 1988. PSI had originally been approached by the Gulbenkian Foundation but several local authorities and the Arts Council contributed towards its funding. The research started from the premise that:

> There is a growing belief that the arts can bring a competitive edge to a city, a region, and a country, as a source of creativity, a magnet for footloose executives and their businesses, and as a means of asserting civic, regional or national identity through the quality of cultural life.[24]

Myerscough and his team demonstrated that the arts could be profitable, and that they could assist in urban regeneration: theories dear to the Council (or at least Government's) heart which it had promulgated through a number of reports, much shorter and glossier than those that debated the direction of the artforms: *Theatre Investment Fund* (1985), *A Great British Success Story* (1985), *Partnership: Making Arts Money Work Harder* (1986), *Better Business for the Arts* (1988). Myerscough's report inspired the later *An Urban Renaissance: Sixteen Case Studies Showing the Role of the Arts in Urban Regeneration* (1989) and set the precedent for the way in which the arts have been expected to earn their funding ever since. *A Great British Success Story*, subtitled *An invitation to invest in the arts*, adopts the kind of breathless rhetoric more in keeping with 1970s public information films:

> The central core of the arts industry depends crucially on financing from the public purse, providing for a consistent and stable support, employment, variety and greater access to all ethnic and social backgrounds. Investment in this central core not only offers returns in improving the quality of life; it contributes greatly to the wider entertainment industry, and it pays back many dividends (which will be revealed later). And while it offers an excellent product now, it also nurtures new talents, stimulates fresh ideas, sows seeds for the future. Rarely in the arts do these research and development costs have to be written off as a wasted investment.[25]

The brochure cites Hull Truck and Inter-Action alongside the National and RSC, Welfare State, Leicester Haymarket and the Thorndike Theatre. Their work is mentioned because of the success of their shows, which either transferred to the West End or undertook regional tours, or in the case of Welfare State and Inter-Action, because they organised large-scale community events. In 2002, Arts Council England published *Measuring the Economic and Social Impact of the Arts*, which reviewed existing work in the area, including François Matarasso's influential *Use or Ornament? The Social Impact of Participation in Arts Programmes*. Soon after the report was published ACE commissioned an economic impact of building based theatre in London and the regions and a social impact study. The publication of the economic impact study and the press which accompanied it coincided nicely with the 2004 Comprehensive Spending Review and allowed them to demonstrate to the government that building based "theatre is worth £2.6bn annually".[26] The social impact study, published in 2006, concluded that:

> The hard evidence for the social impact of theatre lies in the billions of pounds contributed by theatre to the economy of the country. It lies in the large (but unmeasured) sums of money invested by a range of government and non-government agencies in theatre. It is reflected not only in the employment of theatre artists, managers, carpenters and so on, but also in the evidence, found in this study, of changes in behaviour or improvement in skills.[27]

Even social impact is now measured in economic terms. The companies selected for the case studies below explore the way in which four different touring companies have negotiated their way through the funding system since *The Glory of the Garden*.

Local to Global; Regional to National

This book makes frequent mention of "regional", "local" and "national" theatre products and audiences, yet these have very different meanings depending on the user and the context. As Turnbull and others have noted, the Arts Council had no official national theatre policy until 2000, but had no difficulties in designating national companies in the regions in 1986 and in having regional offices, arts associations and eventually, arts boards in the 55 years leading up to this.[28] As we have seen, individuals, companies, buildings and organisations have tried variously to conform to, challenge and quantify this terminology in order to survive, and have done so with varying degrees of success. In this section I want to look at the work of a number of touring companies who are identified, or were identified as, national, regional and local and how they have negotiated these boundaries. For Shepherd and Womack writing in 1996, the organisation of subsidised theatre into regional, touring and national is:

> obviously a hierarchy. The NT and the RSC form the centre, and transitory and homeless touring groups the outer "fringe". In between, subtly competing for relative centrality, then come the Royal Court, the big-city reps, the London club theatres, and the more established touring companies. This concentric arrangement functions as a sort of promotional ladder, each group recruiting writers, directors, actors and occasionally

entire companies who have succeeded on the rung below. One progresses, as it were, from a merely local or sectional audience in the direction of the national stage where one will be addressing, not just the neighbourhood, the region, the avant-garde, or the constituency defined by political or ethnic identity, but *the public*. The "national" theatre audience – this is the most ideologically forceful sense of the category – is taken to be an unconditional one: not anyone in particular, but everybody in general.[29]

Of particular interest here is the concept of the "promotional ladder" and the way in which certain groups have become part of the "national" theatre by being commissioned or hosted by the national companies of the National Theatre and the Royal Shakespeare theatre or by forming an association with one of the *de facto* "national" venues such as the Barbican and the Lowry. Inevitably, what's missing from the following discussion of these groups is an appreciation of their work as performers, a consequence of assessing them against funding priorities rather than on the experience of seeing them. The danger of this approach is that it gives the impression that these groups cynically pursued an agenda allied to funding priorities. This is not the point I'm trying to make. These observations are based on my judgements about why they have been successful in attracting and maintaining funding, rather than whether they made conscious decisions to work in a way that would attract it. It seems equally plausible, given the continuing changes of direction the Arts Council has taken over the period of its existence, that the success of these companies could have shaped Arts Council policies.[30]

Cheek by Jowl – from national to international

Cheek by Jowl's mission is to present classical plays in a fresh and innovative way. Their repertoire is an eclectic one ranging from the first professional production of Racine's *Andromache* in English to *The Three Sisters* in Russian and encompassing Shakespeare and musical theatre on the way. They are one of the few companies founded in the 1980s to have retained their founders, designer Nick Ormerod and director (and writer) Declan Donnellan, and their public funding. Their ten year anniversary in 1991 was marked by a book, written by Simon Reade, exploring the company's history, working practices and phenomenal success. In the preface to the book, critic Michael Ratcliffe charts his passion for the company:

> I followed them out of London whenever possible, to Shrewsbury, Winchester, Chichester, Basildon and Kings Lynn, because Cheek by Jowl

is a national company and audiences from compact communities, palmed off with the second rate for so long, are now expecting nothing but the best.[31]

By the time he wrote this in 1991, Cheek by Jowl were already a major international force, no longer touring to the likes of Shrewsbury and Basildon for a few nights, but spending weeks at the Almeida, Donmar Warehouse and other key London venues. After a sabbatical, and a period based in Russia, they returned to the UK in 2005 as an associate company at the Barbican. In 2006 they received an Arts Council grant of £900,000 for three years to present six productions, three in English and three in Russian. These shows are presented at the Barbican and have also toured to the Lowry, Warwick Arts Centre and several other regional venues. The productions also tour abroad with funds from the British Council. This section examines the company's history and considers the reasons for its continuing success both artistically and commercially.

The company began working on the small-scale touring circuit in 1981, after being spotted by Ruth Marks, then assistant director of touring at the Arts Council, at the Edinburgh Festival. Marks encouraged them to apply for an Arts Council grant, explained how to put together a tour (ring venues up and persuade them to take the show) and advised them to team up with an arts promoter to produce their first play. Although Donnellan and Ormerod were dissatisfied with their first experience of a promoter, they heeded the spirit of Marks' advice and soon approached Barbara Matthews to be their Administrator after she sent them a fan letter. Matthews had worked for the National Student Drama Theatre Company, subsequently set up a company with two friends and had postgraduate qualification in Arts Administration. The combination of the three of them, their passion for the work of the company and their mutual trust ensured the steady foundation and growth of the company. Donnellan and Ormerod gave Matthews complete control of the administrative and financial operations, freeing themselves to focus on the creative output. As Matthews noted in 1991:

> If I say to Declan and Nick "We can't afford it", then they accept it. They don't ask: "Why? Prove it to us. Are you sure?", because they know I only say what I mean.[32]

It might seem strange to attribute the continued success of the company to its decision to employ a professional administrator from the word go, but the Arts Council's archive is littered with correspondence between companies and ACGB staff reminding them of the need for returns, completed paperwork, proper acknowledgement of the ACGB support – and many of these companies no longer survive. Cheek by Jowl demonstrated to its funders time and time again, that it could be trusted with public monies, whether from ACGB or the British Council. It must be one of the only theatre companies to have an appendix of its anniversary publication dedicated to explaining its happy relationship with the Arts Council, and the quality of its work was a useful benchmark for the Council when demonstrating to the government and to other companies what could be achieved on a tight budget. Even before its breakthrough 1986 season of *Vanity Fair* and *Pericles* (given a season at the Donmar Warehouse by Nica Burns), Graham Devlin had identified them as a standout company "establishing a style that is genuinely popular and can expand or contract to fit a space without compromising the integrity of the production".[33] He also recognised their ambition to produce on a larger scale, recommending that greater financial commitment from the Council would allow their ambition to flourish and concluding that:

> Cheek by Jowl have achieved a high national profile over the last two years. The quality of direction and performance in their shows, their distinctive style and their choice of texts makes them one of the very few companies who can bridge the gap between the Theatre Royal circuit and that made up of arts centres and informal venues.[34]

Unusually, the Arts Council acted on Devlin's recommendation (more often than not, reports would be commissioned, endorsed by the artform or touring panel, only to have their budgets slashed at a higher level), and the company were adopted as annual clients in 1987-88 having received several large grants from the various funds implemented in the wake of the *Cork Report*. The appendix "Cheek by Jowl's Arts Council History" is striking in its apparent ignorance of the extent to which it checked all the Council's tick boxes. Recording the first annual grant of £105,000 to tour small-scale venues, Reade also notes:

> In addition, a project grant of an extra £25,000 was made available for an eight week, middle scale tour of Macbeth (a co-production with York Theatre Royal), the Arts Council acknowledging Cheek by Jowl's potential and ambitions to move to a middle scale touring circuit. This middle scale touring money was made available through a development fund, even though Cheek by Jowl didn't actually fall into any of the Arts Council's priority areas.[35]

In fact, they fell into many of them: they were producing high quality productions of classical plays, they were providing much needed middle-scale touring provision, their international focus meant that they could be claimed as part of "the Great British Success story" and they ran an ensemble company so were providing training to young actors as well as retaining those in the middle range. If ever a company had been designed to answer the Drama panel's touring prayers, it was Cheek by Jowl. Little wonder then, that Barbara Matthews subsequently went on to become director of Theatre Strategy at Arts Council England while Ormerod and Donnellan were invited to work in the National Theatre (demonstrating the "promotional ladder" principle) and establish their own company in Russia.

Complicité – negotiating disciplinary boundaries and national borders

Like Cheek by Jowl, Complicité have always had an eye on international horizons. Originally named Theatre de Complicité because they planned to base themselves in France, the company was established in 1983 by Simon McBurney, Annabel Arden and Marcello Magni, all of whom had trained at the LeCoq school and with other mime practitioners in Europe. Their work is influenced and inspired by practitioners across artforms and nations including Pina Bausch, Shostakovich, Nitin Sawney, Tadeusz Kantor, Marukami, Jun'ichiro Tanizaki, Ionesco and Beckett. Their productions tour internationally, with an international cast, through the British Council and their work now appears in the UK in a select number of venues: the Barbican, National Theatre, Warwick Arts Centre and in 2009, in the West End.[36] The focus of their work is physical and visual (rather than textual) devised performance, although most of their work takes a text as its basis. Like all other companies discussed in this section, Complicité have retained their core creative focus in Simon McBurney, have a large and loose set of associates (including the co-founders), and a devoted audience.

The company were originally funded through the Dance department as one of the Council's mime clients, and began as a small-scale touring operation. Their early work used European mime and clowning traditions to explore quintessentially English themes, e.g. *Put It On Your Head* (1983) showed the English at their most awkward at the seaside and *Please, Please, Please* (1986) which focussed on a dysfunctional family Christmas. They were also beneficiaries of the *Cork Report* which recognised the outstanding work being done by mime companies and suggested that they should be transferred to the Drama department. In 1987/88 they featured in Anthony Thorncroft's *Financial Times* piece on

"Business and the Arts", which was reprinted in the Arts Council's *Annual Review*. Thorncroft praised them for an exemplary piece of sponsorship (making such a great marriage between venue and sponsor):

> Beck's Bier is one company that has used sponsorship to fulfil very specific marketing objectives with its support for the mime group Theatre de Complicité. The group performs mainly in pub theatres, bringing Beck's into direct contact with the independent-minded drinker who enjoys alternative comedy with his alternative beer[37]

Thorncroft's inability to fix the company's style (mime and/or alternative comedy) is interestingly at odds with the ease with which he can fix the style of the beer. It also foreshadows the success that stand-up comedy was to have in forging lucrative sponsorship deals with drinks companies (e.g, the Perrier Awards). Securing the sponsorship was a shrewd move on Complicité's part, not only in terms of the revenue brought in by the sponsor, but because it also demonstrated to the Arts Council that they were willing to follow its new directive about seeking partnership funding from business. The next year their grant doubled from £35,000 to £70,000. By 1998 their grant had been at a standstill for five years (along with many other companies), yet they continued to produce with a range of national and international co-producers. Shepherd and Womack's notion of the promotional ladder is again of relevance here as the company moved from the Institute of Contemporary Arts, the Almeida to the National Theatre, the Barbican and the West End.

As the technical and spatial requirements of their work continue to grow, their British touring circuit has diminished, presumably for reasons of space and cost, rather than indifference to their work, which is guaranteed an audience (they are currently one of the companies set by the National Curriculum for Drama). The "Information for Venues" section of their website highlights the spatial and financial challenges many regional theatres might have in booking the company:

> **Touring**
> There is no regular touring schedule and the gaps between tours vary. It is not always possible to see a show before booking it. We try to book the tours ten to twelve months in advance.
> The company tends to travel with large sets and a lot of technical equipment. The number of actors varies from seven to 20. The number of technicians is usually 10. There are usually two administrative staff on the road.

Venue requirements
The minimum stage area is rarely less than 12m x 12m. Because we use a lot of projection we often require an unusually deep stage, up to 18m. Fixed points may be needed for flying sets and/or performers. Open air venues are not usually suitable. It is nearly always necessary for the set to cross the iron / fire curtain.

Performances
A standard fit-up schedule would be two days for the fit-up followed by two days for technical rehearsal with a performance on the evening of the fourth day. The minimum number of performances is two but a minimum of three is preferable. We never perform a matinee on the first or last performance day. We strike and get out directly after the final performance.

Financial matters
Fee rates are show specific and available on request to the Producer. For international touring in addition to the fee, promoters are required to cover the cost of:
Recce visit by the production manager plus one other member of the team;
Freight transportation and freight insurance;
Contribution to cost of technical equipment hired from the UK;
Surtitle system where necessary;
Music and image usage rights;
Writer's royalty where appropriate;
International return flights for company members and local transport where necessary;
Accommodation in minimum 3* rated single hotel rooms;
Per diems in local currency equivalent to the sterling rate requested by the company where necessary;
Visas and work permits where necessary.[38]

These requirements demonstrate one of the problems that the Arts Council has struggled with for the whole of its existence: to create innovative and excellent work is time consuming, resource hungry and expensive. This has not proved a barrier to Complicité's success thanks to the company's shrewd marketing (some of their productions are available as commercial DVDs; their website contains a wealth of information about the company's methods and productions for the students, researchers and critics who write about them). But it does pose a problem for the Arts Council if they are placed in a position of funding companies who can only produce their work in a small number of locations inaccessible to large sections of the UK.

Kneehigh – from local to national

Kneehigh are another example of a long-running company with a long-serving creative team. Founded in Cornwall in 1980 by Mike Shepherd, they began, in Shepherd's words, as a company for children and their families "but we soon found ourselves creating challenging, accessible and anarchic theatre for a diverse local and national audience".[39] The company have created around 80 shows since their inception and have a strong local following, often touring productions around the South West as well as running simultaneous productions across the country, and increasingly around the world. The company is still funded by Arts Council England, South West but is now a familiar name nationally thanks to an increasing number of co-productions with theatres large and small, ranging from the NT and RSC to Battersea Arts Centre and Hall for Cornwall. They rose to national prominence with a production of Nick Darke's *The Riot* in 1999 – the result of a London show of another of Darke's plays *The King of Prussia* (1996) which Trevor Nunn saw and subsequently invited them to the NT. The company had worked with Darke (also a Cornishman with a long history of writing for the local area) as associate writer on a number of shows prior to this, but their relationship didn't survive long after *The Riot* (also their first co-production, this time with Plymouth Theatre Royal). What did survive was their commitment to engaging with the local area in terms of folklore, landscape and audience

Like Cheek by Jowl and Complicité Kneehigh has a USP, a brand, that makes their work popular with audiences and funding bodies alike. Many of their shows began life outdoors in site specific locations (*Tristan and Iseult*, for example, was performed at Restormel Castle and the Minack Theatre in Cornwall before going to the NT); the cast work together as an ensemble for a long period before the show opens (and in many cases return to work with the company on a regular basis); and there is company style which combines physical robustness with live music and songs, and they still practise a kind of rough theatre. One company member describes how:

> We used to joke about the "Kneehigh school of pointing, shouting and running": if in doubt, fill the space, and make a noise. Emma has added a lot of the elements that we always wanted to have there: the darkness, the stillness'.[40]

They hit many Arts Council benchmarks: touring, accessibility, working with children and the local community, co-producing with regional reps, even their physical style is a plus with a Council which is placing increasing emphasis on non-textual work. Like Cheek by Jowl, they seem tailor-made for the current funding emphases. Their national, and increasingly international, exposure has provided them with a growing fanbase, and box-office clout, and is making increasing demands on the company. In 2008 while *Brief Encounter* was touring the country, then running in the West End, then touring again, they were also producing *Don John* with the RSC and reviving *Rapunzel*. For some, their move to a national and international platform is seen as a betrayal of their local roots, for others, particularly theatre journalists and commentators, it is proof of the power of regional theatre. In an interview last year, Shepherd commented that "people like to think of us as a parochial company, just working within our community in Cornwall. [...] But we're too ambitious for that. We want to travel the world."[41] This ambition is already a reality, they already receive British Council funding and their website boasts that:

> Over 120,000 people have seen a Kneehigh production in the past year: nearly 6,000 saw *Rapunzel* in New York, 8,000 saw *Cymbeline* in Brazil, 40,000 saw *A Matter of Life and Death* at the National Theatre and – so far – over 20,000 have seen *Brief Encounter* in the West End.[42]

At the time of writing, the company are also fundraising for their own "nomadic venue", The Asylum, a tent which can be configured in five different ways and pitched in a day on any surface: "truly modern in its conception and yet inspired by ancient building methods and rooted in the idea of circus, troubadour and folk traditions".[43] This will give the company's operation even greater flexibility, allowing them to continue serving rural communities as well as metropolitan areas, and thereby help them to achieve a greater range of targets set by national and local funding bodies.

Eastern Angles – local plays for local people

Eastern Angles represent the other aspect of touring provision that received special attention in the *Cork Report* and subsequent Arts Council initiatives: rural touring. The company, in common with the others discussed here, was founded in the early 1980s, and for similar reasons: lack of drama provision and lack of jobs. Ivan Cutting, one of the founders and artistic director, describes the company's background as:

> Five actors looking for work about 28 years ago, me being a fan of Peter Cheeseman's documentary theatre approach, a gap in the market in this area, keen funding bodies and sheer bloody persistence.[44]

Cutting's enthusiasm for Cheeseman's work at the Victoria Theatre provides a useful context for the work of Eastern Angles. Based at the Sir John Mills Theatre in Ipswich, the company stage new writing and adaptations with an East Anglian focus, and tour them to local venues of all sizes from school and village halls to theatres and arts centres. They also perform site specific pieces at locations all over East Anglia, most recently, *We Didn't Mean to Go to Sea* at Ipswich Dock in 2009. The company first received funding from Suffolk County Council and Eastern Arts in 1983 and currently receives funding from Arts Council England East, Suffolk County Council, Norfolk County Council, Essex County Council, South Norfolk District Council, Mid Suffolk District Council, Babergh District Council, Suffolk Coastal District Council, Kings Lynn & West Norfolk District Council, Waveney District Council, St Edmundsbury Borough Council and the East of England Development Agency. That's a lot of sources for not very much money. In an interview in Whatsonstage.com Cutting described the company's funding as:

> about 40 per cent Arts Council East funding, 40 per cent earned income and 20 per cent other stuff. Not bad for a small-scale touring company. We're pretty entrepreneurial, doing our own Christmas show, hiring our venues and seating and also being self-promoting in the small market towns we visit.[45]

They are widely held up as a model of excellence for rural touring, make a relatively high proportion of earned income and work closely with their closest regional theatre, the New Wolsey in Ipswich, in other words, they fulfil a lot of ACE's criteria, so it came as something of a surprise when, in 2007, Arts Council East threatened to halve the company's subsidy, on the grounds that they:

> serve a limited geographic area, have not widened our touring networks and are, therefore, "sub-regional", and that we have not used their investment to lever additional funds, restricting our ability to develop.[46]

The notion of sub-regional is an intriguing one: surely the whole point of a local touring company is that it is sub-regional: that it serves the local area, rather than a wider community? If ACE was judging them by the same standards as it uses for national touring companies, then Eastern Angles was inevitably going to be found wanting. The company have taken work to the Edinburgh Fringe Festival and transferred a show to London, but that is not their purpose: they exist to provide theatre on local themes for a local audience. In this respect they appear to address two of the priority areas set out in the Council's *National Policy for Theatre in England*:

> theatre must engage with audiences and artists from a broader, more diverse range of backgrounds. It must connect with people who have been excluded, including those living in rural communities.

> we will also encourage the unique local voice of theatre that combines quality with the edge that comes from making work in, and for, a particular community. Theatre companies and agencies should provide a meaningful contribution to the life of the community in which they exist.[47]

One of the other priority areas of the policy is "to develop work of an international quality" and encourage "more international collaboration".[48] It is not difficult to imagine which audience, the international one or the local one, is more lucrative for the companies and the Council in terms of economic impact.

In the end, ACE did not cut Eastern Angles' grant, instead, accompanying the grant allocations of regularly funded organisations in the Eastern region, it notes that "our investment will assist Eastern Angles to increase its artistic impact and extend its reach to new audiences". Subsequently, and presumably mindful of ACE's stipulations, they produced *Getting Here*, a promenade piece set in a bar in the merchant quarter of Ipswich which examined the experiences of migrant workers from Poland, Portugal and the Caribbean, and acted as a host venue for the New Wolsey's *Pulse*, a fringe festival which provides "a platform for the development and presentation of work by regional, British and international artists of vision, nurturing artistic ambition and excellence across a range of artforms"[49]. Eastern Angles may be at a critical point in their history. They could move Kneehigh-like from local engagement and collaborations with their regional theatre to collaborations with national companies and a shot at a greater and more comprehensive funding package, or they can continue to pursue their own, sub-regional, course and continue to seek funding from an array of funding bodies.

Conclusion

At the beginning of the 1980s, where this chapter began, the companies discussed above were small-scale and "alternative", now their practice represents the mainstream. Many of these longstanding companies - Shared Experience, Forced Entertainment and Sphinx, as well as the companies discussed above - have avoided the problems of their building-based peers, particularly in the regions; and they enjoy a much wider level of critical appreciation than those peers. Their product is a more successful commodity in an era of turbo capitalism because it is essentially cosmopolitan in focus and approach. Eastern Angles has the cosmopolitan approach, but its focus is resolutely local. If the franchising of megamusicals around the world is McTheatre, the higher echelons of the touring promotional ladder operate more like a meal cooked by a celebrity chef. It offers a recognisable brand, a hand-crafted and a high quality product using quality ingredients delivered to a discerning audience, but available anywhere if you have the money to pay for it.[50] I don't mean this in a critical way, it's a product that public and funders alike approve of and enjoy, but it is the brand which makes it marketable around the world. They now address, in Shepherd and Womack's terms, *"the public"*, rather than an audience defined by region or political, sexual or ethnic identity. This is manifestly not the case for Eastern Angles, or for regional producing theatres who have access to lesser levels of funding. How and whether the Arts Council and its clients resolve this conundrum remains to be seen.

Notes

[1] Patricia Hollis, *Jennie Lee: A Life* (Oxford: Oxford University Press, 1997), 276
[2] See, for example, Nadine Holdsworth (1997), Baz Kershaw (1993), Maria di Cenzo (1996). What caused many of these touring companies to fold was not just a lack of Arts Council funds, but also the shrinking budgets of their other funders, sometimes Manpower Services Commission, sometimes Youth Opportunities Programmes or other, locally funded schemes.
[3] Richard Eyre and Nicholas Wright, *Changing Stages. A View of British Theatre in the Twentieth Century*, (London: Bloomsbury, 2001), 284.
[4] *Annual Report* 1984/85.
[5] See ACGB/99/54.
[6] See ACGB/38/36.
[7] *The Theatre Today in England and Wales. The Report of the Arts Council Theatre Enquiry*, Arts Council of Great Britain, 1970, p.18. (A copy can be found in ACGB/38/36. Folder 23 of 33).
[8] None of these companies are still in operation.
[9] Of course this is not the complete picture. As discussed by several other contributors to this volume, one of the factors which had crippled regional producing theatres was the emphasis on parity funding (Arts Council money matched by local authority money) at a time when many local and metropolitan councils had their own grants cut and many other pressing calls on their budgets.
[10] See ACGB/96/104 1 of 6 for more information on the development of the Grid system. Also see Baz Kershaw's 'Building an Unstable Pyramid: the Fragmentation

of Alternative Theatre', *New Theatre Quarterly* IX No.36 (1993) for a critique of the system as a means of widening access.

[11] *Theatre IS For All*, Arts Council of Great Britiain, 1986, 67.
[12] Ibid. 22.
[13] Ibid. 22.
[14] Ibid. 98.
[15] The *Cork Report* also recommended that regional theatres take their productions on tour, but this rarely happened, although regional theatres occasionally made money from transferring productions into London.
[16] *Keeping the Show on the Road. Touring theatre in Britain in 1985*, 1985, 16.
[17] *Cork Report*, 26.
[18] Ibid. 26.
[19] 'The Arts Council Touring Franchise and Political Theatre after 1986', Ian Brown, Robert Brannen and Douglas Brown, *New Theatre Quarterly* XVI. No.4 (2000), 385.
[20] *Annual Report* 1986/87.
[21] Ibid.
[22] Ian Brown notes that the panel could draw on the advice of a wide range of senior staff in making their recommendations to the Council.
[23] *Annual Report* 1988/89.
[24] John Myerscough, *The Economic Importance of the Arts in Britain* (London: Policy Studies Institute,1988), 3.
[25] *A Great British Success Story. An invitation to invest in the arts.* ACGB 1985.
[26] Dominic Shellard,*The Economic Impact of UK Theatre* (London: ACE, 2004), 4.
[27] Bill McDonnell and Dominic Shellard *Social Impact Study of UK Theatre* (London: ACE,2006), 30.
[28] The designation of national companies in the regions was also a result of the *Cork Report*.
[29] Simon Shepherd and Peter Womack, *English Drama. A Cultural History* (Oxford: Blackwell, 1996), 311-12.
[30] The relationship between subsidy, policy and practice in British theatre, and the extent to which practitioners have shaped policy is the subject of the AHRC-funded 'Giving a Voice to the Nation': the Arts Council of Great Britain & the Development of Theatre & Performance in Britain 1945-1995.', currently being undertaken by the V&A and the University of Reading.
[31] Michael Ratcliffe, Foreword to Simon Reade's *Cheek by Jowl. Ten Years of Celebration* (Bath: Absolute Classics), 1991, 7.
[32] Matthews quoted in Reade, 19.
[33] Graham Devlin, *Keeping the Show on the Road. Touring theatre in Britain in 1985*, 10.
[34] Ibid. 20.
[35] Reade, 120.
[36] See Jen Harvie's *Staging the UK* (Manchester: Manchester University Press, 2005) for an excellent summary of the way in which Complicité's production

Mnemonic was critiqued for claiming a universal dimension to human experiences, 138-146.
[37] "Business and the Arts. A special report by Antony Thorncroft", *Annual Report* 1988/89, 31.
[38] 'About Us, Information for Promoters and Venues', www.complicite.org/about/booking-touring.html, accessed 1 August 2009.
[39] 'Introduction', www.kneehigh.co.uk/about-us/an_introduction.php, (accessed 1 August 2009).
[40] Maddy Costa, 'Troupe Therapy', 1 Decemeber 2008 www.guardianunlimited.co.uk/stage/dec/01/kneehigh-theatre-cornwall-maddy-costa, (accessed 3/08/09).
[41] Maddy Costa, 'Troupe Therapy', 1 Decemeber 2008 www.guardianunlimited.co.uk/stage/dec/01/kneehigh-theatre-cornwall-maddy-costa, (accessed 3/08/09).
[42] 'Statistics', www.kneehigh.co.uk/about-us/statistics.php, (accessed 1/8/09).
[43] 'The Asylum', www.kneehigh.co.uk/shows-and-projects/the-Asylum.php, (accessed 1/8/09).
[44] 'Ivan Cutting on Eastern Angles', www.whatsonestage.com/interviews/theatre/southeast/E8831247 06548/Ivan+Cutting+on+Eastern+Angles.html, (accessed 3/8/09).
[45] 'Ivan Cutting on Eastern Angles', www.whatsonestage.com/interviews/theatre/southeast/E8831247 06548/Ivan+Cutting+on+Eastern+Angles.html, (accessed 3/8/09).
[46] 'ACE slashes Eastern Angles grant by half', www.thestage.co.uk/news/newsstory.php/19235/ace-slashes-eastern-angles-grant-by-half', (accessed 6/8/09).
[47] ACE, *National Policy for Theatre in England*, (London: ACE, 2000).
[48] 'Our regularly funded organisations', www.artscouncil.org.uk/downloads/rfoeast.08.pdf (accessed 6/8/09).
[49] www.wolseytheatre.co.uk/173/pulse/pulse.html.
[50] See Dan Rebellato 2006 and 2009 for a discussion of McTheatre.

CHAPTER SIX

OPENING UP THE GARDEN: A COMPARISON OF STRATEGIES FOR DEVELOPING INTERCULTURAL ACCESS TO THEATRE IN BIRMINGHAM AND NOTTINGHAM

CLAIRE COCHRANE

It is apt for my purposes that the image of "the glory of the garden" should be taken from Rudyard Kipling's poem. Kipling, the mediator of the experience of empire from the subaltern perspective and author of such memorable lines as "you're a better man than I am Gungha Din", embodied, it seems to me, so much of the ambivalence of white colonial attitudes – the recognition of shared human values and potential brotherhood with the subjugated other—which masked an ineffable belief in white moral and intellectual superiority.[1] This ambivalence, I would suggest, has continued to characterise relations between the leaders of the British arts establishment and successive generations of Black British and British Asian artists who have attempted to achieve viable individual careers and collective enterprises over the past forty years or so.

2006 marked the thirtieth anniversary of Naseem Khan's seminal 1976 report *The Arts Britain Ignores* which was the first authoritative statement on the unacknowledged institutional racism which had led to a chronic lack of resources and support structures for the arts in minority ethnic communities.[2] There was some response in the form of the now defunct Minority Arts Advisory Service (MAAS) but only desultory effects. Eight years later *The Glory of the Garden* flagged up the development of Black and Asian arts as an aim but without any firm strategy as to how that might be achieved. Indeed there was a proposal to cut revenue funding to Temba (founded in 1970) leaving only Black Theatre Co-operative (now NITRO) and Tara Arts with regular support. In 2001 at the Eclipse

Conference held at the Nottingham Playhouse to discuss institutional racism in theatre, the black actor and director Tyrone Huggins described his memory of the *Glory of the Garden* moment: "a terrible thing happened, driven by political will and the ignorant presumption of the arts funding system that it knew what it was doing". For him the effect was the collapse of the small-scale touring that he knew and depended upon as an artist.[3]

I have argued elsewhere that a turning point of some sort was reached in the aftermath of the interracial violence which broke out in the autumn of 1985 in Brixton and Peckham in London, Toxteth in Liverpool and in Handsworth in Birmingham.[4] In Birmingham, the report into what was subsequently dubbed the Handsworth rebellion, commissioned by the West Midlands County Council, revealed deplorable levels of systematic racism in the city which extended far beyond crude street-level discrimination to include a range of institutions, employers and bureaucratic agencies city-wide.[5] Nationwide, and for the steadily increasing numbers of new British citizens who were the product of Britain's former imperial ascendancy, Kipling's assertion that "Our England is a garden that is full of stately views" would have seemed a bitter joke. When, in February 1986, an Arts and Ethnic Minorities Action Plan was launched by the Arts Council, references to a national context of "grave social and cultural problems" make it clear that the recent urban violence had functioned as a timely wake-up call.[6]

For the regional theatres which were either, like Birmingham Rep or Liverpool Playhouse, the venerable survivors of the early twentieth century repertory movement, or had developed as civic theatres in the post-Second World War climate of state and municipal funding linked to building development, such as Nottingham Playhouse and the Coventry Belgrade, the challenge was very great. Not only were they permanently cash-strapped, no more so than in the high noon of Thatcherism when they were constantly exhorted to formulate artistic policy based on strong business principles, but via the funding bodies' strategic objectives, directors also had to consider ways of achieving successful educational and wider community outreach *and* maintain an ambitious, innovative artistic vision. Typically many of the major towns and cities outside London only have one building-based, subsidised producing theatre. If that has to be seen to represent all the different constituencies of interest in the urban environment which it serves, then it is not surprising that the historical record almost invariably lurches between heroic idealism and economic pragmatism. This is certainly the case with Birmingham Rep and Nottingham Playhouse whose attempts to "open up the garden" to Black British and British Asian artists and audiences I want to discuss.

Birmingham Rep became, after the Liverpool Playhouse ceased trading in 1998, the longest surviving of the repertory theatres established at the beginning of the twentieth century. Much of its fame was based on a glamorous past which had seen the launch of the careers of such future luminaries as Laurence Olivier, Ralph Richardson, Peter Brook, Albert Finney and Derek Jacobi. In 1971 the company made a difficult transition to a new, much larger building with a spatially very challenging main auditorium which was frequently impossible to fill. By *The Glory of the Garden* year it had already survived two damaging periods of financial collapse. Under the subsequent leadership of two artistic directors: John Adams (1987-1992) and Bill Alexander (1993-2000) very determined attempts were made to extend audience outreach, especially to minority ethnic communities, and to employ Black and Asian artists. Adams in particular was a pioneer of so-called "colour blind", or integrated, casting. Despite significant artistic achievement, however, the directorates of both ended in professional trauma again largely for economic reasons. [7]

The two men who came in to turn the company around, Jonathan Church as artistic director, and Stuart Rogers as executive director, both had previous connections with Nottingham Playhouse, Rogers as Administrative Director and Church as an associate director. When the riot emanating from the local Sikh community protesting against the Rep's production of Gurpreet Kaur Bhatti's *Behzti* hit the headlines just before Christmas 2005, Rogers and Church had to weather the media storm. Not only did their management ensure that other new British Asian plays could be staged undisturbed in their studio theatre (The Door) in the spring, but most importantly the Rep's main stage commitment to their partnership with Nottingham Playhouse and the New Wolsey Theatre in Ipswich on the Eclipse Theatre production of Roy Williams' *Little Sweet Thing*, was a success for black artists and black audiences. [8]

Nottingham Playhouse, established in 1948, and installed in its present purpose-built theatre in 1963, is decades younger than the Rep. However the two theatres shared in their origins the same ideological and aesthetic goals rooted in early modernism and the problematic "top-down" attitude which tended to encourage coterie audiences. Like the Rep, Nottingham Playhouse "grew" future stars like Judi Dench, Ian McKellen and Zoe Wanamaker. Under successive artistic directors John Neville (1963-68), Stuart Burge (1968-73) and most prominently Richard Eyre (1973-78) who premièred the work of Howard Brenton, David Hare and Trevor

Griffiths, the Playhouse effectively had the status of a regional "pre-national" theatre.[9]

So, like Birmingham, Nottingham provided local theatre aficionados with abundant golden memories. But this was not helpful in creating new audiences from communities hitherto cut off from access to the cultural mainstream because of general socio-economic factors, or indeed "other" non-white cultural heritage. Also Nottingham was not immune to financial crisis. In 1989 the then artistic director Kenneth Alan Taylor had to explain that the Playhouse was "still on a sticky wicket" as it faced the challenge of clearing a large deficit over the following three years. Even programming popular crowd-pleasers like *Hello Dolly, Oliver!* and *Stepping Out* had to fulfil audience expectations of high-quality and costly production values.[10] Indeed Taylor's most enduring legacy to the theatre is a succession of traditional Christmas pantomimes—twenty five to date—all written by him and until comparatively recently starring himself as the Dame—which are vital to filling the theatre's coffers.

The differences in the demographic profile of the two cities are worth noting. Birmingham, while nothing like as huge as London, just about hangs on to its title as Britain's second city with a population at the 2001 census of 977,099. 30% was categorised as non-white as opposed to a national average of 10%, and at present Birmingham is vying with Manchester and Leicester to become in the next decade the first minority-ethnic majority city. In a reversal of the earlier post-Second World War trend, the greater proportion (20%) is of South Asian origin, while 6% is Black or Black British with Black-Caribbeans in the majority.[11] In contrast the total population of Nottinghamshire was reckoned to be 748,510 and the urban areas are predictably more diverse than the extensive rural hinterland. In Nottingham itself, 84.9% of 266,988 was categorised as white. The statistics for the non-white communities again show Asian-heritage people are in the majority (6.49%) but the gap in numbers between them and the African/Caribbean-heritage communities (4.34) is not so great.[12] Like Birmingham, Nottingham has areas of deprivation associated with minority communities. The Lenton, Forest and Radford wards have higher than average numbers of non-white people and it is here that the highest levels of deprivation are to be found.[13] There have been high-profile black citizens in Nottingham, but there is also a history of violence. Nottingham shared in the nationwide flare-up of urban interracial trouble in 1981. In 1958, what has been described as "one of Britain's most bitter and ugliest racial conflicts" broke out and escalated into fighting involving about 1500 people.[14] This in turn provoked further reprisals which resulted in some 4000 whites fighting amongst themselves.

In recent years black on black gang-related crime has been a contributory factor to Nottingham's reputation as the gun capital of the UK—a dubious accolade which civic leaders have battled to reject. [15]

This context and others like it replicated in other cities, places producing theatres in a double-bind. The process of "colouring up" artistic policy involves offering opportunities to ambitious non-white British artists who have grown to expect the same range of artistic challenges enjoyed by their white peers. But it also means focusing resources on the kind of low-profile, almost invisible community-oriented work that subsidised theatres have been increasingly compelled to undertake as a condition of subsidy. This began as far back as the late 1960s with Arts Council initiatives to encourage audience-building, extra-curricular activity with young people.[16]

At the Rep in 1972, the Birmingham Youth Theatre, run by two local teachers who daily encountered the children of migrant families, was invited to use the new Studio Theatre as a performance base. It was a relationship which was to continue until the mid-1980s. Much of the work was devised and increasingly attracted young people from the African and Asian-heritage communities. It was out of this company that actors like Adrian Lester and Joe Dixon emerged and the playwright Nirjay Mahindru.[17] At Nottingham Playhouse in 1973 Richard Eyre's future wife, Sue Birtwhistle, was appointed to lead Roundabout, a Theatre in Education Company which had its own premises, transport, and at that time a staff of sixteen funded from the main Arts Council grant and from earnings for services to the local authorities. [18]

There was no question, given Nottingham's city and county-wide demographic, of the work which included main stage Christmas shows for children, focusing intensively on the needs of minority groups. However as time went by individual productions took on themes such as Vietnamese child refugees and British children sent to farm schools and children's homes in former colonial territories. In 1983 Trevor Griffiths' *Oi for England* about organised racism was staged, while in 1988 *No Longer Kids* was a devised piece which compared young people's aspirations in Soweto with their British counterparts. In a trend which began in the mid-1980s and which was paralleled at Birmingham Rep, these small-scale productions increasingly integrated white and non-white actors. In Birmingham in 1989, Gwenda Hughes who initiated touring productions suitable for all-age community audiences, directed Lisa Evans' *Stamping, Shouting and Singing Home* about an all-black family of women in 1950s' America. Plays were presented in schools and community centres and given a short run in the Rep's Studio.[19]

Studios, however, can be a mixed blessing. Opportunities open up for more challenging or innovative work for small audiences which are deemed not viable on main stages, but can also drain creativity (and financial resources) away from the big spaces. In periods of crisis, they go dark in desperate attempts to concentrate all efforts on saving the core business. This has been the history of Birmingham Rep's small theatre, although in recent years it has been able to maintain The Door, as it is now known, as a venue for home-produced and toured-in new writing. The Writers Attachment Scheme has permitted the nurturing of a series of new plays including Gurpreet Kaur Bhatti's *Behsharam (Shameless)* in 2001 and then in 2005, *Behzti (Dishonour).* [20] Nottingham, without the benefit of a designated in-house studio, has never had the luxury of maintaining consistent programming policies for small-scale productions, although there is a strong record of new work development. In the 1980s and 90s the Ustinov Room (originally the Siddons Room), could function as an alternative performance space. Also there has been an off-site "studio" presence mainly in Shakespeare Street in what is now the Waverley Studio Theatre at Nottingham Trent University. Currently the Playhouse's rehearsal space, the Playroom, is being transformed into a studio theatre and educational workshop venue.

However it was in the access to small performance spaces provided by regional theatres that the London-based Black and Asian companies forged their relationships with the mainstream, albeit for limited audiences. Birmingham Rep first went into co-production with a professional black company in 1985 when Temba presented Nigel Moffat's *Mama Decembra*, followed a year later by a co-production of Tunde Ikoli's version of Gorky's *The Lower Depths* with Foco Novo. Thereafter visiting companies included Tara Arts, Staunch Poets and Players and Black Theatre Co-operative. Indeed John Adams' policy to focus all his energies on the main stage led to specific attempts to fill the studio with guest companies, including the occasional locally-based group struggling to establish itself such as Third Dimension led by Barbadian-born black director and writer (and Roy Williams' mentor) Don Kinch.[21]

In the mid-1990s an attempt to develop a long-term relationship with a British Asian Company began in earnest. Tamasha staged *A Shaft of Sunlight* by Abhijat Joshi in 1994, followed in 1995 by *A Yearning*, a version of Lorca's *Yerma* relocated to Birmingham's Punjabi community. Ayub Khan Din's *East is East* received its first performance by the company in the studio in 1996. The relationship continued to include *A Tainted Dawn* (1997), the joyously successful *Fourteen Songs, Two Weddings and a Funeral* (1998) and *Balti Kings* (1999) all written by the joint directors of Tamasha, Sudha Bhuchar and Kristine Landon-Smith. By that point the local Asian audience had grown to the point where the limited tickets available rapidly sold out. At the same time there were other Asian or Black new plays either developed for community touring like Ray Grewal's *My Dad's Corner Shop* (2000) or Roy Williams' *The Gift* set in Jamaica and premièred in the same year. [22]

Artistic success, or even worthy, if flawed, experiment, in a small space reduces risk, but brings with it another kind of invisibility and a potential for complacency. The question of how the "new British" descendants of migrant families are to become an integral part of the cultural mainstream as represented by the major producing theatres, has much deeper implications about the health of a genuinely multi-cultural society. Colour- blind casting, especially for classic Western drama, is controversial for a number of reasons not least because it can be constructed as another form of colonial incorporation. But the policy puts non-white British actors on big stages, in roles, which they can claim quite reasonably to be part of their heritage. As a result regional theatre audiences have gradually become accustomed to what can be an invigorating defamiliarisation of the traditional repertoire.

In 1987 John Adams kicked off his directorate at the Rep by including black actors in the cast of *The School for Scandal* and provided copious programme notes about the black presence in Britain going back to the eighteenth century. Within a year both Nottingham and Birmingham had staged productions of *A Midsummer Night's Dream* with black actors. In Birmingham where the policy was much more rigorously applied, there were some squawks of outrage when sturdy northern characters in twentieth century classics like *When We Are Married* and *Hobson's Choice*, which Gwenda Hughes directed in 1990 and 1992, were played by black actors. Under Bill Alexander, the casting became less consciously provocative. But in Nottingham in 2005 a decision made by Roundabout director Andrew Breakwell to cast three actors of different ethnicity as the endearing Waterbury siblings in a new stage adaptation of *The Railway Children* gave a well-loved story of the Edwardian era a visible reminder of the global reach of the imperial family.[23]

What failed in Birmingham were attempts to entice audiences from the local Black and Asian communities. Even major artistic successes like Gwenda Hughes' 1994 Olivier-award winning production of the musical *Once On This Island* set in the Caribbean with an all-black cast; and Indhu Rubasingham's energetically multi-cultural adaptation of *The Ramayana* which transferred to the National Theatre in 2000, did not reach their target audiences. The effects of decades of feeling unwelcome and alien in white-filled auditoria were not to be overturned so easily. Big questions had to be asked about the extent to which structural factors in the organisation of theatre had blocked access to the levels of policy-making and control which would enable genuinely collaborative strategies for artistic autonomy and audience development to be put in place.[24]

Eclipse, the conference held at Nottingham Playhouse in June 2001, set out to ask those questions specifically focusing on the need to develop strategies to combat racism in theatre. The driving force behind the initiative was the Executive Director, Venu Dhupa who had been born in Nairobi to an Asian family. When she was appointed in Nottingham in 1997 she was the first non-white woman to hold such a senior post in a regional theatre. Increasingly through the 1990s the idea of using two directors more or less equal in status, but with complementary skills in artistic delivery and business management, had been deployed in theatres as a means of combining artistic effectiveness with entrepreneurial flair. Dhupu succeeded Ruth Mackenzie (1990-97) who had worked with first Pip Broughton and then Martin Duncan as Artistic Directors to create a dynamic international profile for the Playhouse. The company embarked on major European tours, and visiting artists and companies had included Peter Brook, Robert Lepage, The Maly Theatre from St. Petersburg, the Ghana Dance Ensemble and the Market Theatre of Johannesburg. Mackenzie also saved Roundabout, albeit with some ruthless restructuring, as it came under threat from funding bodies.[25]

From 1994 the Playhouse also received financial support from the Arts Council's Black Regional Initiative in Theatre (BRIT) and core staff included a named producer for African or African/Caribbean Arts. African and Asian-heritage music and dance were regularly programmed and there were some attempts at main stage co-production with black companies. In 1997 Roy Shell's *Iced* about the nature of addiction was co-produced with Black Theatre Co-operative. In 2000 there was the first co-production with London's Tricycle Theatre of James Baldwin's *The Amen Corner.* In the run-up to the Eclipse conference, the Shakespeare Street studio theatre presented two tough-minded plays by black writers dealing with racism and exploitation: Colin Prescod's *Banged Up* and Steven Luckie's *Junior's Story.* By then Stuart Brown and Paul Moore were sharing the job of African-Caribbean Arts Producer.

The Eclipse Conference report which was subsequently published by the Arts Council, contained some grim statistics which extended to the conference delegates themselves. The aim of the conference was to target senior managements and resist attempts by theatres to send more junior representatives from education or marketing departments. Of the 125 theatres invited less than a quarter attended with the vast majority not responding at all. There was no representation from the national companies.[26] However the geographical spread of delegates from theatres as far apart as Lancaster and Bolton, Salisbury, Colchester, Brighton and Cornwall did offer some hope of a legacy of nationwide change.

The Arts Council statistics for 1999-2000 on employment in English theatre showed that out of 2,009 staff employed only 80 (4%) were African Caribbean and Asian. The Boyden Report found that only 16 out of 463 board members (3.5) of English producing theatres were African Caribbean and Asian. An ACE survey of 19 arts organisations found that out of 2,900 staff, 177 were of African, Caribbean, Asian or Chinese and of those, unsurprisingly, 100 were working in catering or front of house areas. One was employed at senior management level.[27] Throughout the two days of discussion and presentation, delegate after delegate while acknowledging much that was positive about recent developments, also had horror stories to relate about their own experience.

It would have been clear that there were no straightforward solution to the institutional racism in theatre which the conference had so amply demonstrated. However the convergence of artists, managers and funding agents, especially Isabel Hawson, ACE Senior Officer for Theatre whose remit included BRIT, with Dhupa now working with Giles Croft as the Playhouse Artistic Director, created the necessary impetus which led to the establishment of Eclipse Theatre. Stephanie Sirr took over from Dhupa as Chief Executive in late 2001, but with Croft continued the negotiation to form the Eclipse consortium of Nottingham Playhouse, Bristol Old Vic and the New Wolsey Theatre in Ipswich to enable middle scale touring of black theatre. The plan to present three plays, a classic, an adaptation and a new play over three years with the Eclipse administrative base moving to the theatre responsible for the annual production, suffered a temporary glitch when Bristol Old Vic, entering its own phase of financial crisis, pulled out to be replaced by Birmingham Rep. The London-born black writer, director and producer Steven Luckie was appointed as the Eclipse Theatre producer responsible for managing the relationship between the key agents and institutions; identifying appropriate artistic product and the artists capable of high-quality delivery.[28]

The most visible result was four productions between 2003 and 2006: the 1956 early classic of black theatre *Moon on a Rainbow Shawl* by Trinidadian Errol John, Brecht's *Mother Courage and her Children* in a new adaptation set in West Africa by Oladipo Agboluaje (2004), the Eclipse- commissioned new play by Roy Williams *Little Sweet Thing* (2005) directed by Michael Buffong, and Mustapha Matura's revision of his adaptation of Chekhov's *Three Sisters* set in Trinidad. With each costing in the region of £250,000, the production values were high, each capable of filling the main stages of each venue, including the notoriously cavernous Birmingham Rep stage. By the time Luckie announced his departure in 2006 to pursue other interests, Eclipse Theatre was a well-oiled machine, which crucially did not *lose* the venues any money while building up valuable cultural capital.[29]

The most predictable criticism when *Rainbow Shawl* was produced was that the project lacked contemporary relevance. Where were the new black plays? Luckie was clear that lessons needed to be learnt from past failures; that Eclipse was not aimed at black-only audiences and that the plays, while offering new perspectives, retained an essential congruence with the ethos of each chosen venue. There was a conscious decision to develop *Little Sweet Thing* over three years to give time for appropriate marketing. From the beginning there was a strong element of commercial acumen which benefited from the commitment of each of the Executive Directors, including Sarah Holmes in Ipswich, and the judicious use of a London-based commercial agency, Jane Morgan Associates.

A significant number of the participating artists are effectively members of a black theatre aristocracy. Paulette Randall who directed *Rainbow Shawl* and *Three Sisters* was Artistic Director of Talawa Theatre Company, and in the six months before *Three Sisters* had directed August Wilson's *Gem of the Ocean* at the Tricycle and *What's in The Cat*, a play by Eclipse new writer Linda Brogan at the Contact in Manchester. Josette Bushell-Mingo who directed *Mother Courage*, has played leading roles with the RSC and the National Theatre, starred in Disney's stage production of *The Lion King*, and is also Director of the black-led arts festival PUSH. Veteran black actors whose memories of British theatre stretch back to the 1950s, have included Ram John Holder who played Old Mac in *Rainbow Shawl*, and Carmen Munroe who played Mother Courage. Mustapha Matura in Tyrone Huggins' words is a "grandee" of black theatre whose *Welcome Home Jacko* (1979) was another early classic play about Black British identity.

Little Sweet Thing, set on a mixed London housing estate, used predominantly young black and white actors to play out a story of blighted teenaged lives which would have been very familiar in Nottingham and Birmingham. The patience taken to market Williams' work paid off. The first night in Ipswich played to a full house with substantial numbers of enthusiastic young people in the audience. In Birmingham, the Saturday night performance I attended, had one of the largest black audiences I had ever seen in the main auditorium. The run at the Hampstead Theatre in

London attracted audiences who were 60% non-white. [30]Eclipse had come a long way from the *Rainbow Shawl* first night in Nottingham when the theatre "was dispiritingly cold and empty" and the audience mainly white. The touring circuit increased from five venues for *Rainbow Shawl* to ten for *Little Sweet Thing* and *Three Sisters* when the locations included Bracknell, Eastbourne, and Truro.

The less visible achievements of Eclipse, the Writer's Lab and the Outreach productions, were directly associated with Luckie's tenure. The 2003-4 plan for the Writer's Lab was to select ten new playwrights, match them with five theatres—those in the consortium plus West Yorkshire Theatre and the Contact in Manchester – and encourage new writing for bigger spaces. Paulette Randall and the British Asian director Indhu Rubasingham were part of the development process as well as Lab Mentors, Kully Thiarai, formerly co-Artistic Director at the Leicester Haymarket Theatre and Esther Richardson, Regional Literary Manager for the East Midlands. The Outreach productions – 30 minute two-handers by Juliet Gilkes and Dystin Johnson linked to the Eclipse shows and specifically targeted at young audiences—were all directed by Luckie. [31]

This is a very brief account of a complex, ambitious project which under the new Eclipse Producer, Gemma Emmanuel-Waterton, then entered a new, arguably more controversial phase, less focused on high-profile production. At the time of writing the administrative base has moved from Nottingham to Ipswich. In the meantime at the Playhouse, Bea Udeh, born in London to Nigerian parents and now a BBC Radio Nottingham presenter, is also the BRIT Programme Producer. She works at the grass roots of theatre arts provision for African, Caribbean and dual-heritage young people and adults. In October 2005 the workshops in drama, storytelling, poetry, hip-hop and some elements of black history offered within the framework of the Nubian All-Stars youth theatre for 10-16 year olds culminated in *Lyrically Deep* an evening of "edu-tainment" performed by young people. Since 2004 African-heritage women have facilitated *Femmes Fantastic*, one day events which have included seminars, workshops, food and stand-up comedy. In the midst of the prevailing worries about disaffection and gun crime which leads to so much emphasis on issue-based theatre, simply having fun along with developing a stronger "sense of self" is also a priority.[32] Giles Croft commissioned a full treatment of the Nubian All-Stars play *Misrepresented People* given a rehearsed reading in 2006. There was an aim to develop a fuller integration of youth theatre provision. [33]

So is everything in the garden now coming up roses? Well despite everything which has been achieved since 1984, the answer has to be no, not quite, not yet. There is still the problem of the prevailing whiteness of patterns of employment within the organisational structures of building-based theatres. Immediately before the Glory of the Garden conference, an enquiry at Birmingham Rep elicited the information that there were just eight permanent, non-white members of staff across the different departments. Two senior appointments had been made. One was for the post of Associate Producer with particular responsibility for British minority ethnic programming, and the other was for Marketing Director. In June 2007 in Nottingham, Bea Udeh confessed to feeling isolated amongst an otherwise white management. At that time there were only two non-white members of the core staff and none at senior level since the departure of the former Production Manager to become General Manager at Talawa.

The Eclipse Conference was hosted by Nottingham because, to quote Andrew Breakwell, "we were leading in the field of Race Equality and were concerned to raise questions with our peers". Many of those questions remain unanswered. Why, for example is it considered difficult to secure staff who have the "appropriate qualifications, experience and desire to work in a major regional theatre"? Why is it difficult despite training and placement programmes to recruit black males in particular? Giles Croft, himself, provided a kind of answer in his statement quoted in the Eclipse Conference report: "The problem arises when your own position is under threat and when you are having to look at the way you think...We are nearly all people who find it much easier to spend time with people who feel like us. It is only by stopping and thinking is this right? that we can really begin to change."[34]

Notes

[1] The poem 'Gungha Din' first appeared in Rudyard Kipling, *Barrack-room ballads and other verses* (London Methuen, 1892); 'The Glory of the Garden' first appeared in C.R.L.Fletcher and Rudyard Kipling, *A History of England* (Oxford: Clarendon Press, 1911).

[2] Naseem Khan, *The Arts Britain Ignores: the arts of the ethnic minorities in Britain* (London: The Commission for Racial Equality, 1976).

[3] Arts Council of England, *Eclipse Developing strategies to combat racism in theatre* (London: The Arts Council of England, 2002), 45.

[4] Claire Cochrane, "'A Local Habitation and a Name": The Development of Black and Asian Theatre in Birmingham since the 1970s', in Dimple Godiwala (ed), *Alternatives within the Mainstream British Black and Asian Theatres* (Newcastle: Cambridge Scholars Press, 2006), 153-173; 162-3.

[5] Ibid.

[6] Ibid.
[7] See Claire Cochrane, *The Birmingham Rep: A City's Theatre 1962-2002* (Birmingham: Sir Barry Jackson Trust, 2003).
[8] Cochrane 2006, 151-2, 170-1; see also Anthony Frost, 'Drama in the Age of *Kalyug*: *Behzti* and Sikh self-censorship' in Godiwala, *Alternatives Within the Mainstream*, 205-225.
[9] John Bailey, *A Theatre For All Seasons: Nottingham Playhouse The First Thirty Years 1948-1978* (Stroud: Alan Sutton Publishing/Nottingham Playhouse, 1994) See also the section on Nottingham Playhouse in Anthony Jackson '1958-1983: Six Reps in Focus' in George Rowell and Anthony Jackson *The Repertory Movement A History of Regional Theatre in Britain* (Cambridge: Cambridge University Press, 1984) 131-9.
[10] Kenneth Alan Taylor interviewed in *Nottingham Evening Post*, 9 June 1989.
[11] Cochrane 2006, 158.
[12] Area: Nottingham (Local Authority) Ethnic Group (KS06) Period: Apr01, *Neighbourhood Statistics* http://www.neighbourhood.statistics.gov.uk/dissemination/LeadTableView.do?a=3&b..., (accessed 16 August 2007).
[13] Nottingham Health Action Zone (HAZ) final evaluation report for Changing Faces and Places (CFP). http://www.tin.nhs.uk/EasySite/lib/serveDocument.asp?doc=410&pgid=1248, (accessed 16 August 2007).
[14] Denise Amos, 'Black community history' in *Nottinghamshire Heritage Gateway*, http://www.Thorotonsociety.org.uk/gateway/people/blackcommunity/blackcommunity, (accessed 8 August 2007).
[15] ' Gun Crime' in *Inside Out*, BBC East Midlands, Monday 31 January 2005, http://www.bbc.co.uk/insideout/eastmidlands/series7/gun_crime.shtml, (accessed 17 August 2007).
[16] Cochrane 2003, 36-7.
[17] Cochrane 2006, 161.
[18] 'Roundabout History' on Nottingham Playhouse website http://www.nottinghamplayhouse.co.uk/index.cfm/page/content.index.cfm/cid/38/navid/32/parentid/1.
[19] Cochrane 2006, 132-3.
[20] Ibid. 206.
[21] Cochrane 2006, 164-5.
[22] Full details of key co-productions in Cochrane 2006.
[23] Andrew Breakwell, Director of Roundabout, Nottingham Playhouse answering questions by email, 3 October 2007.
[24] Cochrane 2006, 168.
[25] I am grateful to Derek Graham and the Marketing and Development Department at Nottingham Playhouse for access to production records and press clippings; also for the help of Kitty Parker, the Roundabout Administrator.
[26] *Eclipse*, 5.

[27] Ibid. 9.
[28] For a full account of the background and record of Eclipse Theatre see Tyrone Huggins, *The Eclipse Theatre Story* (London: Arts Council England, 2006).
[29] Conversation with Steven Luckie, 13 August 2007.
[30] Elizabeth Barry and William Boles, 'Beyond Victimhood: Agency and Identity in the Theatre of Roy Williams' in Godiwala, *Alternatives Within the Mainstream*, pp.295-313, 310.
[31] *The Eclipse Theatre Story,* 42-3.
[32] Conversation with Bea Udeh, 14 June 2007.
[33] Andrew Breakwell, 3 October 2007.
[34] *Eclipse,* 7.

I am also grateful for the assistance of Selene Burn, Community Engagement Officer at Birmingham Rep. In May 2009 Bea Udeh representing Nottingham Playhouse accepted the Eclipse Award presented by the Theatrical Management Association for the theatre's outstanding contribution to cultural diversity. Udeh's brainchild PIECES, a BRIT showcase of black comedy, subtitled 'Unity Through Comedy' was singled out for particular praise.

Chapter Seven

I Bet Nicholas Hytner Doesn't Have To Do This: The Role of the Artistic Director in the Regions

Gwenda Hughes

I thought the thing I could most usefully do for this book was try to give you some sense of what running a regional repertory theatre was like. This isn't really an essay. It's more a sort of collage of memos and post-it notes and although some of the correspondence has been edited in the interests of clarity and brevity, the letters are genuine.

Dear Miss Hughes,
My wife and I much enjoyed last night's performance. However, I always look forward to the opportunity of enjoying an ice cream in the interval and was disappointed to find that you are no longer selling Walls ice cream, but have replaced it with what, to my mind is a much inferior brand. I hope that you will consider returning to Walls in the future.

Yours sincerely, Mr. P.K.

Dear Ms Hughes,
I am writing to complain because I couldn't buy a ticket for last Saturday's performance. I am a regular theatregoer and have supported the Vic since the old days in Hartshill Road.

On arrival at the Box Office at a quarter past seven, I was told that there were no seats available for the performance because they had all been sold. I think you should keep 100 tickets for each performance and not sell them in advance, in case people like myself want to come on the night.

Yours sincerely, B.N. (Mrs)

Memo to Artistic Director and General Manager from Front of House

As he was leaving the car park, a man reversed his car into one of the trees. He believes we should pay for the damage as we own the tree. I said I thought it was unlikely that we would, but expect a call from him anyway.

The New Vic Theatre has 600 seats.

We do a lot of work and a lot of different work. We produce nine professional productions a year: new, old, classic, contemporary, with music, without music, the silly and the serious, the illuminating and the celebratory. We have a concert programme: dance, jazz, folk, poetry, comedy, choirs and a popular line in elderly showbiz turns reminiscing with a bloke on piano.

Dear Mrs B.N.
I am sorry you were unable to see the show on Saturday. Your suggestion that we keep back tickets is one that I doubt we will be able to take up. Box office income is a significant part of our overall income and it seems to me it would be foolish to refuse a ticket to someone who definitely wants to buy one, in favour of someone who might or might not. I suggest that in the future you consider booking in advance to avoid another disappointment.

Yours Sincerely,
Gwenda Hughes
Artistic Director

We only go dark for essential maintenance for two to three weeks around April. We have two departments, New Vic Education and New Vic Borderlines whose work accounts for a third of the "engagements" we have with the public each year. Education works within the formal education system and Borderlines with young offenders, children and adults with learning disabilities, children under seven and their families.

Dear Madam,
On Wednesday we had tickets for the show. We decided to have a meal at the Vic before going into the performance. Sadly, our relaxing meal was ruined by a conversation at one of the tables in the restaurant. We believe it was a humanist society, a group of ten whose conversation dominated the whole restaurant area. Living wills, humanist funerals etc. being the main agenda of business from 6.10pm until 7.20pm. My husband and I will not be dining again at the Vic and may look elsewhere for future theatre events. Up to this point we have been great supporters of the Vic.

Yours sincerely, F.H. (Mrs)

Dear Mrs F.H.
I was sorry to hear that your evening was spoiled by conversations taking place in the restaurant area. It is not our policy to hire out the public restaurant area to private groups, but neither can we regulate the conversations that members of the public engage in whilst there. I can appreciate that you found the subject of their conversation upsetting, but hope you will appreciate that I could not attempt to stipulate to members of the public what they could or couldn't discuss in the public areas of the building. I hope you will reconsider your decision about dining at the Vic again in the future.

Yours Sincerely,
Gwenda Hughes
Artistic Director

Talking about the regions as we are today, Stoke on Trent is about as regional as it gets. To the side of the M6, it is stuck in between the temptations of Manchester and Birmingham. It's difficult to get across, because the big ring road isn't a ring road at all, but a cut-straight-through-the-middle road. Without a car, it's quite hard to leave after 9.30 at night.
When you get off the train at Stoke station, you find that you aren't in, aren't even near, the city centre because Stoke Station is in Stoke, and Stoke on Trent city centre is in Hanley and you can see that, with the best will in the world, it's a not pretty place.

Stoke on Trent is a made-up city: an artificial construct of six rival, fiercely independent towns: Fenton, Longton, Stoke, Hanley, Tunstall, Burslem.

On the edge of this reluctant family of squabbling siblings, in an urban wildlife garden, with a pond and tadpoles, is a beautiful, purpose built theatre-in-the-round. Its existence is due, largely, to the single-mindedness and determination of one person, Peter Cheeseman, the Director for over thirty years. If you build it they will come - a lovely, absurd act of faith and folly. And miraculously they do come, from North Staffordshire, Shropshire, Derbyshire, the Moorlands and beyond. Except of course, when they don't.

To whom it might concern,
I am writing in response to the standard of service at the coffee bar when I visited on the 9th June. There was a piece of eaten chewing gum on a carton of juice for sale, which several people commented on.

Dear Miss M.
I have looked into the matter of the piece of chewing gum that you referred to and think that what you may have seen was the glue used to attach the straw to the carton. Please be assured that we maintain hygiene to the highest standards.

Yours Sincerely,
Gwenda Hughes
Artistic Director

Memo to Artistic Director from General Manager
Re: complaint from D.R.

I received a phone call from D.R. who was the person named on the show report as leaving the performance of TRAVELS WITH MY AUNT on Monday. Ms. R was voicing a complaint that there was no proper scenery, although she had realised that this was a theatre-in- the-round, that a member of the cast had as she said an unpleasant stain on the crotch of his trousers, and she was extremely disappointed that there were only four cast members and they were all dressed in cream suits rather than dressed as the image in the brochure. I have passed on to wardrobe the laundering complaint, but they could find no such stain. I don't think there are any further outstanding issues.

Our turnover is two and a half million pounds. This includes funding from Arts Council, West Midlands, Newcastle under Lyme Borough Council, Staffordshire County Council and Stoke City Council. Our average wage is £17, 500.

When I started at the Vic I went to see the important people in the three local authorities to introduce myself. "What would you like to see change at the theatre?" I asked, to demonstrate what an open, friendly, altogether reasonable person I was. The response can be summarised thus: at the first they said, "the problem we have with the Vic is that they are always doing plays about miners. We want more proper, classical work"; at the second they said, "the problem we have at the Vic is that it's for posh people, the gin and tonic crowd. We want more things about ordinary people". And at the third, I asked the Mayor I think it was, "So what do you think about the Vic?' "You should do more snooker" was the reply.

Dear Madam,
My family have been to see the children's Christmas production at the New Vic for many years. All performances have been most enjoyable but our enjoyment of A CHRISTMAS CAROL was seriously marred by the fact that when booking to see the show I was not able to book the front row seats. Having been to the theatre for a while one becomes used to the seats

that one likes and we have found that the front row seats by Century Oils Door suit us best. I was told that in this production the front row seats were not being used. Imagine my disappointment on Saturday when I walked into the auditorium and saw that people were using the front seats. I have two boys and I particularly like them to sit at the front so that their field of vision is not minimised. We also like the fact that when sitting on the front one is nearer to the cast - indeed their clothes often waft you and for us, the children especially, this adds a certain amount of magic. Not being given the seats we really wanted very much upset me. Indeed it was the only occasion all year that my husband has accompanied us such are his work commitments at the weekend. Indeed I became quite shaky and tense which was picked up by the children. The happiness was taken from the afternoon. My husband and I were bothered on the journey home and the children were crying.

"The happiness was taken from the afternoon." I love words. My formative theatre years were spent in the TIE teams and socialist/ feminist companies and collectives of the 70's and early 80's. I am conditioned to talk of theatre workers, of our "industry", of actors or performers but never actresses. There is a whole raft of vocabulary designed to shift the perception of us, and our perception of ourselves, away from wafty flakes in dressing gowns, although a part of me has always been comfortable with being in show business, in the happiness business. I do miss the rather austere, obsessive rigour of our examination of language back then however: we are not girls or ladies, we are women; I am not queer, I am gay, but now I'm owning queer again; that character is a Native American not Indian; we are mixed race not half-caste and so on round and around.

Dear Mr K.C.
Thank you for your letter concerning your recent visit to see PERFECT DAYS. We are always disappointed when members of our audience don't enjoy a particular production.
I find it difficult to answer the specific points you make as I am a little unsure about the substance of your complaint. You say that there was no warning about what sort of play it was but I am at a loss to identify which aspects of the play required a 'warning". Try as I might, other than a little strong language I can find nothing in the play that could give offence.
Your letter mentions the Scottish accents and 'sexuality" and you say that you and your wife "are not that way inclined", although it is unclear as to whether this refers to the "sexuality" or being Scottish. I am reluctant to believe that you object to the play because one of the characters depicted is gay. Nor, I hope are you suggesting that we publish warnings if any of the characters in our productions are gay.

Yours Sincerely,
Gwenda Hughes
Artistic Director

Nowadays my mouth is full of words I wish weren't there. A foreign language that I find harsh and unattractive, but in which I have become fluent: slippage, exit strategy, RDA's, SRB's, blue sky thinking, additionality. Hmm. ADDITIONALITY!
"Hello, this is the New Vic Theatre... we were wondering if we could have some more money because we can certainly use it. Education and Borderlines are really overstretched, we need to replace the air conditioning and the wage levels aren't good. Rather poor in fact...Oh I see...yes I understand...additional...yes...The thing is, we're doing an awful lot at the moment, I'm not sure we could do much extra...we're already very tired...additionality ...yes...So we couldn't have some money to do what we're doing better or to pay people better? ...No... no...OK...Thank you anyway."

And there are other words that seem to me to have become untethered from their value: quality, innovation, access, diversity. Important, precious things certainly, but seemingly now more significant in their repetition than their meaning like a chant or mantra: nam yoho renge quyo, nam yoho renge quyo, Lord Jesus Christ have mercy upon me a miserable sinner, quality, innovation, access, diversity, quality, innovation, access, diversity.

What's to blame for this? An American corporate management-speak virus? New Labour, whose relationship with the language of truth and the truth of language has always, it appears, been flexible, a little slippery? They are culpable in so many other ways, why not in this? All I know is that it leaves me profoundly unsettled, but not clever enough to articulate why. Certainly, I feel (I cannot prove, but I feel) that since the latest restructuring the face of the Arts Council has turned away from us, the practitioners and artists, toward the shiny, sparkly lights of Westminster. I feel (I cannot prove, but I feel) that the Arts Council now might just as well be a department in the DCMS. It used to be a relationship that was committed, argumentative, sometimes constructive, sometimes not, with slammed doors and tears, and big hugs to make up, imperfect, infuriating but close nevertheless. Now we are distant, hardly ever meet up really; a letter at Christmas, a post card from the holiday, and an apology for forgetting the birthday. Our phone conversations are short and getting shorter, our discourse inert, lifeless like our words.

Quality *n*: Degree or level of excellence; characteristic; something that is special in a person or thing.

Innovation *n*: something newly introduced, such as a new method or device

Access *n*: the act of approaching or entering; the state or condition of being approachable; the right or privilege to approach, enter or make use of something; an attack of emotion.

Diversity *n*: the state or quality of being different or varied; a point of difference.

"The state or quality of being different." Please talk to us, the artists. Listen to us. We seek out and celebrate something that is special in a person or thing. We newly introduce ideas, thoughts, feelings and change in the people we engage with. We work hard at the state or condition of being approachable because we believe in the right or privilege to approach, enter or make use of our artistry, our craft, our building and resources. We have loads of attacks of emotion. And absolutely and entirely what we are about, what theatre is for, is to engender in people the state or quality of being different: to imagine beyond ourselves, to try on someone else's skin and walk around in it and begin to understand what it's like to be not-us. It's what we do. Listen to us. Talk to us.

> Dear Dr. S.
> I was saddened to receive your letter this morning. I am sorry that you and your wife were so disappointed by Northern Broadsides' production of RICHARD III.
>
> I am perplexed as to how I might answer your complaint about the use of northern accents in the production. I could argue that it was entirely valid to hear a variety of Lancashire and Yorkshire accents in a trilogy of plays entitled THE WARS OF THE ROSES. Certainly that would be as, if not more valid than your suggestion of London accents, because, you say, the plays were performed there and because it is the seat of government. However, I do not offer this argument since all the company's work is performed with northern accents because the use of a "northern voice" is the *raison d'etre* of the company, hence their name, Northern Broadsides. Barrie Rutter's distinctive approach to theatre is fuelled by his passion for language and his unceasing celebration of the richness and muscularity of the northern voice. It is what Barrie and the company are famed and celebrated for nationally and internationally.
>
> To be frank, your letter gives the impression, with its reference to Bolton Wanderers and its repetition of an old cliché, "By 'eck, I'll go to the foot of our stairs" that your objection is not to the use of a northern voice

speaking Shakespeare, but a northern working class voice doing so. In my opinion, the work of Shakespeare, or any great artist, is not "owned" by any one place, nation, culture or class. In so far as the work is owned by anyone or any thing, it is owned by the world in all its richness and infinite variety. Neither do I believe that there are "correct" and "incorrect" or "appropriate" and "inappropriate" voices for Shakespeare. There is Shakespeare, the world's playwright and there are people and their voices, also full of richness and infinite variety. The latter should not be excluded from exploring the former.

Yours Sincerely,
Gwenda Hughes
Artistic Director

Dear Barrie,
Please find enclosed a copy of a letter of complaint and my reply.

Yours Sincerely,
Gwenda Hughes
Artistic Director

Dear Gwenda,
Thank you for the copies. Your reply was very diplomatic. I would have just told him to fuck off.

Love Rutter

Extract from *The Glory of the Garden, a strategy for a decade, Arts Council of England 1984*:

We are not people who believe London knows best.

Extract from letter To Gerry Robinson,
ACE
Re: Restructuring and Prospectus For Change Document. 1999

I find the proposition that the new organisation, based in London, will have "a single authoritative voice" more than a little chilling. That and the suggested structure of a controlling centre of power with a second tier that will only be able to take "decisions delegated to them by Council and the New Executive Team" sits oddly with ACE's commitment to decentralisation. I do not doubt the sincerity of intention that the relationships between the Chief Executive and the Executive Team will be based on "respect and trust" but a hierarchy that relies only on good intentions of decency without formal checks and balances on the centre of power, embedded within the structure itself, is open to abuse when, as can happen, the respect and trust break down.

The new structure is predicated on a single authoritative voice being a good thing. Why? Shouldn't we be encouraging a plurality of authoritative voices as long as the relationships between those listening and those listened to, are clear and coherent? What happens when that single authoritative voice is wrong?

The replacement of the Regional Arts Boards by regional advisory boards, however "strong" represents a diminution of the power of the regional arts voice within the arts funding system. Long-standing accusations of "Londoncentricity" within ACE are a result of the lived experience of many of us who live and work outside the capital. With the best will in the world, I can not see how the removal of the RABs and the concentration of power in London will do anything but exacerbate the problem in spite of the declared commitment to continuing the process of decentralisation.

These days it is easy to take a cheap shot at any public document by accusing it of "spin". However the proposition that the new arrangements will "properly address democratic needs", makes me feel distinctly spinned at. I'm sure a system which makes the arts regions co-terminous with government planning regions makes neat, logical sense but does not necessarily address democratic needs any more than standing next to a musician on the bus will make one musical.

Yours sincerely,
Gwenda Hughes

Dear Sir,
Could you please let me know the dates and times of the performances of the Alan Ayckbourn play JOKING APART, due at your theatre this coming October.

Yours faithfully, A. W.

P.S. Have you noticed that your postcode ST5 could be interpreted thus: - 5 is the fifth letter of the alphabet, i.e. E so ST5 becomes STE short for Stephen.
OJG has the letters OJ. Turn to JO the start of Joseph.
So ST5 OJG = Stephen Joseph (Alan Ayckbourn's theatre in Scarborough)

I was on the Steering Committee for the Boyden Report that led to the Theatre Review, which led to some more money for some of us, for which we are extremely grateful. Two things in the Report have stayed with me:

that building based producing theatres are among the most over regulated businesses in the UK; that all those years of struggle and under-funding had left directors "not battle hardened, but battle weary". About a month after I wrote the following letter in Spring 2005, I told our Board of my intention to leave at the end of 2006. Not because I had another job, not because I don't respect, admire and care about the people I work with. I do beyond measure. I adore larking about a rehearsal room with actors. Unlike a lot of directors, I really, really like management. But I am indeed battle weary and need to lie down somewhere quiet for a little while.

Dear Mr. S,

>Your letter is without doubt, one of the most pleasant and polite letters of complaint I've ever had. I am saddened that you think we are just concerned with putting "bums on seats" through our programming. I also share your sadness at the death of Arthur Miller.

>I take the job of making the organisation financially stable very seriously, because it is public money we are spending and because I am responsible for the employment of over seventy employees. These are not louche, arty types like me who expect to have periods of unemployment because we work in the theatre and also expect to move to where the work is, but the cleaners, the caterers, the box office staff, the administrative staff, the carpenters, the costume makers. These are local people, many of whom have worked at the Vic for years. If the theatre closes, these jobs are lost. That is not something to be taken lightly. Neither is the loss of the ninety or so freelance contracts (actors, designers, choreographers, directors etc.) available here each year.

>I don't mean to be rude, but there is a kind of intellectual snobbery around the use of the dismissive phrase "bums on seats". What is wrong with wanting and trying to sell as many tickets as possible for work we have spent a long time creating? What is wrong with wanting as many people as possible to engage with a company that, after all, they are paying for through their taxes? Why is it an ignoble ambition to want a full theatre?

>It is a myth that putting "bums on seats" inevitably means "dumbing down". Last year was the best ever in the history of this building, with record sales for *Amadeus* and *To Kill a Mockingbird*, both works of serious intent and purpose. Even a new play *Once We Are Mothers*, hardly a laughter fest with its stories of grief, disability and the Bosnian war did creditably well at the box office.
>I don't think any theatre that has produced, among others, *Kiss Of The Spiderwoman, Top Girls, Broken Glass, Who's Afraid of Virginia Woolf, Blue Remembered Hills, Translations, Dealer's Choice, Privates on*

Parade, *The Duchess of Malfi*, *Sizwe Banzi is Dead* and three operas can be said to be going for easy, comfortable entertainment.

Of course I programme lighter material. This theatre is for everyone and that is a passionately held belief at the heart of our artistic policy. It is for committed playgoers like you and also for those who just fancy an occasional, diverting night out at something like *Stepping Out*. It is for the young offenders, the people with learning disabilities, the asylum seekers and others at the margins of our community that we work with through our Borderlines Programme. It is for those who saw *Broken Glass*, but equally for the school children that worked over the last six months on a Holocaust Memorial presentation, performed to a full house earlier this month.

Mr. S. your letter clearly came from the heart and so does this reply. I care deeply about theatre. After all I have worked in it for over thirty years now and believe me, no one goes into a career in subsidised theatre for the big bucks. I am writing as someone who slept with a handwritten letter from Arthur Miller under her pillow like a lovesick teenager a few years back, but we can't do *All My Sons* all the time.

Everybody at the New Vic has worked hard against some very difficult odds to make this a successful theatre. *Stepping Out* was enjoyed by hundreds of people and even if some of our plays are not to your taste, better that than a closed and empty building.

Yours Sincerely,
Gwenda Hughes
Artistic Director

I've been packing up my office and packing up, sentimentally, my memories: the asylum seekers who saw *Four Nights in Knaresborough* and for whom that story of four men trapped in a tower in a cold, damp, inhospitable, foreign country, surrounded by people who hate them, had particular meaning; the young girl who ran away from her foster home to the Vic because it represented for her a place of safety; the young offender sharing a cup of tea with the professional actor playing Billy in *Kes* and whose life might have been a model for the character; the elderly woman who thanked me after *The Kiss of the Spiderwoman* because she said it had profoundly altered her view of homosexuals and the volunteer who said, " the problem I have with you Gwenda is that when you talk about the Vic you don't sound like a director, you sound like a social worker."

If I were to write to Mr.S now, I think I'd write him a love letter. I'd write them all love letters: postcode man, the ice cream couple, stains on the trousers woman. Because I do love them and I'm grateful to them from the bottom of my heart, even the angry, the rude and the downright barmy, because they are the reason why we do what we do.

I'd apologise again to the wafting lady but I'd say that on balance I believe that for most people we've put more happiness into their afternoons and evenings than we've taken away.

One final thing: when I looked up quality in my dictionary the words that then follow are these: qualm *n.* misgiving, pang of conscience; quandary *n.* state of perplexity, difficult situation; quango *n.* administrative body with senior members appointed by the government. Quality, qualm, quandary, quango; that's not a bad description of what it's like to run a regional repertory theatre. It is also, however, a privilege and I shall miss it.

Chapter Eight

Salisbury Playhouse: Anatomy of a Theatre in Crisis[1]

Olivia Turnbull

Since its creation after the Second World War, the Salisbury Playhouse, originally known as the Arts Theatre, has played a vital and successful role in the small, rural community in the heart of Wessex. After the Arts Council pulled out of direct management of the theatre in 1951, a plea to the local community for greater support produced a thriving theatre that, by the beginning of the 1980s, boasted the highest regular attendance rates of any British regional theatre and operated a 100-seater studio theatre, a permanent Theatre-in-Education company, and a youth group alongside its main house productions. In 1995, however, a huge accumulated deficit and falling attendances saw the theatre on the brink of ruin and forced to go dark for a period of seven months. The following article investigates the issues at the heart of the Playhouse's decline, and relates the events to the ongoing problems endemic to many of the country's regional theatres during the Conservative administration.

> At a public meeting in December 1994, Bonnar-Keenlyside, the consultants called in to review the Playhouse's operations, revealed their findings in one brief sentence: 'Everything that could go wrong, went wrong.'[2]

At the time, the Playhouse was carrying an operational deficit of almost £300,000, something put down primarily as a consequence of long-term underfunding and plummeting box office revenue. However, this figure almost doubled when considered in terms of the accumulated deficit. Taking into account the problems of the dilapidated, twenty-year old building, untouched since its construction in 1976 and now deemed "unsafe" by surveyors, the total deficit was estimated as lying somewhere between £300,000 and £600,000.[3] Based on the consultants' recommendations, the Playhouse was closed for a period of seven months in order to make a saving of £100,000 in costs, revise existing operations and receive extensive refurbishment financed by Southern Arts and the Arts Council. The Playhouse's period of darkness witnessed the loss of fifty-eight jobs and the replacement of the entire board and executive.

Until the appointment of chief executive Deborah Paige in 1991, the official line was that the Salisbury Playhouse ran a very successful operation, claiming the highest attendance figures of any regional theatre then operating nationally, with houses averaging 84% capacity. The reality of the situation however, was somewhat different with attendance figures long showing signs of decline. The older end of the audience who had been committed theatregoers since the 1950s were literally dying off; others were becoming increasingly unhappy with the standards of production under David Horlock, the Playhouse's artistic director from 1982 to 1990.[4] Thanks however, to an antiquated and inefficient administrative system that was organized manually, lacked the involvement of a fully qualified accountant, and employed only a part-time bookkeeper, the discrepancy between attendance figures and financial capacity was potentially huge. Above all, such a discrepancy could be traced to the hefty number of complimentary tickets regularly given out to loyal patrons and friends of the staff, a situation not alleviated by deals that financially benefited large coach parties and those who bought into the subscription scheme more than they did the theatre. Unfortunately, the same system meant that the extent of the problems was impossible to substantiate. The lack of a computerized box office before 1991 for instance, meant an audience profile could not be built up from anything more than sporadic audience surveys compiled, on average, once every three years. Similarly, systematic statistical records were not kept. As such, the viability of the subscription scheme was never properly monitored or the number of comps given out in any one season noted.

Any attempts to improve this situation came up against the impenetrable force of the "one-man-show" conducted by David Horlock, true as much of the legacy he left following his sudden death in 1990 as during his tenure at the Playhouse. During Horlock's time as artistic director, his power was so absolute that even the board of directors were unable to get access to the books. In turn, his local popularity and the circumstances of his death in a car accident ensured that subsequent management was loathe to speak ill of his administration in anyway, including making public any problems that had begun at the theatre under his charge.[5] Even when problems began to spiral under Deborah Paige, it was believed speaking out would only make matters worse.[6] But this meant the problems inherited by his successor were not limited to a sizeable £125,000 operating deficit, but included the legacy he left in people's minds of the "good old days." When administrative, not to mention artistic, changes were subsequently made to the Playhouse system, they were inevitably therefore a hard sell to the local community. Ironically, given the problems caused by the inefficiency of the previous system, any improvements were greeted with hostility, and used to blacken the new management's reputation. Over the following years, they found themselves constantly compared unfavourably to David Horlock. While such circumstances were in many ways unique to Salisbury, in others they simply aggravated problems common to many of England's regional theatres during the Thatcher and Major years.

As with many regional theatres, at the heart of its troubles was the perennial issue of funding: Salisbury Playhouse blamed many of the problems that led to its closure on long-term low levels of subsidy. Since the mid-1980s, annual budgets were based on attendance figures, and as noted, these officially averaged 84%. These were the figures on which grants were allocated by the major funding bodies – the Arts Council (the Playhouse was devolved to the Southern Arts Board in 1992), Wiltshire County Council, and Salisbury District Council. Notwithstanding the vast discrepancy between official audiences and the income such figures should have generated, a history of good attendances translated into smaller grants, with the Playhouse widely perceived to be a victim of its own success. From 1984, total subsidies meant the Playhouse had been expected to earn in the region of 72 percent of its income, far less than theatres of comparable size, operation and catchment area.[7] And it was openly acknowledged by the Playhouse and funding bodies alike that this was not a case of particular generosity to other theatres.

If the Playhouse was a victim of its own success, its funding woes were added to by the changing policies of funding bodies trying to cope with new governmental directives and pressures during this period. The Arts Council's policy of parity funding, intended to force reluctant local authorities to pull their weight and provide more sustained support for local theatres, proved as big an albatross for Salisbury as it did for many of its compatriots. Throughout its lifetime, support from local authorities had never come near to matching central funding and had proved a serious source of tension between the funding partners. Always problematic, it became increasingly so after the Arts Council adopted parity funding as a formal policy in 1986 following the Cork Report. On three separate occasions during the 1980s, the Playhouse found their Arts Council grant frozen or in jeopardy as the central body attempted to pressure local authorities to bring their support up to equal levels.[8] In 1981, Arts Council provision accounted for 84% of the Playhouse's subsidy. Despite ongoing pleas for increased contributions from their partners, the following decade saw little improvement, and by 1991, combined local authority contributions amounted to only 37% of the Arts Council's. The difficult relationship between the various partners was not helped by a series of broken promises by the local authorities. In 1992, for instance, Wiltshire County Council had agreed to increase their contribution by £15,000 over two years, but as on numerous previous occasions, failed to do so. Rather, partly in response to the national recession, the County Council's grant was actually frozen. At the time of the Playhouse's closure in 1995, funding was still far from at parity levels, with local authorities collectively contributing over £120,000 less than Southern Arts. Taken on its own, as detailed more fully later, the fallout from such a disparity was extensive, consistently compromising forward planning and programming, and ensuring a constant stalemate in the Boardroom when any potential solutions were put forward to address the theatre's problems.

After years of failing to improve the issue of funding for the Playhouse, the Arts Council was finally relieved of its burden when it delegated responsibility for the theatre to Southern Arts Board in 1992. Publicly presented as part of the larger strategy of devolution of theatres to regional funding bodies more immediately invested in local theatres' operations and interests, in the case of the Playhouse, the move was widely interpreted as a case of passing the buck by an Arts Council beleaguered by client casualties and bad press. Certainly, the Playhouse's management held deep-seated reservations about any potential benefits, not least because while the Arts Council had a slush fund, Southern Arts had no flexibility in its budget whatsoever. And, in the middle of a recession, devolution inevitably coincided with a freeze on government spending on the arts. So as Arts Council grants to regional arts boards were frozen, so, in turn, were the grants made through the regional funding bodies to the theatres. In the financial years 1993/4 and 1994/5, the Playhouse thus received standstill funding not only from the County Council, but from Southern Arts, and the theatre's already inadequate subsidy was further devalued in real terms. With the increasing inadequacy of annual subsidies, the Playhouse had to rely ever more heavily on alternative ways of generating income to cover rising production costs. First amongst these was earned income from the box office, but as noted earlier, this had long been declining, and as a result of earlier changes made to accommodate problems caused by low levels of subsidy, by 1993, attendances had gone into freefall.

From the 1960s, when Local Authority support had become an increasing staple of regional theatre funding, the requirement for theatres to be all things to all masters had become an increasing burden. While the Arts Council had long emphasized quality programming and an adventurous artistic policy, local authorities were traditionally more interested in obvious returns for the local community in terms of educational and outreach programmes. Thus supporting a wide range of activities was a condition of funding, and with maintaining funding from one partner dependent on sustaining adequate support from the others, the pressure to keep all areas of the Playhouse's operation alive were heavy.

At the beginning of the 1990s, in addition to its main house productions, Salisbury Playhouse ran a studio theatre, the Salberg, a TIE department called Theatrescope, and an affiliated youth programme, Stage '65.[9] Following Deborah Paige's arrival in 1991, years of inefficient administration and a subsidy that did not allow the theatre to support all the activities it was expected to sustain, combined with escalating production costs to create a situation in which the theatre found it increasingly difficult to continue running the various activities at existing levels. The inherited deficit, which escalated to £125,000 during the period of confusion following David Horlock's death, meant that within six months of Deborah Paige's arrival, cuts had to be made.

The first area to be affected was the TIE department. Here, the traditional practice of taking productions out to schools was abandoned in favour of a reduced, more economical in-house programme which provided workshops at the Playhouse based around the current production in the main auditorium. Initially, the cuts to the TIE program were far less severe than at many other regional theatres, with the Playhouse only reducing Theatrescope rather than cutting it altogether. This did nothing to alleviate the huge outcry from the local community, however. In part, their outrage could be understood given such changes put the onus of bringing children to the theatre on the schools, something the 1988 Education Reform Act which left schools managing their own grants had made difficult. Entailing a loss of six of the eight jobs in the TIE department, the controversy surrounding the cuts was heightened by the fact that these staff had traditionally run the affiliated youth programme, Stage '65, which therefore also had to be restructured on a more modest level.

To say the cuts to Theatrescope and Stage '65 were badly received is an understatement, and the letters pages of the local *Salisbury Journal* were dominated by furious parents:

> Why do the children of Salisbury and district, who are tomorrow's audience, have to bear such a large part of the cuts?....The theatre is being short-sighted and shooting itself in the foot.[10]

The result was a mass boycott by those previously involved with the youth programme, particularly friends and relatives of the children affected who represented a substantial part of the Playhouse's regular audience. Consequently, while the reductions to the Young People's Theatre and TIE programmes initially cleared £80,000 of the Playhouse's deficit, the related falling revenue from the box office almost immediately meant that the deficit began to mount again.

Without question a significant influence, diminishing audiences were obviously not a consequence exclusively of such cuts. The decline in the box office was a gradual but consistent trend over two years, and while it coincided with the cuts to the youth and educational programmes, it was also aggravated by the delayed effects of the national recession. While necessitating a freeze on already inadequate grants, insult was added to injury when it also ensured a fall in commercial sponsorship and ticket sales. In something of a vicious circle, low levels of subsidy had forced the Playhouse to raise ticket prices at an annual rate of 10% since 1982. While noted as an ongoing problem in falling attendances, it became particularly serious when patrons were affected by the recession. Particularly badly affected was the subscription scheme. The Playhouse's success in selling seasonal passes had accounted for a substantial part of the theatre's high attendances over the previous decade, and the theatre was heavily reliant on the associated coach parties that brought people from regions as far away as Cheltenham and Oxford, and regularly packed the main house at matinees and weekends. During the recession, paying for individual tickets was considered less risky than paying for an entire season. With rising unemployment, a poor economy, and high inflation, "people were increasingly wary about handing over £60 at a time."[11] Problematic enough, many customers' feelings of apprehension intensified out of concern that were they to continue subscribing to the theatre, it might not be for the type of programme they wanted to see.

When Paige was initially brought in to the theatre from working on the London circuit, it was partly with the idea that she might improve artistic standards and provide a programme that was a little more adventurous than the Playhouse's traditional fare. While arguments subsequently raged over whether she ever actually tried to do this, nevertheless, there was mounting hostility from the Playhouse's older audience to the "sophisticated and avant-garde" programming she had supposedly introduced.[12] Accusations of "Kulture Vultures" were levelled at Paige and her management by members of a committed audience used to "a staple diet of Ben Travers, Agatha Christie, Kenneth Horne, Alan Ayckbourn, et al" - such playwrights had dominated the programmes of her predecessors, David Horlock, Roger Clissold, and Reggie Salberg, and had earned the Playhouse a reputation for "Strip, strip, hurray" and "proscenium curtains and box set" productions.[13] Criticisms of the Playhouse's supposed new artistic policy sat alongside complaints about the cuts to the youth and educational programmes dominated the local media:

> Experimental theatre should be abandoned. It is a total commercial and artistic waste of time....Playhouse-goers want productions which will lift their spirits, provide enjoyment and be fun. They don't want to be forced to understand the angst and despair of kitchen sink artists who belong in the kitchen or down the plughole.[14]

> We don't go to the theatre to be educated – we go to relax and be entertained.[15]

Despite such protests, Paige maintained there had been no deliberate change in artistic policy. Despite the Board of Directors' concern to be more adventurous, her plan had been "to continue more or less the same sort of programming policy, but to work on improving standards of direction, design and casting."[16] As such, where changes were made, they were less to the Playhouse's programming than in the production values of the dramas. Even this was limited. Examination of individual criticisms and interviews with Paige and Allanah Lucas, the administrative and development director, reveals that concern was only really connected to four main house productions: *Down and Out in Paris and London, The Europeans, Celestina* and *The Office Party,* the last three of which were all staged in the 1991/2 season. However, the fact that a mere four productions, staged over the course of two seasons during which time more than twenty plays were mounted, could cause such an outcry brings up the question of the limitations of artistic policy in English regional theatres during this period. Here, the sense of ownership and parochial attitudes often endemic to the old and loyal audiences militated against the possibility of trying anything different no matter what the Arts Council/Southern Arts might have said. As the Chair of the Board Nick Bourne, asserted at the time, "in the provinces, people resent change."[17]

In Salisbury, this problem was particularly acute with regard to the body of loyal theatregoers, whose profile was itself generating a certain amount of anxiety at the theatre even before Horlock's death. Audience profiles gathered by the Playhouse in 1992/3, using the newly-installed computerized system, revealed that almost 80% of the regular audience were over fifty years of age and from social class AB. Notwithstanding the decline in attendance figures, comparisons with surveys conducted sporadically over the previous decade showed there had been little change or development in the profile of the audience. Basically, Salisbury's audience had been dying off and the theatre had not developed a new one along the way. As such, on her appointment, Paige was encouraged to consider the need to attract and develop a new, younger audience alongside the existing, loyal patrons. Consequently, as she acknowledged, if there were any attempts to be more adventurous, they came primarily through her efforts to employ a more contemporary and varied style of repertory in an effort to attract a wider range of people.

Following the national move away from weekly repertory in the 1960s, limited finances and facilities have traditionally worked against the staging of audience-specific productions in Britain's regional theatres. Since the 1960s, the average run of a main house production in a provincial theatre has been three or four weeks. The increased dependence on earned income that began under Margaret Thatcher, combined with escalating production costs and low levels of subsidy, meant that consistent artistic success became increasingly important for regional theatres in the 1990s. Even one unpopular production could prove potentially fatal. In the case of the Playhouse, this was particularly true with regard to its older audience and the baggage of feelings they brought with them in regard to the theatre. As one such individual put it, "the Playhouse was built with massive donations from the public."[18]

The Playhouse's loyal audience had been largely responsible for creating the theatre after the Arts Council pulled out of direct management in 1951. Similarly, they had been involved in supporting it in the ensuing years, raising the capital for a new building in the 1970s that allowed the theatre to be moved from its original site in a converted chapel to its present location in the purpose-built venue near the centre of town. Inevitably, strong proprietorial feelings developed towards the Playhouse, which translated into very specific ideas of how it should be run and how much say the local community should have in those decisions:

> The audience wanted to return to something perceived as the good old days, and looked back as a way of going forward.[19]

> I say "our Playhouse" because it was built with subscriptions from many local theatre lovers and businesses, coupled with efforts from a number of dedicated people....The average age of theatergoers is well over 40 and

they remember the excellent performances in the past form the likes of Nancy Herod, Sonia Woolley, Lionel Guyatt and many others.[20]

For the Playhouse, the challenges posed by such strong feelings went far beyond a simple resistance to change or specific way of doing things. The local community's history of investment in the Playhouse translated into a belief that official decisions about the operations of the theatre, ranging from artistic policy to education and youth programmes, should be taken with specific, if not exclusive reference to them. Consequently, any alterations about which they were not directly consulted gave rise to feelings of alienation and exclusion, articulated in accusations of high-handed and tactless behaviour by senior management. As a representative comment from the *Salisbury Journal* says: "Miss Paige has shown a total disregard for the tastes of her audience."[21]

In practice, Paige's efforts to attract a specifically younger audience were only realized in one main house production. Unfortunately, as the consultants noted, "the problems began the summer *The Office Party* was staged and *Celestina* put on."[22] *The Office Party*, a modern comedy by John Godber, who at the time of the Playhouse production in 1992 was the fourth most performed playwright in Britain, was actually a huge popular success. Such was the drama's appeal that it actually broke box office records at the Playhouse, and on that occasion brought in the target younger audiences. But as Paige commented in hindsight, "it was possibly a little too contemporary," and "not homely enough" for the conservative, older audience.[23] For instance, it contained some strong language, which gave rise to numerous complaints published in the local paper protesting that it "was so full of four letter words, [it] was an embarrassment to those with female or young company."[24]

Taken exclusively, the damage might have been contained. However, what Paige conceded to be "an error in scheduling" meant that *The Office Party* was staged immediately before a received production of *Celestina*, a little-known Spanish Renaissance drama which was considered to be experimental because it was performed in modern dress, against a contemporary set using non-realism acting styles. The subject matter of the play also was highly sexual and called for some scenes of nudity. Ironically, given that many criticisms focused on the postmodern concept of a Renaissance play being performed against a modern setting, further complaints were raised by the use of Tudor English. This was variously described by spectators as "complete gibberish" and "gobbledy gook."

The departure from conservative styles of straightforward proscenium realism in two successive productions apparently gave credence to the suspicion that Paige was imposing an avant-garde, educational programme of productions that were not "what regular theatregoers want to see, but what the producers think is good for them."[25] Moreover, what was conceded as an error in scheduling also meant that these two productions were presented mid-season, the period which can traditionally determine the success of an entire season in a regional theatre, either by repairing any damage already incurred from unpopular productions and boosting sales for the remainder of the season, or vice versa. In this case, ticket sales dropped at an alarming rate as loyal patrons began to desert the Playhouse, despite a particularly safe repertory for the rest of the year.

If the safe repertory was not enough of a concession to persuade the traditional body of theatregoers to keep attending, neither was it conducive to developing the new, younger audiences first targeted by *The Office Party*. Any chance of sustaining this new group was immediately undermined by the simultaneous announcement that it would be necessary to cut the Playhouse's youth theatre activities.

Many of the complainants considered their protests were made in the interests of saving the theatre. While ignorant of many of the administrative challenges faced by senior management however, the vocal members of the local community were perhaps equally unaware of the damage they themselves were doing through such vociferous criticism. Of the voluble public outcry, Paige commented, "I regret that people feel able to criticize in the way they have done, which I think has ultimately been very destructive to the Playhouse."[26] This sentiment was echoed by the arts editor of the *Salisbury Journal*, where most such complaints were published:

> If [the Playhouse] closes, I will blame those "friends", whose strident criticism, the point of which I never could grasp, created a climate to turn off potential audiences.[27]

The devastating effects of such vocal grievances obviously were further detrimental but not limited to box office sales. Under these circumstances, the increasingly unpalatable working conditions characteristic of so many regional theatres during this period became so bad at Salisbury Playhouse that in 1994 the entire executive resigned in protest.[28] Although problems with internal management, particularly between the chief executive and the board, played an important role in this, both Paige and Lucas emphasized that external, often stinging personal criticism, which in the case of the artistic director ultimately resulted in calls for her resignation, created unbearable working conditions where management was practically blackmailed into submission. The situation saw the executive caught in an impossible position: in an attempt to appease the community and reduce the declining audience figures, Paige resorted back into the terrain of safe traditional repertory in the last season before the theatre's closure. But this was to the extent that the consultants criticized her for being "disproportionately affected by perceived public failures resulting in retrenchment,"[29] and it was offered that had Paige defined and continued with a definite new artistic style, she might have successfully developed a new audience, even if at the expense of the old one.

From the time of Paige's arrival in 1991 until the theatre's closure in 1995, criticism focused heavily on senior management. Accusations such as "[the Playhouse] has now suffered the sad decline inevitable when an arrogant management sets out to educate its customers, and by patronizing them cuts off their goodwill and its own revenue stream," made the possibility of doing a good job extremely difficult.[30] Nevertheless, a lack of diplomacy in the new management's handling of the changes did not help the situation, such that in their findings, the deemed the Playhouse's handling of public relations "to have been a failure."[31]

The need for senior management to ingratiate themselves with the local population is a vital part of the English regional theatre operation. One audience member at Salisbury Playhouse commented in 1994, "theatre is not a one-way business – it needs to build on a real support between community and theatre, and the more personal the relationship comes to be, the greater the success." [32] Such a sentiment has become increasingly important for the nation's regional theatres as many of the older traditions with which audiences can identify have gradually disappeared. The seasonal employment of a resident ensemble company provides a good example of one method that the country's regional theatres historically employed to allow the local community to feel more involved in the theatre's operations, but that by the 1980s had been typically phased out:

> When we had a resident company, if the play was a doubtful draw, a lot of people would go to see what Roger Hume, Stephanie Cole, Robert Frost, Christine Edmonds, or whoever their favourite was might be doing that week/month/production. In fact, a couple of people have said to me recently "nice to see Stephanie Cole is coming back", meaning not Stephanie Cole the famous TV star, but our Steph Cole.[33]

In the absence of such conventions, the responsibility of being an ambassador to the community falls squarely on the shoulders of senior management. Unfortunately for the Playhouse, as Paige admitted, she was not a great diplomat.

Before arriving at the Playhouse, Paige was faced with an enormous task based on the popularity and circumstances of the death of her predecessor. "It was Deborah Paige's misfortune to succeed to the post while we mourned David Horlock," and there was no question that she could ever live up to his reputation.[34] Nevertheless, in the eyes of the community, Paige did not help herself by failing to move up to Salisbury from London, or make any attempts to take any active part in the local community. Had she done so and been seen to care about the feelings of local theatregoers, the traditional audience might have felt less "incensed as traditions were trampled and changes imposed upon them rather than negotiated."[35] The same principle could be applied to certain members of the new staff Paige brought with her, such as marketing director Danny Moar, whose "aggressive marketing methods were alien to Salisbury."[36] With the memory of Horlock so fresh in people's minds, Paige's approach encouraged nostalgic memories of the past, such that many complaints in the local paper harped on the good old days as a model of what the Playhouse should aspire to:

> How many remember, like me, the days when the auditorium was full, the director was known by everyone, and he played an active part in our community?[37]

> Reggie Salberg, Roger Clissold, David Horlock promised and delivered commitment to the community...dwelling in the city they identified with local issues. Recognised, greeted in the street, they responded and respected people as individuals. Aspiring to, and achieving high fund-raising targets, they were encouraged and inspired by personal effort.[38]

Partly as a consequence of this situation, and certainly an important factor in the failure of public relations, was a fundamental lack of communication between senior management and the public. This was true of almost all of the theatre's operations. Artistic policy, for instance, was described by the consultants as "unfocused, uncommunicated, and misunderstood."[39] As such, it was not just the productions the loyal audience disliked, but the motivations they perceived to be behind them. As a consequence of retaining her London base, her perceived alterations to artistic policy, and the new administrative positions that were created on her arrival, including the introduction of a marketing director and an administrative and development director. Paige was widely regarded as an ambitious woman who was simply using her appointment at the Playhouse to climb the career ladder. Since Paige never explicitly corrected them on this, the traditional audience became "predisposed to hate anything like [*Celestina*] because Deborah had brought it in."[40] So strong was local resentment that even Paige's successes were turned back on her. It was generally recognised that following her arrival, there was a "marked improvement in the quality of productions" at the Playhouse, something reiterated in the national press, where certain of Paige's productions received critical acclaim.[41] But what should have been a focus of local pride became one of resentment when artistic quality was perceived as providing evidence of Paige's personal ambition: "The much vaunted regional and national acclaim will count for nothing without local support." [42] and "The Playhouse exists primarily for the people of Salisbury and the surrounding area." [43] As such, "artistic successes were not commensurate with box office successes," and Paige herself finally conceded that the local population "liked [a production] better when it was a bit more homely, even if this meant the standard of production wasn't so high."[44] Both the received productions *Celestina* and *The Europeans* fell into this category. Both were postmodern in their aesthetics and acclaimed in the national papers. Paige was indicted for the productions which were perceived locally as evidence of her experimental policy, largely because of the Playhouse's failure to communicate that these had been brought in from outside. Such was the hostility Paige personally engendered in the local community that by the time this mistake was realized, attempts to rectify the situation simply added fuel to the fire. A public statement asserting that Paige and the Playhouse management had little control over the content of the productions simply resulted in an outcry that the productions were not home produced, something which had been a traditional source of pride to theatregoers in the past.

Similarly, while some opposition to the changes to the youth programmes in Theatrescope and Stage '65 could be expected, the overwhelming resentment they caused must be partially attributed to the Playhouse's public relations failure. The lack of rapport between the theatre and public meant that the new management underestimated the popularity of the youth programmes. Consequently, cuts were made very quickly, without reference either to the teaching profession or local funding bodies. Moreover, they were only made public after they had been implemented, resulting in a widespread feeling of a *fait accompli:*

> Perhaps the most worrying aspect of the whole issue is the way the cuts were made public only after they happened, too late for anything to be done about them.[45]

While there was a recognition of the need to avoid talking badly of the previous administration, there was equally a wholesale failure to communicate to the public the financial necessity of making cutbacks. This was particularly true in the case of Stage '65. The announcement about the reduction of the youth programme was made immediately following a sell-out production of *West Side Story* that the youth group had performed in the main house, and which had generated over £6,000 at the Playhouse box office:

> With direct and indirect grants for the youth theatre and TIE, the Playhouse receives £130,000m plus £7,000 Stage '65 subscriptions – not to mention profits from productions. *West Side Story* - had 99.9% occupancy.[46]

Factually, this information is far from accurate. Annual membership fees of just over £10 for each of the two hundred members of Stage '65's would have generated just over £2,000 per year. This sum accounted for less than one-third of even one of the seven professional TIE members' salaries, and took no account of the capital costs of running the operation. These included two large-scale, main house productions the youth group performed each year. Moreover, despite the unofficial emphases of the various funding partners, separate grants were never specifically allocated for specific departments or projects. Had the situation been different, the Playhouse might have been able to make a stronger case to the funding bodies for additional capital, and to explain the necessity of the cuts to the public. Given the circumstances however, such figures as noted here cannot be entirely substantiated or discounted by either side. Consequently, the general belief that Stage '65 traditionally generated a profit for the Playhouse, combined with an emphasis on the efficacy of the programme, meant senior management were unable to prevent "a suspicion in many people's minds that TIE and Stage '65 are being sacrificed for Miss Paige's artistic ambition."[47] Similarly few people recognised that "the cuts which are currently causing so much distress are only part of a series of stringent measures affecting all departments of the theatre."[48] Aggravating the suspicion was the evident fact that the money spent on paperwork was simultaneously escalating as the administration department increased in size under Paige's lead.

Paige's overhaul of the system of administration, including the appointment of a marketing director in a newly created position, and a qualified full-time accountant, constituted an attempt by the chief executive to establish a more efficient and cost-effective operation in the Playhouse. These changes had the full backing of the board of directors with regard to the burgeoning but unknown deficit left over from the previous administration, and the theatre's signal failure to develop a new, younger audience. Nevertheless, increased administrative costs partly contributed to the fact that the budget for production costs was reduced from £750,000 in 1989/90 to £660,000 in 1994/5, a figure that was reduced further when inflation was taken into consideration. Combined with the hostility in the community and rumours of a mounting deficit, an increasingly costly administration department ensured that any efforts by the Playhouse to explain the reasons behind the new system failed to make an impact. Thus, while attempts to explain via the local paper that "comparisons [regarding the size and budget of the administration] were being made with twenty years ago," these were drowned out by the much louder complaints about "the seemingly endless list of administrators."[49]

Perhaps the public would have been more inclined to listen had the Playhouse presented a united front. While the fact that many of the theatre's problems could not be attributed to the Paige administration was never adequately communicated, internal tensions within the theatre were played out in the public eye – something encouraged by the vocal criticism carried out in the local media. Summing up the theatre's problems, the consultants criticized the board of directors as:

1. Divided and not acting corporately
2. Openly split and unsupportive
3. [Displaying] poor financial understanding and management.[50]

Certainly, the need to maintain a harmonious and supportive relationship between the board and chief executive is demonstrated by the consequences of its failure to the Salisbury Playhouse.

At the time of Paige's arrival, the existing board operated under the auspices of a system which imposed no time limit on the length of service. Annual general meetings at which new members were elected or re-elected were only open to existing and former board members, who were equally the only people allowed to nominate and vote on those standing for election. The inevitable result was a self-perpetuating oligarchy dominated by a significant number of members who had served over ten years, including former artistic director Reggie Salberg.[51] This element shared a nostalgic idea of the past and the sympathy of the Playhouse's loyal audience, and consequently carried strong ideas about what the theatre's priorities should be and how it should be run. Many of these ran contrary to those presented by Paige. And where these tensions should have been worked out in private, this was rarely the case.

In addition to confusion over the original reasons for appointing Deborah Paige, who was recommended by a select committee of only three members from a board of sixteen, the board was constantly in conflict with itself over questions of artistic programming, alterations to Theatrescope and Stage '65, and to the system of management.[52] Decisions were difficult to make internally because of the excessive size of the board, which delayed and increased the difficulty of agreeing on a coherent policy, and its nature and composition. Under normal circumstances, the board only met once a month for two hours. Complicating matters, in addition to the long-serving element who were heavily involved with the operations of the theatre, membership also included a number of well-respected professionals from outside the immediate local community who had little knowledge of either theatre in general, or the Playhouse in particular, beyond the professional interest merited by their responsibility as a board member. For such reasons, the full implications of the changes proposed for Theatrescope and Stage '65, and those allegedly made to artistic policy, were only appreciated by a minority of the board. Consequently, when they were voted through, those who had been unhappy with the decision aired their dirty linen in public. Reggie Salberg, for example, expressed his views over Paige's artistic policy on numerous occasions:

> When she arrived she put in the wrong programme and we lost a lot of people.....Her policy of exciting theatre did not work, but the programming has gone too far the other way now. I personally would be happy if she resigned.[53]

Because of his popularity in the local community, his sympathy with the views of the most vocal protestors, and his record of long service at the Playhouse, Salberg's comments arguably carried more weight than anything Paige could say to counter them:

> Modesty prevented [Reggie Salberg] from pointing out that he and his successor were not only experienced professionals who knew how to fill a theatre, but were blessed with personalities that enabled them to work in mutual confidence with the board and also made them popular and respected in the city.[54]

Similar sentiments were voiced about other committed board members from the local community such as Veronica Stewart and Richard Leutchford who were both equally outspoken in their criticism of Paige. Their resignations in the midst of such debates incensed public feeling further, with the overwhelming opinion being that they had been badly treated by the Playhouse's current management.

While poorly-contained divisions within the board created adverse publicity, so did their handling of many of the theatre's affairs. A series of unsanctioned leaks over the Playhouse's proposed closure caused the consultants to criticize the board as "poor ambassadors for the theatre" and almost certainly expedited the closure through an adverse affect on ticket sales:

> The leaks annoyed the theatre – already saddled with a six-figure debt as a result of funding difficulties and poor audience figures – because of the danger that audiences will start to drift away a year early.[55]

While on the one hand the board members were considered to be too outspoken, they were equally criticized for excessive secrecy, in part because they failed to communicate the theatre's problems and financial situation to the public, knowledge which the local community regarded as their right. On certain occasions, such information was deliberately withheld by the board because it would have involved publicly contradicting certain of their own members, which many felt would simply aggravate speculation over internal divisions. In hindsight, the decision not to speak out was recognised as just fuelling the rumours. For instance, feelings ran high over the fact that it took over two years of media pressure to extract publicly the financial position of the theatre from the board, which prevented the local community – and their official representatives, the "Friends of the Playhouse" – from the opportunity to actively help. When the consultants condemned the board for failing to retain either "external or internal confidence" and called for their complete replacement, public response overwhelmingly concurred:

> We are told that the board is to be replaced; many think that it has been weak, secretive and largely to blame for the current situation.[56]

Echoes of the animosity between the board of the Nottingham Playhouse and John Neville in the 1960s can be seen in the board's dealings with Paige. Their own internal divisions and failure to anticipate adequately the extent of the animosity that changes to the theatre's programme would generate meant that the outsider Paige was never properly briefed, but was still squarely blamed for a series of situations in which they were equally culpable. The increasingly unpleasant working conditions for practitioners in regional theatres which had become an acknowledged problem nationally at this time were clearly aggravated here by the board's failure to support their chief executive, who resigned in 1994 in protest at their treatment:

> I wasn't prepared to work for a board which didn't have confidence in me but weren't forthcoming about what I had done. [The resignation] followed a meeting where members had called for my contract to be terminated. Unfair dismissal?[57]

Such a situation was made worse by the interference of local funding bodies, some of which had representatives sitting on the board. One of the individuals who called for Paige's resignation was the representative for Wiltshire County Council. Wiltshire traditionally insisted on having a councillor on the board as a condition of funding. By 1994, confidence in the Playhouse had dropped so alarmingly that the County Council refused to hand over a loan of £58,000 despite an existing agreement with the other two funding bodies. Their condition for releasing the agreed amount was the dismissal of the current senior management and consultation/power of veto over artistic policy and all appointments of senior management in the future. While such calls for Paige's dismissal were contractually illegal, equally the board was legally bound to make their own decisions on such matters. As Antony Fanshawe, chair of the board of directors, 1993-4, commented:

> Wiltshire must have known it was setting a condition that we could not possibly accept because it was seeking to take away the board's power and put the board in an invidious position.[58]

The implications of allowing funding bodies to interfere with artistic policy in this way were considered potentially devastating. Commenting on the situation, Southern Arts, an organization that operated under the "arm's length principle" and only reserved the right to have a representative present at Playhouse meetings, said:

> It is our belief that the theatre would be in an extremely vulnerable position were it to lose at this crucial time the artistic vision and continuity for which it has rightly gained a national reputation.[59]

In one sense it could be argued that Salisbury Playhouse had already been a victim of such a practice. The inclusion of Wiltshire County Council's representative on the board consistently delayed and increased the difficulty of making and following through policies that might have eased the crisis. Possible measures that could generate income were constantly brought back to questions of expenditure. Inevitably, a representative from a funding body was vocal in insisting that immediate financial considerations be addressed first to reduce the deficit. However, any decisions that were made to accommodate such demands had negative long-term implications. The decision to slash the marketing department's budget to under £20,000 in 1994, for instance, when "it should have been doubled" to address the problem of poor public relations with the community, directly stemmed from Wiltshire County Council's demands to reduce the deficit.[60]

Bringing the situation full circle, such ongoing problems once again brought the issue of parity funding to the fore again. Although Salisbury District Council and Southern Arts agreed to continue their support through the period of closure, the financial situation was so dire that it was recognised that the Playhouse could not continue to operate, even by going dark for several months, without the full backing of all funding bodies. This was particularly true after Hampshire County Council withdrew the small subsidy they had previously provided to the Playhouse during the recession. For this reason, Southern Arts made their "support conditional on the continuing support of the local authorities" effectively having to resort to threats to force Wiltshire County Council to comply with its part of the agreement:

> Should the theatre close permanently, Southern Arts' grant of £242,900 would be lost to Wiltshire and possibly to the region. The current crisis in arts funding and in regional theatres in particular, means that there are others only too ready to take up and use that money for their own survival plans.[61]

In the event, this situation was only finally resolved by the intervention of the local Member of Parliament and junior heritage minister for 1993, Robert Key, who persuaded Wiltshire to forward the loan and the Arts Council to pay off the Playhouse's deficit. After a period of seven months being dark, the Playhouse reopened in September 1995. During this time, the building was completely refurbished through funds provided by Southern Arts and Salisbury District Council, and following the recommendations of the consultants, the entire executive and board were replaced. Under the new terms of agreement recommended by the consultants, board members were limited to serving a maximum of two terms of five years. The new artistic director, Jonathan Church, meantime, moved down from Derby to live in Salisbury, and opened with a production of *Tess of the d'Urbervilles*. In his first interview with the *Salisbury Journal,* Church commented, "I have no desire to shock people....my aim is to illuminate."[62]

170   Chapter Eight

Notes

[1] This chapter also appears in Olivia Turnbull, *Bringing Down the House: The Crisis in Britain's Regional Theatres* (Bristol: Intellect, 2008), it is reproduced here with the permission of the publishers.
[2] Comment made by Hilary Keenlyside at a public meeting held at the theatre on 15 December 1994, in which the results of consultants Bonnar-Keenlyside's investigations and recommendations about the operations of the Salisbury Playhouse were revealed.
[3] Statistics and information supplied by Allanah Lucas, Salisbury Playhouse administrative and development director, and Southern Arts.
[4] David Horlock was artistic director of Salisbury Playhouse from 1982 to 1990.
[5] Nick Bourne, chairman, Salisbury Playhouse board of directors, 1991-3, speaking in an interview with the author, 10 January 2002.
[6] Paige was appointed as chief executive. The role incorporated responsibility for artistic and financial policy, something that was problematic since the responsibilities of one job were often in direct contradiction to the requirements of the other.
[7] Information and statistics supplied in Salisbury Playhouse. Reggie Salberg, artistic director of Salisbury Playhouse, 1955-76, "Our Future in Danger," audience pamphlet (Salisbury: Salisbury Playhouse, 1984).
[8] The 1986 Cork Report included Salisbury Playhouse as one of the theatres as being in imminent danger of closure.
[9] Stage '65 was so-called because it was founded in 1965.
[10] Hugo Stewart, *Salisbury Journal*, 12 November 1991.
[11] Allanah Lucas. Interview, December 2002.
[12] Robert Hawkins, *Salisbury Journal*, 22 February 1993.
[13] Comments taken from various letters published in the *Salisbury Journal* in 1994.
[14] Timothy Strand, *Salisbury Journal*, 24 November 1994.
[15] D.G.W. Brind, *Salisbury Journal*, 24 November 1994.
[16] Deborah Paige, Chief Executive, Salisbury Playhouse, 1991-4. Letter to author, 1996.
[17] Nick Bourne, interview, January 2002.
[18] Karen Johnstone, *Salisbury Journal*, 4 August 1994.
[19] Dee Adcock, *Salisbury Journal* assistant arts editor, speaking on *Southern Eye*, B.B.C. South, December 1994.
[20] Jim Soutar, *Salisbury Journal*, 10 August 1994.
[21] John and Mary Pinder, *Salisbury Journal*, 24 November 1994.
[22] Hilary Keenlyside, speaking at Salisbury Playhouse public meeting, 15 December 1994.
[23] Paige, 1996.
[24] Derek Jones, *Salisbury Journal*, 21 May 1992.
[25] Marie Stride, *Salisbury Journal*, 10 August 1994.
[26] Paige, 1996.
[27] Peter Blacklock, Arts Editor, *Salisbury Times*, 10 November 1994.

[28] This included the chief executive, the administrative and development director, and the marketing director.
[29] Bonnar-Keenlyside, "Salisbury Playhouse Business Plan," consultants' report, November 1994.
[30] Margaret McClean, *Salisbury Journal*, 1 December 1994.
[31] Bonnar-Keenlyside, "Salisbury Playhouse Business Plan," November 1994.
[32] Ena Wootton, *Salisbury Journal*, 28 July 1994.
[33] Bette Anderson, *Salisbury Journal*, 22 November 1994.
[34] Marie Stride, *Salisbury Journal*, 12 August 1994.
[35] Ibid.
[36] Ibid.
[37] Elizabeth Colston, *Salisbury Journal*, 1 November 1994.
[38] Marie Stride, *Salisbury Journal*, 12 August 1994.
[39] Bonnar-Keenlyside, November 1994.
[40] Lucas. Interview, December 2002.
[41] Bonnar-Keenlyside, November 1994.
[42] Peter W. Docherty, *Salisbury Journal*, 1 August 1991.
[43] Sidney Vines, *Salisbury Journal*, 13 August 1994.
[44] Paige, 1996.
[45] Paul Gahan, *Salisbury Journal*, 25 July 1991.
[46] Christine Leversuch, *Salisbury Journal*, 11 July 1991.
[47] Philip Sayer, Letters Page, *Salisbury Journal*, 8 July 1991.
[48] Nick Bourne, quoted in the *Salisbury Journal*, 2 December 1991.
[49] Antony Fanshawe, speaking at Salisbury Playhouse public meeting, 15 December 1994.
[50] Bonnar-Keenlyside, November 1994.
[51] Antony Fanshawe, speaking at Salisbury Playhouse public meeting, 15 December 1994.
[52] Hilary Keenlyside, speaking at Salisbury Playhouse public meeting, 15 December 1994.
[53] Reggie Salberg, speaking on *Southern Eye*, B.B.C. South, December 1994.
[54] Roger Hamilton, *Salisbury Journal*, 24 November 1994.
[55] Peter Blacklock, *Salisbury Times*, 10 November 1994.
[56] Correspondence from "Friends of Salisbury Playhouse" to Antony Fanshawe, November, 1994 Supplied by Antony Fanshawe.
[57] Paige, 1996.
[58] Antony Fanshawe, interview, January 2002.
[59] Sue Robertson, Executive Director, Southern Arts,"To All Leaders of Political Parties in Wiltshire", (memorandum), 9 November 1994.
[60] Allanah Lucas, interview, December 2002.
[61] Sue Robertson, 9 November 1994.
[62] Jonathan Church, artistic director, Salisbury Playhouse, 1995-2000, "Playhouse Gifts to Welcome New Duo", *Salisbury Journal*, 1 June 1995.

CHAPTER NINE

STRANGE BEDFELLOWS: MAKING A COMMERCIAL SUCCESS OF A SUBSIDISED THEATRE

ROS MERKIN

> It seemed merely intolerable that the theatres of a great city should be no more than booths for the entertainment of travelling companies from London. We must, if we were civilised, have our *own* theatre, in which we could produce the plays we wanted to see, the plays that London would never give us and in which, in the course of time, we might perhaps hope to produce plays that would affect and criticise our own life instead of being content with the drawing room (or bedroom) comedies of sophisticated London Society.[1]

> In the past Liverpool Playhouse has been safe, middle-of-the road rep. The pressures are building up to force it in that direction once again.[2]

In January 1991, Joe Orton's *Loot* was playing at Liverpool Playhouse. It was to be a prescient piece of programming as the 80-year theatre, with debts of £800,000, was put into Administration and given three months to sort out its finances or face closure. A campaign was launched, declaring, "It's Too Good to Lose". 27,000 postcards were sent to Arts Council Chair Peter Palumbo and to the leader of the local council. Michael Hesletine, who had become known as the Minister for Merseyside in the wake of the riots ten years previously, launched an appeal from the stage of the theatre for £1.5 million, and accepted a cheque from Littlewoods who had promised the theatre £250,000 over five years. The insolvency expert appointed to try and save the theatre cancelled Red Star Brouhaha, an international youth festival and a forthcoming production by Beryl Bainbridge and hoped, rather wistfully, that there may well be a millionaire who would like to save the Playhouse.[3] Ironically for a theatre that was founded by citizens' subscriptions in order to get away from commercialism, his pleas were answered in the form of producer and impresario Bill Kenwright, who signed a deal to take responsibility for the theatre for the next five years. It was a deal that was to raise questions and concerns, unsurprising given the characterisation of him as a very successful "wheeler dealer."[4] There was a fear that he would turn the Playhouse into a West End test venue, "a kind of seaside repertory circuit", or a venue for his touring shows, silting it up with "second-rate tosh".[5] There was anxiety that the theatre would lose its identity and would no longer be a local theatre for the city, as Robert Hewison noted:

> The issue is not simply one of money, but of local identity. In our increasingly homogenised towns and cities, the theatre can be a beacon of difference. Just as long as the plays it puts on are not the sort of bland productions that all too often wend their way from Aberdeen to Norwich, and sometimes the West End.[6]

There was a concern that impresarios were "inadequate custodians of Reithian principles" – a concern that ignored the fact that Reithian principles had long since disappeared from the Government and Arts Council's agendas.[7] In retrospect, his tenure at the Playhouse has been seen as being, in the long-term, "ambiguous".[8] This chapter looks at the story of those five years, and at the often vexed question of the relationship between the subsidised and commercial theatre.

We tend towards a bi-polar approach to the kinds of theatre that exist in England. Both provide art and entertainment but one is motivated by money and the other (in the best of all possible worlds) by the more philanthropic desire to create art and help people understand life. In reality, these two are not separate strands (many of the regional subsidised theatres have their roots in the profits made by tea, sugar and margarine or as was the case in Liverpool from the profits of numerous businessmen in the city) but as Cameron Mackintosh has argued, they "have been totally interdependent for decades."[9] It was a point reinforced by the Society of London Theatre in *The Wyndham Report* (1998) which argued that the strength of the West End was based on a healthy working relationship between commercial and grant-aided sectors of the English theatre ecology and further emphasised in their 1999 follow-up, *After Wyndham*, which emphasised the vigorous "two-way traffic with regional theatre", arguing that the benefits worked both ways.[10] The Arts Council has been happy to use this sense of beneficial interdependence to argue for subsidy with Lord Gowrie seeing Cameron Mackintosh's article in the Council's *Annual Report* of 1995-96 as "one of the most powerful pieces of advocacy – unanswerable even – for sustaining, not cutting" government funding.[11] Nor was the relationship seen to be a return to the regions acting as homes for a "smudged carbon-copy of last year's West-End success".[12] If anything, the boot was to be on the other foot.

Throughout the 1980s, many theatres aspired to commercial transfers to boost their shrinking budgets and to meet increasing demands for raising money not dependent on the public purse. The ACGB *Annual Report* even listed transfers as a badge of honour citing twenty-five in 1980-1, eighteen in 1982-83 and eighteen in 1983-4, proudly announcing that three of these (*Stepping Out* from Leatherhead, *Up'n'Under* from Hull Truck and *The Hired Man* from Leicester Haymarket) had won Olivier and *Evening Standard* awards. That year, Leicester Haymarket was the clear winner in the transfer market with five productions providing *The Aspern Papers*, Peter Nichols' *Passion Play, Pygmalion* and *West Side Story* alongside *The Hired Man.*

Some, like John Peter in *The Times*, were unsure that a local event put together with a commercial future in mind was always wrong; in fact, it may have become a necessity. The Leicester Haymarket, he argued:

> is the only proper theatre in its town: it gets its subsidy to provide everything from Shakespeare to Cole Porter. The Studio Theatre serves as its 'off-Broadway'.... Such a theatre needs every penny it can get: it is a civic amenity, like buses and job centres. But no: I hear that its Arts Council grant will only increase by one per cent which in real terms means a cut of 2-3%. On the other hand, if *High Society* is a success it will bring them in up to £100,000 a year. I think, with my tongue only halfway in my cheek, that Mrs Thatcher has done such theatres some good. She has stiffened their sinews, summoned up their blood.[13]

For others, there were potential problems afoot, especially the move from simple transfers to co-productions with commercial producers. The most often cited offender here is *Les Miserables*, a joint venture between the RSC and Cameron Mackintosh, which had the disastrous side effect, in Michael Billington's view, that "beleaguered subsidised companies came to regard the musical as a permanent goldmine".[14] Whilst on the surface, this was a classic public-private partnership (much admired by both the Tories and New Labour) in which "the brand name and technical expertise of the RSC were allied to the commercial flair of a West End showman" it set a "dangerous precedent" giving commercial producers a say in (and power over) the programming and policy of subsidised companies, thus totally changing "the rules of the theatrical game". It might have fitted with the Thatcherite policy of stealthy privatisation of nationalised industries, but it meant subsidised companies were increasingly being judged by "the fundamental criterion of commercial theatre: is it a hit or a flop?"[15]

Les Miserables was also in the spotlight over Trevor Nunn's earnings and one of the issues *The Cork Report* (1986) was asked to look into was the question of "gains" made by commercial transfers which at the time were operating by "the law of the jungle". This had been provoked by an acrimonious row which blew up in July 1986 over accusations that Trevor Nunn and Peter Hall were amassing personal fortunes by launching new productions at subsidised theatres and then transferring them to commercial venues (Hall, for example, was said to have made £2 million from the transfer of Shaffer's *Amadeus* to Broadway through receiving 4% of the box office while the National only received 1% and Nunn was said to have amassed more than £60,000 to date from the transfer of *Les Miserables* whilst the RSC had not yet recouped its £300,000 production costs). Fears abounded that they were 'neglecting their jobs' (paid for by the taxpayer) although Nunn and Hall insisted that the deals were "vetted down to the last comma by our boards and then by the Arts Council".[16] Both made known their anger at the perceived inaccuracies of the attack and Hall attempted to set the record straight with a more detached look at the issue. For him, subsidised theatres up and down the country had regularly exploited their successful productions by transferring them to commercial theatres – an "honourable practice" which had been:

> approved by theatre boards, sanctified by the Arts Council and welcomed by commercial managements. With state subsidy steadily dwindling, the practice has intensified; a reason I suspect for the present controversy. All of us are now continually exhorted by government and Arts Council to increase our self-earned income in every possible way, which chiefly means moving our most popular work into the West End and then hopefully to Broadway. Lord Birkett, in a letter to *The Times* last Thursday, wrote that 'the transfer of successful subsidised productions to commercial theatres is not a matter of greed, it is essential'. So indeed it is. For such transfers, apart from freeing space in our subsidised repertoires, allowing us to introduce new work, often and blessedly cause large sums of life-giving money to flow not only to the commercial organisation now staging the production, but also to the originating subsidised theatre, inevitably badly strapped for cash. The main beneficiary has to be the latter. Subsidy put the play on initially.[17]

This was a problem that would not go away (Nunn was being questioned again in 2001 about his co-production of *My Fair Lady*, again with Cameron Mackintosh, and the National was under seemingly constant fire during his time there for its 'populist' repertoire) and in 2003 the Arts

Council produced a report by Robert Cogo-Fawcett which provided subsidised theatres with guidelines for operating with commercial managements. He acknowledges that "commercial managements have often been characterised as predators on the subsidised sector" although the Arts Council itself embraced the need to "acknowledge and exploit the synergies between the subsidised and commercial sector" in its 2000 *National Policy for Theatre in England.*[18]

All of these concerns (and more) were to follow Kenwright's arrival at the Playhouse. For it is one thing to enter into an agreement to transfer or co-produce a show, and another to take charge as a commercial management of a theatre funded by public money. Tensions between artistic and commercial values were nothing new at the Playhouse. "Battles royal took place in the boardroom every Thursday", noted the founder Basil Dean, "Suggestions put forward at the behest of the chairman were usually thought too advanced. Commercial plays to redress an adverse verdict at the box office were torn quietly apart by university members".[19] Nor was Kenwright's involvement in subsidised theatre anything new. Hailed by many as one of the saving forces behind regional theatre in the 1980s with his touring shows, he had immediately offered the Playhouse three shows, including two by Willy Russell, to fill the gap when the Administrators had stepped in. He had worked with the Playhouse in previous years on co-productions, including a 1990 production of August Wilson's *Fences*, a play which a regional repertory company would never have been able to afford to produce or even to have got the rights to without the involvement of a commercial partner and the promise that brought of a West End transfer. He was also, at the same time, running another subsidised theatre, the Thorndike in Leatherhead, where he had stepped in to save it the previous year when it too was threatened with closure.[20] And he was to come under fire there (as he later did in Liverpool), when the Yvonne Arnaud Theatre at Guildford, one of the other "Surrey Cluster" theatres, was struggling financially, for encouraging the Arts Council and local authorities to give him money to tour what were perceived as West End productions.[21]

Kenwright's relationship with Liverpool and therefore his programming of the theatre was, however, different from his relationship to Surrey. This was his hometown (he had once appeared as a stoat on the stage of the Playhouse). It was a "romantic" (and just) intervention thought Michael Coveney and Kenwright's attachment to his city was evident in his letter for the first season's brochure:

> When I heard at the start of the year that the Playhouse had gone into Administration, I felt I wanted to do something – anything – to make a

contribution towards retaining the Playhouse as a theatre for the people of Merseyside. My reasons were simple. I have a great love for Liverpool, and a great love for the theatre, and it is very important to me that the place that I love retains the thing that I love.[22]

That sense of romanticism and "instinctive populism", appropriate for someone characterised as a soap actor (he had played Gordon Clegg in *Coronation Street*), was to personify part of Kenwright's approach to the programming of the Playhouse.

From the outset, Kenwright promised three things to the people of the city: plays for the city, plays to be produced with an eye to transfer or a tour, and good quality touring product to be bought in. The promise was also that the theatre would remain a producing house, and the agreement he signed, giving him artistic control whilst still retaining the services of Ian Kellgren (the theatre's artistic director), ensured at least six in-house productions every twelve months. Many of these in-house productions (seven in total over the five years) were nostalgia shows, singalong songbooks based on the lives of often dead and sometimes local stars. The first of these, *Good Rockin' Tonite* (October 1991), was a celebration of the life and work of Jack Good (who also wrote and directed the show), the musical producer responsible for television shows such as *Oh Boy!* and *Boy Meets Girl*. *Be Bop a Lula* (August 1993) had a longer pedigree. Commissioned by the Playhouse in 1980 and written by Bill Morrison, it had its first performance in 1988 and told the story of the legendary 1960 British Tour of Gene Vincent and Eddie Cochran, focusing on one of their most celebrated concerts at the Liverpool Empire.[23] The most successful of these shows was undoubtedly one that started life as *Only the Lonely* (August 1993; restaged August 1994) and later became *The Roy Orbison Story* which transferred to the Piccadilly in September 1994 and was still touring in 2003. In August 1994, a return, from two summer's previously, of *Imagine*, described as being a new musical based on Bob Eaton's hugely successful *Lennon* (staged at the Everyman Theatre in Liverpool in 1982) but in fact it was a show that had "taken Bob Eaton's moving musical biography of *Lennon* and thrown away the book".[24] The following summer, it was the turn of another local boy, this time the "Elvis of Birkenhead", Billy Fury in a show called *The Sound of Fury* (June 1995). By this time, Robin Thornber had had enough. "Surely" he sighed, "these rock nostalgia shows have had their day even in Liverpool, where they are the last surviving industry".[25] But Kenwright was not quite finished and August 1996 saw the arrival of *Ferry 'Cross the Mersey* which stood out by boasting the presence on stage of Gerry Marsden playing himself. One other Kenwright developed show which, whilst not a musical about a dead or local pop star, had as much of a nostalgic glow to it as any was Alun Owen's *No Trams to Lime Street*, produced in 1995, the year of Owen's death. Originally written in 1959, it had been broadcast as an *Armchair Theatre* production (directed by Ted Kotcheff and starring Billie Whitelaw) and as a *Wednesday Play* in 1970. Kenwright saw this story of three merchant seamen looking for the tramlined cobbled Liverpool they had left, as a wonderful piece of Liverpool joy. He added music and billed it as Liverpool's own *On the Town*. No wonder Thornber was still sighing that nostalgia was still Liverpool's biggest growth industry.[26]

Kenwright was unapologetic about his use of nostalgia or his use of music:

> If you've got it, flaunt it. Just as Stoke capitalises on its potteries, so we must capitalise on our musical past. If we don't we're fools. It's a key to our ability to thrive again.[27]

Liverpool was certainly a city proud of its musical past and, proving Thornber right, it was starting to build a tourism industry based on its pop heritage. *The Beatles Story*, the only permanent Beatles themed visitor attraction, had been opened in 1990 to be joined later by the National Trust's purchase of the childhood homes of both John Lennon and Paul McCartney; by 2009 the Visit Liverpool website could proclaim to potential visitors: "It's impossible to imagine Liverpool without music – or music without Liverpool".[28] In this environment, Kenwright's capitalisation on the city's musical past can be seen as following a path that was increasingly in tune with both the city's needs and the additional agenda of the Arts Council to provide economic value from tourism. While many of these summer shows were attacked by the critics for being short on script and storyline, for being "a cheap and cheerful form of showbizzery", a pale shadow of the real thing, for a city that had weathered (and still was weathering) a recession, these 'feelgood' shows had something to offer a local audience as well as the tourists, as Glen Walford, artistic director of the Everyman in the early 1980s pointed out: "If you live in a tower block you know how miserable it is – you don't want to see shows about it."[29] Even hard-bitten critics could be pulled in to enjoying a "wonderfully nostalgic treat" or admitting they were "rather life affirming at the last."[30] They were also quick to point out another phenomenon associated with these shows; they played to an ageing audience with the theatre "alarmingly" taking on the air of a rest home as the audience clapped along.[31] So, whilst these shows might fulfil the brief of creating local new work at the Playhouse and at the same time providing money from tours and transfers and tourists, the theatre needed something else to bring in a younger audience.

Nor was it one long nostalgia-fest at the Playhouse. Other commercial productions designed for touring (or as part of Kenwright tours) or co-productions with the Thorndike and other subsidised theatres also found their way on to its stage. Variously, over the five years, the theatre saw the perennial Liverpool favourite *Blood Brothers* (prior to a transfer to Toronto and then Broadway), Tom Elliot's *Feed* about a music hall entertainer and two Godber shows: *On the Piste* and *Up'n'Under*. The Peter Hall Company, with whom Kenwright had a long association, came with *Lysistrata* and Frederick Lonsdale's comedy *On Approval*. Classics also appeared with a production of *The Cherry Orchard* in association with Leicester Haymarket and the RSC with *Les Liasons Dangereuses*. The stage also saw its fair share of big names; Tom Conti both directed and starred in *Present Laughter*, Eric Sykes appeared in Stoppard's *Rough Crossing* and Susannah York in Daphne du Maurier's *September Tide*. A lot of money was lost on a production of Poliakoff's *Sienna Red* and also on a production of Jim Cartwright's *Stone Free* which had originated at Bolton as *Five Miles High*. Christmas was taken care of by musicals – *Oklahoma!*, *Annie* and Kenwright's own *Robin, Prince of Sherwood*. Not all popular shows were designed to tour. Dave Simpson's *Raving Beauties*, for example, a comedy about the backstage antics as five contestants vied for the title of 'Miss Golden Gate', reappeared in the city twice, as a show chosen specifically for the Playhouse. On the surface then, this was classic, safe rep designed to earn the theatre some money and keep the doors open, and Kenwright's opening show, *Steppin' Out*, timed to coincide with the opening of his film version, should have suggested that this was the path he would follow. In this sense, it was little different to many regional theatres up and down the country at the time which were playing safe to keep their heads above water.

But the Playhouse under Kenwright was also set to undertake some more risky and experimental ventures, as Ian Kellgren warned the local press at the outset of the first season: "Don't expect bills of bland and easy fare. This is not a programme of take-outs. It's a feast".[32] On the main stage, some interesting choices were made: a stage version of *The Cabinet of Dr Caligari* in 1995; a new one man *Shirley Valentine* in the shape of Dennis Lumborg's *One Fine Day* (1995), about a Liverpool steel worker accused of abusing his children, which transferred, with enthusiastic reviews, to the Albery as result of Stephen Fry's disappearance.[33] There was a production of Robert Bolt's *A Man for All Seasons* (1991) at Liverpool's Anglican Cathedral and there was Andrew Sherlock's *Fall from Grace* (1994) a story of three generations of Irish immigrants, complete with a large community chorus. Undoubtedly though, the runaway critical success of Kenwright's main-stage shows was *Medea* (1993), a re-staging of Jonathan Kent's production originally seen at the Almeida. It might have included Diana Rigg as an attraction but it was a long way from the kind of popular touring shows many had envisaged and a long way from Diana Rigg's role of Emma Peel in *The Avengers*. It forced Robin Thornber, who had been a harsh critic of Kenwright's, to admit that "this time he has picked up a 'product' which is classic British theatre at its best" and to assure his readers that it was "the most intellectually honest and compelling production I've seen of a classically awkward text and a dazzling display of sheer theatrical virtuosity."[34]

Nor was it just on the main stage that there was excitement. In his agreement with the theatre, Kenwright had undertaken to ensure the continuation of the Youth Art programme and to make all reasonable endeavours to provide a programme in the Studio (both contingent on the availability of public funding) and at the outset, this seemed to be happening. In his first season, the international youth festival was reinstated along with the production of Beryl Bainbridge's *An Awfully Big Adventure*, the play deemed too expensive and too risky by the administrator the previous year. In the Studio, the first two seasons did indeed provide Kellgren's promised feast of new work and as the main theatre:

> responds to harsh economic times with ever more commercial programming, it is good to be able to welcome this alternative, newly refurbished and, more importantly open to new voices.[35]

Starting with a co-production with Altered States of Andrew Cullen's *Self-Catering* in October 1992 (later to find its way to the Cockpit), the season followed with the British debut of Phyllis Nagy's *Weldon Rising*. The latter was a co-production with the Royal Court Upstairs and moved there in December of that year. They rounded off 1992 with the first British performance of Denise Chalem's *At 50 She Discovered the Sea*, in a short season that had *The Guardian* celebrating that it showed what a leap of faith could do and placed "Liverpool Playhouse where it belongs – with the innovators".[36]

January 1993 started with a three-week 'New Developments' season, three new plays by Merseyside writers which included *Boy* by Shaun Duggan, Cheryl Martin's *Home for the Holidays* and *The Dark Side*, by Liam Lloyd, the Playhouse's writer in residence. This was followed by involvement with Springboards, a collaboration between theatres round the country (including Birmingham Rep, Salisbury Playhouse, Leicester Haymarket and the National Theatre Studio) to showcase new studio based work and in Liverpool this included Gregory Motton's *A Message for the Broken Hearted* and Judith Johnson's *Somewhere*. The latter was to be part of the final showcase at the Cottesloe. Whilst the impetus of the new work in the studio was never carried through (finances never again allowed for this kind of work during Kenwright's time, despite applications being made for grants), the performance of eight contemporary premieres in seven months suggested there was a will to support new writing, if only the money had been there.

There is of course a key question about Kenwright's time at the Playhouse: did it work? The closure of the Playhouse in 1998 with debts of £800,000 after barely eighteen months of reverting to a more traditional repertory theatre under Richard Williams, would suggest that it was a failed experiment. Of course, he had kept the theatre open, and while it closed in January 1998, it was to be re-opened in December 2000, run jointly with the Everyman theatre – and is still being run jointly today with increasing profile and increasing success, helped in part by Liverpool being Capital of Culture in 2008 and in part by a general renaissance being enjoyed by the city. It is doubtful if it would have been possible to re-open it at this juncture if it had been closed in 1991. He was certainly also responsible for raising the profile and credibility of the theatre nationally, for increasing audience numbers, box office takings and the numbers of performances a year. However, there clearly were also large elements of failure.

Some of these failures were accidental. The cancellation of the premiere of John Osborne's *Déjà Vu* was one case in point. It was to have starred Peter O'Toole and to have been the main attraction (and selling point) of the first season, but arguments between the writer and the actor over the length of the play led to its postponement and its replacement with a hastily produced *Woman in White*. Whilst this did do well for the theatre, it was never going to be the national jewel in the Playhouse's crown that Osborne's long awaited sequel to *Look Back in Anger* would have provided. Other reasons for failure lie at the door of audience expectations raised by the scale and the stars of Kenwright's productions. In the two years that followed his departure, Richard Williams, as the new artistic director, could not hope to match these and, accordingly, audiences were disappointed. In many ways, the theatre had lost a sense of its own identity. The scale of the productions also caused concern about escalating production costs during Kenwright's time, although he was always at pains to point out that the problem was not the original budgets but the inability of the Playhouse to keep to them.

The agreement that was entered in to was, unsurprisingly, drawn up hurriedly and never seemed to have been quite understood on either side. There were constant issues with management and communication; Kenwright was in effect an absentee landlord based in London and although he was often at Board meetings, day to day running was left with the old Playhouse personnel, including Ian Kellgren, until he eventually left in January 1995. Planning was problematic given two different approaches and attitudes. Kenwright was happy to wait to see how the box-office was doing before confirming shows, the Playhouse staff were more used to longer term planning and thinking. Confusions and disagreements between all concerned were one of the reasons the Playhouse went into administration a second time. Protracted discussions ensued with Kenwright's company about quite how much the Playhouse owed him.[37] Unsurprisingly, the Arts Council would not release money except in small monthly allowances and the local authorities and Littlewoods were unwilling to give money until this was resolved and until they could be sure that public money was not going to go straight into paying off debts.

It would, however, be harsh to lay the entire blame at Kenwright's feet. The roots of the problems at the Playhouse went back at least as far as the abolition of the metropolitan county councils and the continuing insistence by the Arts Council on parity funding, despite the particular and deep rooted problems facing the city. From as early as 1984, Merseyside Arts, in their response to *Glory of the Garden*, had been arguing that whilst Liverpool had a strong tradition of municipal investment in the arts, a degree of caution needed to be exercised by the Arts Council when assessing development proposals in the light of "hoped-for" local authority responses because there was "increasing uncertainty as to the future roles of local government and the resources to be made available to this sector within the foreseeable future."[38]

Whilst over the next few years, the Arts Council did show some patience and tried to persuade and encourage the local councils to meet their funding requirements, they were also not above a bit of sabre rattling as well. "I did suggest that in the brave new world beyond Wilding", they wrote to Merseyside Arts in 1989, "there might be no further funds for Merseyside unless the local authorities were able to join us in a proper partnership...."[39] At the point of the crisis in 1991, Brian Rix was admonishing:

> In Liverpool, the Arts Council has been negotiating for the past four years because it was not possible to sustain an original disparity of £9 for £1, Arts Council to local authority funding. Neither can the disparity of £5 for £1, which still exists, be sustained. Nevertheless, just as a chink of light has appeared in Arts Council negotiations with our colleagues on Merseyside, the long-deferred crunch has come. It can only be stated categorically: the Arts Council has no spare cash. If the Playhouse is such an artistic and well-loved Elysium, local patronage will have to be seen and counted and surely this is not too much to ask, even in these storm-tossed dog days of the community charge.[40]

He concluded: "The Arts Council cannot afford in these stringent times to impose a theatre on a reluctant local authority."[41] At this juncture the city was £750 million in debt and facing a strike over redundancies at the council. The tussles went on right through the period when Kenwright was in charge; in 1993 Ian Brown, then drama director at the Arts Council, was writing to the Board to explain that it would be "entirely unrealistic and impolitic for the Arts Council to release funding except as a match for local authority funding".[42] The Council had to look as though it meant business.

The issue was never to be resolved, despite special pleading in the press. Michael Coveney saw Liverpool as "an exceptional case, still reeling like no other British city from the double blow of abolition and the disruption of Derek Hatton's Militant-dominated ruling party."[43] *The Guardian* was equally forceful in making the case in 1991, the year of Kenwright's arrival:

> ...it is clearly time for the Arts Council to reconsider this policy of rewarding the rich and penalising the poor. Is it reasonable to expect local authorities like Liverpool to increase their contributions at a time when they are being told by the Department of the Environment to cut back their spending? It can equally well be argued that it is the depressed areas of the country which are most in need of central government investment in cultural activities. In fact, the Playhouse's artistic director, Ian Kellgren, points out that it is the Arts Council's reduction in funding that has brought his theatre to its knees. Local authorities, he says, don't provide enough support. "Our local authority funding is now less than in 1986".[44]

Such protests seemed to cut little ice. The Arts Council withheld money or refused applications for contingency or stabilisation funding. In 1990, most theatres found themselves in receipt of an 8% increase (many with enhancement money on top), the Playhouse received standstill funding.[45] In 1993, with Kenwright in place, the theatre was put on annual funding, in 1995 its grant was reduced and just prior to its closure in 1998, it was in receipt of monthly handouts. This, combined with late payments and reductions and withdrawals from local authorities (who saw the Arts Council's lack of commitment as a sign of a lack of confidence in the city and the theatre), meant the theatre was quite often operating on a hand to mouth existence. Kenwright did provide extra working capital when it was needed, but at no point did the theatre receive the annual grant of £800,000 which had formed the basis of his agreement. Nor was its original debt ever dealt with.

The problems were compounded by the existence of two producing theatres (the Playhouse and the Everyman) in the city. The character of the Everyman, founded in 1964, was very different to that of the Playhouse. Whilst the Playhouse had always retained a sense of being a traditional theatre with an audience drawn from the outlying and wealthier areas of the city (and beyond), the Everyman was home to new writing, a younger audience and had an altogether edgier and poorer aura. However, by the early 90s, it too was struggling and trying to stay afloat under the directorship of John Doyle by offering a programme heavily reliant on Shakespeare and other classics. Whilst the Arts Council argued that it was committed to a producing theatre in Liverpool "what remains to be seen is whether the city can support two producing companies", others saw "a manipulative plot by the Arts Council to close the Playhouse or the more informal, raggedy Everyman" as underlying their unwillingness to solve the financial stalemate.[46] Much of the 90s saw an undignified squabble between the two and when the Everyman was forced to close at the end of 1993 with its grant cut by half, there were accusations that Kenwright had "secured a commitment from the funding bodies which now means there isn't enough cash to run two producing theatres in the city. The Everyman...is effectively losing its grant to an entrepreneur in a neighbouring theatre."[47] The Everyman did re-open three months later, thanks to the owners of the bistro downstairs, but essentially, at least for a while, it was to be a receiving house and the whole story was not to be resolved until 2000 when the theatres merged, whilst still maintaining their own buildings and their own identities – by which time the whole question of parity funding, which had in many ways borne the brunt of responsibility for the mess the theatres in Liverpool came to find themselves in, had strangely and quietly been dropped.

What then are the lessons we might draw from this example of commercial and subsidised co-operation? It is certainly an almost unique moment of co-operation (Kenwright's tenure at the Thorndike being the only other sustained example to date), situated at a time when the argument was for theatres to accept business practices and models (as the introduction to this book notes). It is one example of what can happen when we go down that route. Yet it also suggests a far more complex picture than one that simply draws the battle lines between them (the commercial) and us (the subsidised). If repertory theatres "were created as a result of the rebellion of individuals or groups of individuals" against the "the commercial play and the commercial production" as Grace Wyndham Goldie argued in her 1935 history of the (then) Liverpool repertory Theatre, Kenwright was indeed a strange bedfellow.[48]

Notes

[1] Ramsay Muir, Professor of Modern History at Liverpool University and a director of Liverpool Repertory Theatre 1911-1913, quoted in Grace Wyndham Goldie, *The Liverpool Repertory Theatre* (London, Hodder and Stoughton, 1935), 23-24.
[2] Jules Wright, artistic director, Liverpool Playhouse, 1985-1986, quoted in Helen Chappell, "It Lacks Heart, Spirit and Soul", *Guardian,* April 23, 1986.
[3] Ronald Faux, "Theatre Acts Out Its Toughest Role", *Times*, January 11th, 1991.
[4] Claire Armistead, "Mersey Maverick", *Guardian*, January 29, 1993.
[5] Sheridan Morley, "They're Singing in the Train", *International Herald Tribune*, August 21,1996; Robert Fox quoted in Michael Coveney, "One for the Money", *Observer,* June 16, 1996.
[6] Robert Hewison, "In Search of More Local Heroes", *Sunday Times*, July 24, 1994.
[7] Jim Hiley, "Angels Need Not Be Afraid", *Times*, June 25, 1990.
[8] Olivia Turnbull, *Bringing Down the House* (Bristol: Intellect, 2008), 180.
[9] *Annual Review 1995-6*, 12.
[10] Society of London Theatre, *After Wyndham: Key Issues in London Theatre* (London: Society of London Theatre, 1999), 4.
[11] *Annual Review* 1995-6, 5.
[12] Rowell and Jackson: *The Repertory Movement* (Cambridge: CUP, 1984), 3. An interesting contemporary example of complex collaboration can be seen in Kneehigh's *Brief Encounter* (2008) which was created in association with Birmingham Rep, remounted with support from the Royal and Derngate in Northampton and then presented in the West End and toured by commercial producers. See: ACE: *Achieving Great Art for Everyone: Consultation Paper*, Appendix *Theatre: Achievements, Challenges and Opportunities*: 2 (available at http://www.artscouncil.org.uk/consultation/).
[13] John Peter, "Moving in the Best Society", Times, March 1, 1987.
[14] Michael Billington, *State of the Nation* (London: Faber & Faber, 2007), 285.
[15] Ibid. 291.
[16] Gavin Bell, "Arts Council Meet on Hall-Nunn Row", *Times,* June 30, 1986.
[17] Peter Hall, "Why This Show Must Go On", *Times,* July 6 1986.

[18] Richard Cogo-Fawcett, *Relationships Between Subsidised and Commercial Theatre* (London: ACE, 2003), 1 and ACE, *National Policy for Theatre in England* (London: ACE, 2000), 6.
[19] Quoted in Robin Thornber, "Critical Stage at the Playhouse", *Guardian*, February 11, 1991.
[20] For details of Bill Kenwright's involvement with the Thorndike see Turnbull, 137-143.
[21] Phil Gibby, "Kenwright Backed Theatre Should Bale Out Arnaud", *Stage*, March 3, 1994.
[22] Bill Kenwright, *Liverpool Playhouse Season Brochure* 1991-92, Liverpool Playhouse Archive, Liverpool Central Library; Michael Coveney, "Port at Sea on a Rising Tide of Debt", *Observer*, February 24, 1991.
[23] It was the death of Cochran, killed in a car crash in Chippenham, which was one of the reasons for the tour becoming legendary. Vincent was also seriously injured in the crash.
[24] Robin Thornber, Review of *Imagine*, *Guardian*, July 28, 1992.
[25] Robin Thornber, Review of *Sound of Fury*, *Guardian*, July 5,1995.
[26] Robin Thornber, Review of *No Trams to Lime Street*, *Guardian*, October 18, 1995.
[27] Alan Jackson, "A Splendid Time is Guaranteed For All", *Times*, February 17, 1996.
[28] visitLiverpool, http://www.visitliverpool.com/site/what-to-do (accessed 1/9/09).
[29] Glen Walford, *Arts Alive*, October 1964; Claire Armistead, "Send in the Clones", *Guardian*, September 28, 1994.
[30] Sheridan Morley, "They're Singing in the Train", *International Herald Tribune*, August 21, 1996; Kate Bassett, "Mersey Beaten by Tat", *Times*, August 14, 1996. Both are reviewing *Ferry 'Cross the Mersey*.
[31] Kate Bassett, "Mersey Beaten by Tat", *Times*, August 14, 1996.
[32] *Birkenhead News*, September 4, 1991.
[33] For Stephen Fry's disappearance and details of Lumborg's play see Angella Johnson, "Fry Quits Drama After Duff Reviews", *Guardian*, February 23,1995; Giles Coren, "The Steely Bard from Crewe", *Times* April 12, 1995.
[34] Robin Thornber, Review of *Medea*, *Guardian*, September 21, 1993.
[35] Les Smith, Review of *Self Catering*, *Guardian*, October 5, 1992.
[36] Les Smith, Review of *At 50 She Discovered the Sea*, *Guardian*, December 1, 1992.
[37] The amount, which became known by the theatre as the "debt of honour" varied from £50,000 to £373,000, although Kenwright claimed he had lost up to £2 million over the five years.
[38] Merseyside Arts, *A Development Strategy*, June 1984, 84 in ACGB Archives, ACGB/111/20.
[39] Letter from Graham Marchant to Peter Booth, director of Merseyside Arts, 13th February 1989 in ACGB Archives, ACGB/111/20.
[40] Brian Rix, "A Scheme to Avoid Disaster", *Times*, January 17, 1991.
[41] Ibid.

[42] Letter from Ian Brown to Liverpool Playhouse, 1st March 1993, Liverpool Playhouse Archive.
[43] Michael Coveney, "Port at Sea on a Rising Tide of Debt", *Observer,* February 24, 1991.
[44] Robin Thornber, "Critical Stage at the Playhouse", *Guardian,* February 11, 1991.
[45] Both Liverpool theatres received a 0% increase along with Bristol Old Vic whilst Sheffield Crucible found its grant cut by 17%. All were theatres in cities affected by abolition of metropolitan councils.
[46] Patric Gilchrist, North West Arts Board, quoted in David Ward, "Liverpool Playhouse to Close After 130 years", *Guardian* October 9,1997; Michael Coveney, "Port at Sea on a Rising Tide of Debt", *Observer,* February 24, 1991.
[47] Robin Thornber, Review of *The Gambler, Guardian* 14th May 1993.
[48] Goldie, 11.

Chapter Ten

Enjoying and Achieving: The Future of Participation in Building-Based Theatre

James Blackman

In the conclusion of *The Repertory Movement: A History of Regional Theatre in Britain* Anthony Jackson asks a question that could be considered to be at the heart of the wider debate surrounding the future of education, learning and participation in building–based theatres. He asks [should theatre]:

> have a social mission, political, educational or otherwise, responding to perceived needs rather than apparent wants; or should it be the venue for an aesthetic experience that cannot be encompassed by the criteria or obligations associated with other social services or public utilities.[1]

In the current arts funding climate many would agree that this question does feel somewhat dated. Whilst New Labour did significantly re-invest in the arts this investment came with significant funding criteria that sought greater justification for its funding and a clearer sense of measurable outcomes.

However, whilst on the surface Jackson's argument seems to have aged, his recognition of the educational powers of theatre and how these powers are justified and delivered as part of a theatre's core vision still hold great relevance today.

There is not the space to track the history of education and community interventions in building-based theatres since Jackson and Rowell last summarised it in their book. This chapter will seek to explore the changing relationship between building-based theatre education departments, the formal and informal education sectors, and perhaps most importantly – children and young people.

There are of course many different types of intervention that theatres can have with children and young people. Many will experience our art form for the first time as part of a school trip, usually coming to see a production in the lead up to the winter break. Alongside these more traditional methods of engagement the last 15 years have seen a significant increase in the number of young people participating in theatre out of school hours. These activities are not linked to school-based learning and it is these very interventions that theatre educators are having to question. What are their core values and how much longer can they exist within a changing funding climate?

In 2003 the government published a green paper called *Every Child Matters*.[2] This was published alongside the formal response to the report into the death of Victoria Climbié. This young girl was horrifically abused and tortured, and eventually killed by her great aunt and the man with whom they lived. The green paper prompted an unprecedented debate amongst those who worked with children and young people. It called for a massive overhaul of how services are provided, how the children and young people's workforce operate together and how schools, colleges, social workers and the community and voluntary sector come together to work in partnership. The government published five key aims that the sector was required to achieve for every child, regardless of their background or circumstances. The aims were that every child had the support they needed to: be healthy, stay safe, enjoy and achieve, make a positive contribution and achieve economic well-being.

It is these five outcomes that are now vigorously tested in OFSTED inspections, Joint Area Reviews of local authorities and, perhaps of most relevance to this chapter, the outcomes are applied to almost all funding for activities within other sectors, including the arts. The outcome at the heart of the current shift in arts education practice in theatres is 'Enjoy and Achieve'.

Most young people who participate in the arts do so because they enjoy it. These young people first learn the skills that enable them to take part in this enriching activity at a class, workshop, youth theatre or in a play. Classes like these have always been popular because they are unthreatening, open to all ages and abilities and provide a pleasurable alternative to formal structures experienced at school. The Every Child Matters outcome of 'Enjoy and Achieve' has called this type of activity to account and is arguing that there is not a clear enough sense of 'achievement'.

This non-accredited learning is increasingly at risk. Unlike accredited courses, non-accredited arts programmes do not always provide the tangible benefits that are so attractive to policy-makers and potential funders. Although the benefits of such classes - increased self-esteem, new friends and new skills - are obvious to all those involved, they do not appear to have the immediate economic impact most politicians are seeking. Consequently, organisations offering courses and programmes in their traditional format are being forced to provide evidence of skills-related outcomes and contributions to social inclusion, community cohesion and public health. Those that fail to do so, for whatever reason, face the inevitable risk of not being able to find funding for their work.

The benefits of voluntary (non-accredited) arts participation are many and varied. Attending an arts workshop or class, or participating in arts activity - putting on a play, singing in a choir, staging an exhibition - can help people sustain independence and enjoy social interaction on a regular basis. Activities like these raise confidence and enable the cultivation of skills that are used every day - at work, in the home and in their community. Additionally, they suit our multicultural and ageing population; many people prefer to learn where there is no bureaucracy and formal qualifications. These participatory opportunities give those who might be wary of education (due to lack of opportunities or bad experiences in earlier life) a safe place to learn, without the pressure of exams and marking systems. They provide learners with the chance to experience achievement, perhaps for the first time in their lives.

In an education system driven by accreditation it can be argued that too much time and money is spent on demonstrating acquired skills and collecting evidence - resources that could be better spent on fostering the humanising aspects of participatory arts and widening opportunities to learn informally. The arts sector is well placed to deliver these opportunities to those who wish to learn simply for the love of it.

There is a strong argument within the children and young peoples' workforce that the 'Enjoy and Achieve' outcome would be best split so that children and young people are able to 'enjoy' and 'achieve' separately rather than the providers of services being required to find a method of measuring success and achievement alongside the enjoyment.

Whilst this argument is valid there are many who believe that the theatre sector can provide a vital role in delivering accredited learning for young people in their individual regions. What the Labour government has been good at assessing, and is starting to tackle, is that for many thousands of young people the traditional route of achievement (GCSEs, followed by A Levels, followed by a degree) is not suitable. This model of achievement is delivered exclusively in the formal education sector and if a young person does not happen to fit this model, for any number of socio-economic reasons, and therefore does not attend school, then they are deemed not in education, employment or training (NEET). This NEET cohort has been growing.[3] At the end of 2005 there were approximately 220,000 16-18 year olds (which equates to 11% of the total population of that age group) who were classified as NEET. This was a 1% increase on the 10% recorded in 2004. The government now has a commitment to reduce the NEET cohort to 8% of the total 16-18 population by 2010.

Recently, theatres and other arts organisations have started working with NEET young people to provide them with a framework of achievement, progression and support in an environment totally different from that of school. The results of these artistic interventions have been very positive. As well as increasing participants' soft skills (self esteem, confidence and time-keeping) theatres have been starting to deliver accredited learning so that the participants are equipped with a formal qualification at the end of the programme.

The funding for this work comes primarily from the Learning and Skills Council[4] and the European Social Fund.[5] This funding has worked exclusively with young people outside the school system, those who are NEET and/or socially excluded. Working with this cohort has, of course, its challenges. The government describes that

> Social exclusion happens when people or places suffer from a series of problems such as unemployment, discrimination, poor skills, low income, poor housing, high crime, ill health, and family breakdown. When such problems combine they can create a vicious circle.[6]

This description enables us to create a clear picture of the young people participating in these arts programmes. They are indeed hard-to-reach, they present with a huge variety of needs and behaviours, they have been excluded, not only by their school, but also more often, from their community.

As a way of further enabling an understanding of the type of activities being offered, below is a short case study of a groundbreaking programme being delivered by the Lyric Hammersmith.

The START Project – A Case Study

The START programme at the Lyric Hammersmith is a unique education programme delivering nationally recognised qualifications in literacy and numeracy to disadvantaged young Londoners aged between 13 and 19.

The programme engages young people who are NEET including refugee and asylum seekers, young people from black and minority ethnic backgrounds, offenders, ex-offenders and those young people who classify themselves as having a disability. They are referred from youth offending teams, pupil referral units, the Connexions service, children's services departments, schools and other community/voluntary sector organisations. Each year the project involves three terms of activity broken down into 160 sessions (53 per term) benefiting over 120 young people. The Lyric's innovative approach to the advancement of education has been providing quantifiable results for those who genuinely cannot engage with the formal education sector.

Within the London boroughs in which the Lyric works, there are over 190,000 young people aged 11-19. Although these areas have a vibrant economy and unemployment is falling, there are pockets of poverty, including some wards featuring in the top 5% of deprived areas in the country.

The Lyric piloted the START project throughout 2006-2007 and witnessed outstanding responses to this area of work. Many of the learners entered the programme with reading and numerical skill levels of 5/6 year olds. Through the distinctive approach, coupled with a bespoke programme of learning, the Lyric were able to progress them to levels much nearer the national average for young people of their age. 96% of all young people on the programme achieved a nationally recognised City and Guilds qualification between levels 1 and 2.

The programme is run in partnership with experienced arts-in-education specialists, key skills tutors, and professional performers and includes dance, performance poetry, drama and movement. The Lyric Hammersmith works closely with the local Connexions service to provide a high level of information, advice and guidance on progression routes back into education or, where appropriate, into employment or training.

To their knowledge the Lyric is the only arts based organisation in the UK delivering work of this kind.

The young people in the case study above are without doubt in need of intervention. More often than not these interventions are radical in approach and hugely different from the environment in which they failed. It is an environment that is kinaesthetic in approach, that is accepting of difference, and that is familiar with struggling. One could argue these are all key features of the theatre industry.

Despite all of these thematic similarities this type of accredited learning, coupled with the niche it is marketed to, does place theatre practitioners in completely new ground. It calls on us to have a skills language, to talk-the-talk of education and learning first, before we talk about our art form. To engage with the desired outcomes before we consider how they will be achieved and to make the activity through which these outcomes are delivered learner centred and not art form centred.

It also presents different challenges in terms of appropriately dealing with learners and beneficiaries. As an example, a colleague in a well-regarded regional theatre recently e-mailed me to say that over the duration of their accredited Summer Arts programme they had had five visits from the police, two violent incidents and one arrest.

With the sector engaging with beneficiaries of this kind, coupled with the change in delivery mechanisms, does theatre in education need to reconsider itself?

Theatre, education and social work are all too often considered as very separate commodities. Yet what is apparent is that the practice of accredited learning in theatres can allow both an artistic experience and an educative participation to have long-lasting, quantifiable and useful effect on a beneficiary. The debate that surrounds the validity of theatre, education and social work are not new ones. In Tony Jackson's paper *The Dialogic and the Aesthetic: Some Reflections on Theatre as a Learning Medium* he cleverly refers to how Bertolt Brecht wrote about a similar problem he faced in the 1930s:

> Generally it is felt to be a very sharp distinction between learning and amusing oneself. The first may be useful, but only the second is pleasant... Well, all that can be said is that the contrast between learning and amusing oneself is not laid down by divine rule; it is not one that has always been and must continue to be... Theatre remains theatre, even when it is instructive theatre, and in so far as it is good theatre it will amuse.[7]

It is difficult to argue that theatre-in-education, creative learning and arts participation has not been part of a "massive cultural experiment".[8] Our society, and the rules that govern it, have undergone substantial change over the past forty years and theatre in education has always, in one way or another, sought to represent these changes.

David Pammenter in the collection of essays *Learning through Theatre: New Perspectives on Theatre-in-Education* writes that "We cannot pretend that the socio-political factors that govern the lives of adults are different for children"[9] and so, if access to knowledge is an important freedom as the UN Convention on the Rights of the Child states, - "we must make these factors accessible to the young so that they may explore and challenge them if they choose".[10] It is this point that could be considered at the heart of the *Every Child Matters* outcome of 'Enjoy and

Achieve' and theatres across the country will need to make important choices about how their participatory programmes assist in its delivery.

When considering these changes in practice, and specifically the practice within building-based theatres, it is vitally important that educators, artists and managers have a clear sense of why this new form of practice is valuable not only to the learners but also the theatre building. The theatre workforce has a massive leap to take in the diversity of its workforce. The Cultural and Creative Skills Council recently published figures that showed that 94.7% of arts employees are white.[11] Activities that engage young people from outside the formal education sector can help to open the doors of opportunity for young people from a wide variety of communities. The government's 2005 White Paper *14-19 Education and Skills*[12] highlights clearly that the NEET cohort is diverse in its broadest sense. Providing pathways for young people to enter our sector from these groups will only enrich our artistic offer and ensure an authentic contemporary voice. Furthermore, one of the biggest daily concerns for a building-based theatre is audience. Educators in building-based settings have a key responsibility to promoting theatre-going and introducing participants to the live, professional art form.

Over the coming years theatres up and down the country will be making important decisions about the future direction of their education activities. We have a government with an agenda that is very clear. To better equip our children and young people with the skills they need to join a workforce and to reward and fund those organisations that best assist in delivering this outcome. Where the government needs to take a bigger leap is in realising that theatre and arts education practitioners can be leaders in turning their ambitions into reality and this might be even more pertinent if we find the UK with a conservative administration in 2010.

Evidence suggests that the sector can deliver accredited qualifications to disenfranchised sections of our communities who are desperately in need of intervention, a second chance, and more often than not, a certificate to prove they can read, count and communicate.

The future looks promising. We have, for the first time, a ten-year strategy for positive activities,[13] a move towards child centred, rather than schools centred funding and, at Arts Council England, a three-year programme to develop youth and participatory theatre and the first appointment of a Head of Young People at Risk. There is also an ever-increasing commitment from Artistic Directors to the existence of education and learning departments in building-based theatres.

For centuries theatre has existed as a public service and in more recent decades this has been recognised with public money. We stand now at a point of change, where theatres and arts organisations can receive additional public funds to deliver other public services. Services that will indeed call into question the remit of our buildings. Changes that will make us question and re-consider our core organisational values and which will change the nature of our day-to-day operation. However these changes do not have the potential to weaken the art form, or negatively alter an organisation's artistic integrity. Far from it. The artist has always been an educator, a storyteller and a deliverer of knowledge transfer - these are processes that take place between actor and audience every night, in every theatre, during every performance. Evidence suggests that when theatre-makers, educators and young people come together in a creative collaboration it is at this point that life-changing effects take place. When this happens the words 'actor', 'audience', 'learner' and 'beneficiary' are united beneath the proscenium arch as a single word yet to be discovered.

Notes

[1] Rowell, G & Jackson, A *The Repertory Movement: A History of Regional Theatre in Britain,* (Cambridge: Cambridge University Press, 1984).
[2] Http://publications.everychildmatters.gov.uk/eOrderingDownload/CM5860.pdf.
[3] www.dcsf.gov.uk/14-19.
[4] www.lsc.gov.uk.
[5] www.esf.gov.uk.
[6] www.socialexclusionunit.gov.uk.
[7] Anthony Jackson, "The Dialogic and the Aesthetic: Some Reflections on Theatre as a Learning Medium.", *The Journal of Aesthetic Education* - Volume 39, Number 4, Winter 2005, 104-118.
[8] Baz Kershaw, *The Politics of Performance: Radical Theatre as Cultural Intervention*, (London: Routledge, 1992).
[9] Jackson, Tony. *Learning Through Theatre: New Perspectives on Theatre in Education*, (London: Routledge, 1993) 60.
[10] Jackson, Tony. *Learning Through Theatre: New Perspectives on Theatre in Education*, (London: Routledge 1993) 60.
[11] Bewick, Tom. http://www.ccskills.org.uk/media/cms/documents/pdf/TOMS_SPEECH.pdf (Cultural and Creative Skills Council, 2006).
[12] Department for Children School and Families, *14-19 Education and Skills White Paper* Available at: http://www.dfes.gov.uk/14-19/documents/14-19whitepaper.pdf.
[13] Department for Children, Schools and Families *Aiming High for Young People: A Ten Year Strategy for Positive Activities* (July 2007).

CONCLUSION

"WHAT'S POSSIBLE AND WHO CARES?": THE FUTURE OF REGIONAL THEATRE

KATE DORNEY

At the September 2006 conference that inspired this book, many practitioners spoke of a sense of uncertainty about the future of regional producing theatre. The optimism of Boyden and the Theatre Review of 2000, and the accompanying £25 million of extra funding provided to address Arts Council England's (ACE) eight key objectives, which once again made regional theatre an inviting place to work, had given way to pessimism in the light of the Department of Culture Media and Sport's (DCMS) 2005 announcement that funding would be frozen until 2008.[1] As organisations faced their umpteenth decrease in funding, it became clear that the brave new strategies would have to be delivered with no extra resources beyond the initial lump-sums.

At the beginning of 2007 the Government gave warning to arts organisations that the Comprehensive Spending Review might result in a drop in funding as spending on health, education and the London Olympics was prioritised. Added to falling revenue from lottery ticket sales, the outlook for state-subsidised companies was bleak. ACE, realising once again that it had more clients than it could adequately fund, decided to conduct a review of all its regularly funded organisations (RFOs), determined that, unlike in the days of *Glory of the Garden*, this time there would be no equal misery for all. It announced that it would remove 194 clients from its portfolio of RFOs and reduce funding to a further 27 in order to add 90 new companies and increase funding for those staying on the books. Christopher Frayling, then Chairman of ACE, argued that there was "no room for old blood if we keep a fixed playing field". In an uncanny echo of the 1980 Christmas cuts, this was announced in December 2007 and organisations were given until the 15th January to appeal. Amongst them (alongside the Bush Theatre and the Orange Tree in London) were Derby Playhouse, the Northcott at Exeter (who received their notification the day before they were to re-open following a part-Arts Council funded refurbishment), and Bristol Old Vic. Of these, two were already in trouble. Derby had closed at the start of December 2007, following months of speculation over its health. Bristol had closed rather abruptly in August 2007, ostensibly for refurbishment, towards which the ACE had allocated £2 million. In the face of criticism the Council continued to assert that the cuts were necessary to ensure adequate funding to its other clients (new and existing). When the result of the Comprehensive Spending Review was finally announced (three months later than expected), ACE was awarded a 3.3% uplift in funding, but continued to stick to its plan, to the fury of its clients. Not all of them opposed the principle, which had been raised during the evidence gathering of the Culture, Media and Sport Select Committee Report on Theatre, but many objected to the methodology. The Select Committee had flagged up:

> the concern expressed by the Independent Theatre Council, and by some of the theatres who gave evidence to us, that the Arts Council seems to be entrenched in its existing funding programme. We believe that a more dynamic approach is needed in rewarding new entrants, and existing theatre groups, who have innovative ideas while being far more critical of those recipients of funding who have failed to develop their original potential to fulfil their commitments.[2]

The Council's efforts to address it led to what Genista McIntosh described as: "ACE battling for its reputation against some of the most damaging publicity in its 60 year history".[3]

In January 2008 Peter Hewitt, ACE's outgoing Chief Executive, was called to a public meeting at the Young Vic and faced a vote of no confidence. In yet another piece of unfortunate timing, the McMaster report, *Supporting Excellence in the Arts: From Measurement to Judgement*, was published the following day. The report had been commissioned at the beginning of 2007 by newly appointed Culture Secretary James Purnell to review the target driven culture which dominated arts funding and programming. The report found social objectives had been attained or promoted at the expense of excellence and innovation, and that the burden of administration related to grants took up more time than actually producing the work that companies had been funded for in the first place. The fact that McMaster came on the heels of ACE's review of RFOs once again created the impression that the Council and government were not working together and further damaged its credibility within the sector. Hewitt came to the end of his term and was replaced by Alan Davey who immediately commissioned Genista McIntosh's *Lessons Learned* report about the fall-out of the 2007/8 cuts. The result was the announcement of a new "light touch" assessment system with clients being assessed by "peers" rather than increasingly remote art form officers. ACE have now recruited the first members of these peer review panels and are hoping to regain industry confidence as a result of the new artistic assessment process.[4] The episode provides a timely reminder that it's not only regional theatre which is portrayed as being in a constant cycle of crisis and recovery, so too is the Arts Council.

Local/regional

Although the story of British regional theatre cannot ever be wholly divided from the story of the Arts Council, subsidy at regional and local level is also a crucial component in the development, sustainability and success of regional theatre. As flagships for civic pride, tourist attractions, job providers and education resources, the ideal of regional theatre is to play a significant part in the local community and attract national attention. Tony Jackson has observed in this volume and elsewhere that, "the raising of standards, and the relationship of theatre to its community" are recurrent themes in the aspirations and assessments of theatre in the regions from 19th century repertory through to the present. From urban regeneration in Liverpool, fostering community identity in Staffordshire and East Anglia, reflecting changing ethnic demographics in Birmingham, Leicester and Nottingham, all alongside providing a "good night out", subsidised theatres in the regions are tasked with fulfilling a variety of roles. Arguably perhaps, a greater number of roles than their London based counterparts where responsibility for these things can be shared. Among the attractions offered by touring versions of West End musicals and long-running shows, productions from touring companies like Out-of-Joint, Tamasha, Kneehigh, Shared Experience, Frantic Assembly, English Touring Theatre and Northern Broadsides and an assortment of professional, semi-professional and amateur shows, an ERPT must produce shows that are excellent (for ACE), educational (for the Local Authority), popular (for both funders) and challenging, and that draw in new audiences as well as retaining existing ones. As Gwenda Hughes has shown above, local audiences have high expectations of their local theatre on a number of levels, and not solely related to the artistic output. Hughes' provocative title (which directly addresses and acknowledges the long-standing hostility between the centre and the regions) "I Bet Nick Hytner Doesn't Have To Do This" resonates on a number of levels. It's highly unlikely, for example, that Hytner personally answers complaints about ice-cream or parking: the scale of the organisation makes it possible for it to be someone else's immediate problem. Also Hytner's audience is hugely diverse ranging from local residents, those from Greater London, the regions and overseas tourists. For the most part these groups probably don't have the same sense that their taxes, local and national are contributing to the running of the building, choice of ice cream and parking provision and therefore don't feel the same sense of ownership. This in itself is an interesting conundrum: a National Theatre that belongs to no one and everyone rather than a regional theatre which (some) people see as a manifestation of civic pride and achievement. In Hughes' case, her regular audience is obviously drawn was from a narrower section of the population, and it's highly likely that the older members of the audience contributed to the building of it, or at least remember it as a landmark local event. The Vic's history is embedded in the community, it was and is a key feature of its organisation, and this has its downside, as both Hughes' and Turnbull's pieces attest. Their essays also highlight the problems of scale: in the case of both theatres, there are other theatres nearby with bigger budgets, different repertoires and casts. These issues have also been forcefully raised by the debates around Bristol Old Vic which I will be using here as a case study for a model of a 21st century ERPT.

One of the requirements of ACE's national theatre policy is "regional distinctiveness" which should:

> encourage the unique local voice of theatre that combines quality with the edge that comes from making work in, and for, a particular community. Theatre companies and agencies should provide a meaningful contribution to the life of the community in which they exist.[5]

The key term here is "community" rather than "region". As ever, the Arts Council doesn't really define what "regional" means beyond being a way of delineating an administrative area. "Community" is much more elastic admitting a range of ages, classes, ethnicities and experience and also, crucially, in terms of DCMS objectives, suggesting "participation" as well as edification. The resurrected Bristol Old Vic (BOV) is responding directly to ACE and DCMS's directives in the way it's framing itself, driven not only by these directives but also by the wishes of local artists and audiences who attended the public meetings and events organised after the closure and which have now become part of the new model of working.

BOV's re-emergence serves as a template for the issues surrounding ERPTs in the new century: the burden of the building, methods of community engagement, creating a repertoire and training and developing staff. BOV first ran into difficulties in the 1980s as local authority funding failed to keep pace with inflation and ACE susbidy. The post-Glory requirement of parity funding resulted in the Council reducing the theatre's grant, and it continued to suffer from a lack of funds until given a stabilisation package in 2001. In 2003 David Farr and Simon Reade were appointed joint artistic directors joining the cohort of young professionals who, post-Theatre Review, found the idea of working in the regions both palatable and viable. They had previously worked together as Artistic Director and Literary Manager of the Gate Theatre, Notting Hill and affirmed their intention to continue the European ethos of the Gate by running Bristol along the lines of a European regional theatre and to "redefine the whole idea of theatre outside London not as regional reps but as they are in any self-respecting European country: cultural powerhouses, national state theatres."[6] In the same interview they spoke of a desire to produce an "ambitious" programme of "radical productions" and to situate the theatre at the heart of the cultural renaissance that Bristol was undergoing with the continued success of Shakespeare at the Tobacco Factory, Aardman animation and work on the fringe. Both being writers, they also declared their commitment to new writing, reflected in the programming by a number of adaptations of classic texts including *Paradise Lost, Great Expectations* and the world premiere of Carol Ann Duffy's *Beasts and Beauties* dramatized by Tim Supple and Melly Still. They also continued the theatre's already established relationship with Kneehigh. In 2004 Farr left to take over the Lyric Theatre Hammersmith and Reade continued as sole artistic director with co-productions between the two theatres as a notable feature of this new direction (and in line with ACE recommendations about sharing resources, minimising production costs and touring shows). In the eyes of the London critics Reade and Farr had "rescued" BOV and once again made it into a nationally important theatre. Reade had weighed into a number of debates about the vibrancy of regional theatre in the press, notably responding to Mark Ravenhill's *Guardian* piece about the difficulty of getting second productions of new plays on outside London with an impassioned piece asserting that:

> For many of us, rehashing a recently produced new play is not an enticing prospect. The playwright may like the royalties, but they, like their audiences, will know that the reproduction is unlikely to be as good as the original. We'd rather produce something that's new for the very first time, not second-hand.[7]

He ended the article with a plea for theatre to pull together nationally in the face of more cuts in public spending and to look to Europe for models of collaboration.

However, when Reade announced his departure in 2007, and shortly after the board announced the closure of the theatre for refurbishment (along with the shedding of all but a skeleton staff), a very different, and local, story emerged. Despite the board's claim that the suddenness of the closure was due to a £1m donation from the Linbury Trust which, alongside money from ACE and the lottery, had made it possible to begin refurbishment work immediately, the project appeared to be largely unplanned. The next season's programme had been advertised and included high profile projects such as Kenneth Branagh directing and starring in *Ivanov*, Kneehigh's Christmas show and a collaboration with Headlong and Lyric Hammersmith. The fact that Reade did not break news of the closure of the theatre and the attendant redundancies in to his staff contributed to negative feelings towards him and the theatre's board in the local press. A clear narrative never emerged from this period, it was said that audience figures had dropped to 30% of the house, chair of the board Rupert Rhymes blamed ACE for the closure, the Council denied responsibility and tried to focus instead on finding a replacement for Rhymes, Reade said nothing, and Philip Hedley publicly speculated that he had signed a gagging order.[8] As this book goes to press, a similar story is unfolding in Exeter.

The local story that did emerge, much of it via Lyn Gardner's *Guardian* blog, was that the work produced under Reade's tenure received far better reviews from the national press than from the local audience. Reade appeared to have been unpopular with local audiences and was accused (along with Farr) of cronyism, metropolitanism and of failing to involve the local theatre community in their planning and programming. At an early public meeting Rhymes spoke of an audience who had defected to Bath, and as concern grew locally and nationally that BOV might never operate again as a producing venue, ACE commissioned Peter Boyden to work with local development agency Theatre Bristol (TB) to "investigate what it might take to produce a performance culture of ambition in the city".[9] Their assessment of the theatre's recent history was, unsurprisingly, more even-handed than those who had posted comments on Gardner's blog but it clearly identified the difficulties faced by the board and director(s):

> The decision to close the Theatre Royal, the country's oldest continuously working theatre, and mothball the company followed a long period during which sequential BOV managements struggled to find a sustainable

artistic, production and financial model for the King Street complex and its production facilities. During the winter and spring of 2007 costs rose and earned income declined to the point at which it was no longer possible to continue trading. What should be the city/region's creative engine for live performance had fallen silent.[10]

The involvement of Theatre Bristol and the appointment of Dick Penny (already Managing Director of Bristol's Watershed media centre and a former associate director of BOV and of the Boyden Report seems to have set BOV on a new and radical course in terms of opening the theatre and its resources up to the local communities. This new model is driven by the vision of TB.

In Dec 2006 Theatre Bristol had organised an Open Space event entitled *What's possible and who cares?* to discuss the future of performance in the city, a subject of much debate since dreams for the Heritage Lottery funded Performing Arts Centre on the waterfront had come to nothing. The success of the event led them to plan a series of seminars for autumn 2007 to follow up the issues raised and discuss them with other successful artists from across the UK. Before the seminar series could begin, the closure of BOV prompted them to host a second event *So, where to do we go from here?*. The event "laid the foundations on which to rebuild a fit-for-purpose performance culture for a thriving city".[11] ACE commissioned Theatre Bristol to run an "extensive programme of seminars, consultation and research designed to raise the collective ambition of the sector".[12] They organised seminars with John Fox (Welfare State); Lucy Neal (LIFT); Pax Nindi (formerly ACE's senior combined arts officer and Artistic Director of St Paul's Carnival Bristol); Tony Reekie (Imaginate); John McGrath (Contact Theatre); Jonathan Church (Chichester Festival Theatre) and Dick Penny (BOV/Watershed Media). They held open meetings and one-to-one consultations with practitioners across the art-forms, with academics, and with workers in other parts of the creative industry in order to try and determine the opportunities available in Bristol to both practitioners and audiences and also to identify what it lacked.

The report, *Bristol Live: A Performance Culture of Ambition*, which resulted from the seminars and consultations revealed that the city's key strengths were the number of creative workers in the city across art-forms and at a variety of different scales, the size of the potential audience (1.34m people within a 45 minute drive) and a thriving circus and festival culture. The key weaknesses were the lack of suitable performance venues, particularly for mid-scale theatre and dance, and the lack of community venues.[13] The report also articulated a vision of performance which combined the McMaster values of excellence and ambition with the government's emphasis on performance as an agent of social change through participation. In a section entitled "Public Investment for Public Benefit. Why should we invest our money in performance", the report asserts: "a performance culture of ambition (seeking social and economic as well as cultural dividends) depends on making good choices about public investment". [14]In this section the rhetoric is designed to appeal to local pride but also echoes the national agenda of "Creative Britain": "Bristolians deserve the best"; "we want to produce national 'hot ticket' work in Bristol that people get on trains to come and see"; "we want to grow worldclass talent in the city".[15] The sentiments are not new or radical, but in the context of reduced budgets at local, regional and national levels, selling BOV as the hub of a new "performance culture of ambition" was critical to convincing all the funding bodies that its resurrection was viable and represented a shrewd investment as the subsidy would no longer be solely for the theatre, but for the performance community. And it was on these terms that BOV reopened with a clear mission, expressed in the Directors' Report as: "To delight, surprise and inspire the people of Bristol with excellent live theatre in an environment of creativity, welcome and adventure".[16] One of the features of the new regime was an agreement for a series of co-productions between BOV and TB which would showcase the work of Bristol-based artists and performers.

Local Engagement

Determination to engage on a local level has been key to BOV's new strategy. Dick Penny's chairmanship has been characterised by public meetings acknowledging "we need to know what you think and what your hopes for the theatre are". He also emphasised, even before the new directors were appointed, that the refurbishment would be planned in consultation with the public. Soon after his arrival he oversaw the recruitment of new trustees including local writer Catherine Johnson, actor and Equity spokesman Patrick Duggan and Jenny Gentles, director of communications at the Drum Birmingham. One of the theatre's first shows after reopening was the premiere of Johnson's *Suspension* in the Studio. The play used local landmark, Clifton Suspension Bridge, to address the universal issue of parents and children, written by a local writer with a global profile (as a result of *Mamma Mia!*). When Tom Morris and Emma Stenning were appointed as Artistic and Executive Directors BOV's hopes of bringing world class talent to Bristol as well as developing local artists looked even more hopeful. Stenning came from running Manchester International Festival, Morris from an Associate Director post at the National where he had co-directed the hugely successful *War Horse* and *Every Good Boy Deserves Favour* as well as working with Kneehigh on *A Matter of Life and Death.* Morris and Stenning had previously worked together running Battersea Arts Centre bringing together an amazingly diverse range of artists from Kneehigh and Punchdrunk through to NIE and puppetry, winning hosts of awards and fighting off closure by Wandsworth Borough Council. When Morris addressed a public meeting to lay out their new vision, it seemed plausible when he spoke of the:

> extraordinary ferment of activity from the artistic community within the city and how BOV aims to give opportunities to that community through collaboration. Alongside this is a wide range of opportunities for young people within the theatre and an invitation for non-professionals of all ages to also get involved.[17]

Of course his invocation of a local artistic community serving the wider local community, his invitation to young people and non-professionals of all ages to participate in theatre-making is straight from TB's report, but it is being followed through. One of the earliest pieces of programming announced by Morris and Stenning was Bristol Jam, the UK's first ever festival of improvisation, which they described as a "tiny riot of improvised performance of some of the artforms which flourish across Bristol".[18] Thus far, BOV has held true to its new mission, in the year since its doors reopened, the theatres have hosted local touring companies, youth and community shows, co-produced *Uncle Vanya* with Shakespeare at the Tobacco Factory, in a production which has pleased local and national critics, before receiving Christmas shows from Kneehigh and Bristol-based Travelling Light. Morris and Stenning announced their first full season in November 2009 which includes a new production of Churchill's *Far Away*, and *Juliet and Her Romeo*, a project which Morris has been developing for over 10 years, about lovers in their 80s being prevented from marrying by children fearful for their inheritances. Also announced were visiting shows from the Royal Court and National Theatre, and productions by Fevered Sleep and Sound and Fury.

It seems an ambitious programme for a regional theatre, but one that is likely to engage Bristol's local creative community. The question mark over the other audiences is partially because, as *Bristol Live* acknowledged, despite the criticisms previously levelled at BOV in terms of its engagement with local audiences: "very little is known about the habits and wishes of Bristol audiences" because of a lack of research into the area.[19] The report also identified the need for "pathways" for audiences as there seemed to be little crossover between audiences for one venue or performance type and others. The clearest articulation of BOV's audience I have been able to find was expressed in a letter to *The Times* in October 2007 by Ray Price, Chair of Bristol Old Vic Theatre Club. Price wrote of his membership's fear that BOV would not reopen as a producing theatre, but would instead fall prey to small-scale touring companies, community theatre groups and alternative theatre. This fear suggests the kind of conservative approach that regional theatre directors cite as stopping them from reinventing their programme, but Price ended by stating:

> We are a knowledgeable and discerning audience. We know that in the current funding climate some co-productions are essential and indeed desirable. We understand that theatre must be inclusive. We are willing to engage with challenging and provocative new writing. We also like to be amused and entertained.[20]

Morris and Stenning look as though they will be able to provide both, and their approach also incorporates a new element of community engagement over and above the work produced on the stage. "The Memory of Theatre" installation which collects theatre-going memories from Bristolians will assist in the continuing historicization and narrativization which appears to be so crucial to the survival of regional theatre. In its darkest hours, BOV, like many other theatres before it, drew on, and was described in terms of, its glorious past. No newspaper article was complete without a mention of the high profile actors who had begun their career there, or about its status as the first subsidised theatre in the UK, or that, until its closure, it was the oldest surviving continually producing theatre in Britain. Of course all these elements are significant, but the key to BOV and other ERPT's survival is the narratives they can weave about their future. As Lyn Gardner pointed out, the old justifications no longer convince:

> There is an argument that the regions are the prime training ground of the theatre industry. This is as outmoded as the idea that working on a regional newspaper serves as an apprenticeship for Fleet Street. [...]
> So if these theatres are no longer at the heart of training, and are increasingly expensive to run, do they still serve a purpose in our theatre culture? I, along with the very large swathes of the population they serve, would say a resounding yes. But it's a yes that comes with a proviso: these buildings and their management need to recognise that British theatre is changing. The old idea of a regional theatre as the flagship around which the rest of the city revolves is dying; it is now only one element in a flotilla

of activity. If these buildings want to keep their place in our theatre culture, they need to breathe out - and engage a wider community - as well as in.[21]

In terms of the theatre ecology, ERPTs must evolve or die, but not, it seems, in an atmosphere of public and professional indifference. Theatre Bristol's provocative title for their first event about the state of theatre in Bristol, "What's possible and who cares?" proved that a great many people did care and believed that a renaissance was possible. Like the Devoted and Disgruntled events first facilitated by Improbable Theatre in 2005, a new model seems to be evolving in which ACE is a partner in the shaping of new policies rather than the prime motivator.

Notes

[1] Culture, Media and Sport Select Committee Report on Theatre, 5th Report. http://www.publications.parliament.uk/pa/cm200405/cmselect/cmc accessed 25/10/2006

[2] Government Response to the Culture, Media and Sport Select Committee Report on Theatre (HC-254-1) Session 2004-2005, para 75

[3] *A Review of Arts Council England's RFO Investment Strategy 2007/2008*, p.14. Published as an Annex to Alan Davey's *A Review of Arts Council England's RFO Investment Strategy: Lessons Learned*. London: ACE, 2008

[4] I am one of them, alongside former ACGB Drama panel member Paul Allen. For a full list of assessors see http://www.artscouncil.org.uk/funding/regular-funding-organisations/artistic-assessment/.

[5] Ibid, 6

[6] Farr, theatrevoice.com 19.12.03

[7] Reade, Pride and Prejudice, Guardian 11/01/07

[8] Hedley, *Stage* 26.6.07

[9] *Bristol Live: A Performance Culture of Ambition. A Discussion Paper*, 1

[10] Ibid., 1

[11] Ibid., 1

[12] Ibid, 1

[13] Ibid, 3

[14] Ibid., 3

[15] Ibid., 3

[16] The Bristol Old Vic Ltd Directors' Report and Consolidated Financial Statement Year Ended March 2008, 5

[17] BOV Press Release, 17.9.09

[18] BOV Press Release, undated.

[19] Ibid, 2

[20] *Times* 6 October 2007.

[21] The Guardian April 27, 2009 Monday 'The bold, the old and the obsolete' Lyn Gardner

Appendix A

Revenue Funding to ERPT 1984/85

Theatres in italics are London based companies

Alternative Theatre Company (Bush)	*114,320*
Basingstoke: Horseshoe Theatre	72,000
Birmingham Repertory Theatre	430,500
Bristol Old Vic	457,650
Caryl Jenner productions	*200,000*
Cheltenham Everyman	22,000
Chester Gateway	87,500
Churchill Theatre Trust	90,500
Croydon Alternatives Theatre Co	73,500
Colchester Mercury	185,000
Coventry: Belgrade Theatre Trust	197,000
Crucible Theatre Trust	471,000
Derby Playhouse	167,500
English Stage Company	*506,727*
Farnham Repertory Co	128,000
Greenwich Theatre	133,500
Guildford: Yvonne Arnaud	136,000
Half Moon	*99,500*
Hampstead Theatre	*107,000*
Harrogate: White Rose Theatre Trust	132,500
Hornchurch Theatre	148,000
King's Head Theatre	*55,000*
Lancaster: Duke's Playhouse	126,500
Leatherhead: Thorndike Theatre	159,000
Leeds Theatre Trust	235,000
Leicester Theatre Trust	323,000
Liverpool Repertory Theatre	313,500
Liverpool Everyman Theatre	156,000
Manchester Young People's Theatre	128,500
Newcastle-Under-Lyme; Stoke-on-Trent and North Staffordshire Theatre Trust	174,500

Northcott Devon Theatre and Arts Centre	206,500
Northampton Repertory Players	95,500
Nottingham Theatre Trust	428,625
Octagon Theatre Bolton	133,000
Oldham Coliseum	108,000
Oval House	55,500
Oxford: Anvil Productions	239,000
Pioneer Theatres	180,625
Polka Children's Theatre	113,950
Richmond Fringe Ltd	63,500
Royal Exchange Theatre Co	580,500
Salisbury Arts Theatre	142,583
Scarborough Theatre	113,000
Soho Theatre Company	*63,125*
Southend: Palace Theatre	87,500
Theatre Royal (Plymouth)	222,000
Tyne and Wear Theatre Trust	210,500
Wakefield Tricycle Co ltd	89,125
Watford Civic Theatre Trust	97,500
Wolsey Theatre (Ipswich)	148,000
Worcester Arts Association	90,500
Worthing: Connaught Theatre	76,000
York Citizens Theatre Trust	202,500
Young Vic Theatre Co	*227,125*

RAA Grants

Eastern Arts	889,775
East Midlands Arts	1,061,119
Greater London Arts	1,583,722
Lincolnshire and Humberside	591,050
Merseyside	583,903
Northern Arts	1,983,659
North West Arts	1,031,953
Southern Arts	995,088
South East Arts	628,991
South West Arts	970,894
West Midlands Arts	1,221,727
Yorkshire Arts/Yorkshire and Humberside Arts Board	841,602

APPENDIX B

REVENUE FUNDING TO ERPTS: 2008-09

Almeida	1,002,943
Alternative Theatre Company (Bush)	503,998
Battersea Arts Centre	635,000
Belgrade Theatre, Coventry	1,002,045
Birmingham Repertory Theatre	1,723,752
Bristol Old Vic	578,000
Chichester Festival Theatre	1,572,180
Colchester Mercury	791,059
Contact Theatre, Manchester	886,506
Derby City Council [1]	742,810
Donmar Warehouse	513,500
English Stage Company (Royal Court)	2,189,628
Everyman Theatre, Cheltenham	384,190
Gate Theatre	290,212
Half Moon	206,010
Hampstead Theatre	890,000
Hull Truck Theatre [2]	532,690
Leicester Theatre Trust	1,751,555
Live Theatre (Newcastle)	554,837
Liverpool Everyman and Playhouse Theatre	1,571,310
Lyric Hammersmith	963,542
New Victoria Theatre, Stoke	948,810
Mercury Theatre, Colchester	812,418
New Wolsey Theatre, Ipswich	723,927
Northampton Theatre Trusts	715,960
Northern Stage	1,227,993
Northcott Theatre, Exeter	547,236

---

[1] Money to ensure the long term future of producing theatre in Derby and to produce a viable model
[2] Classed as both a touring and building based producing theatre given its new building

Nottingham Theatre Trust	1,378,405
Nuffield Theatre, Southampton	591,106
Octagon Theatre Bolton	586,725
Oldham Coliseum	485,463
Oxford Playhouse	285,472
Queens Theatre, Hornchurch	281,908
Richmond Fringe Ltd (Orange Tree)	371,597
Roundhouse	1,000,000
Royal Exchange Theatre Co	2,373,089
Salisbury Playhouse	859,148
Sheffield Theatres [3]	1,301,117
Soho Theatre Company	662,965
Stephen Joseph Theatre, Scarborough	678,210
Theatre Royal (Plymouth)	1,206,271
Theatre Royal, Stratford East	854,078
Theatre by the Lake, Keswick	448,491
Tricycle Theatre	742,358
Watermill Theatre	319,008
Watford Palace	737,028
West Yorkshire Playhouse	1,533,147
York Theatre Royal	580,080
Young Vic Theatre Co	1,511,095
Yvonne Arnaud Theatre, Guildford [4]	447,799

National Theatre: 18,715,432
Royal Shakespeare Company: 15,179,676

---

[3] Incorporating Crucible, Lyceum and the Studio
[4] Currently, its final year of funding

APPENDIX C

ARTS COUNCIL SPENDING IN THE REGIONS 1984-1988

(Source: ACGB: *Glory Reflected: a Progress Report on Glory of the Garden* (1989)

Region	Total Subsidy: 84/5	Total Subsidy: 87/88	% of Total: 84/5	% of total: 87/88	% change	% change; inflation adjusted
Eastern	2,646,000	3,458,568	3.65	4.04	30.71	17.30
East Midlands	3,300,000	5,077,408	4.55	5.94	53.86	38.08
Greater London	34,807,000	34,697,322	48.02	40.57	-0.32	-10.54
Lincs & Humberside	1,008,800	1,784,927	1.39	2.09	72.08	59.92
Merseyside	2,212,000	2,526,241	3.05	2.95	14.21	2.49
Northern	3,491,000	4,357,928	4.82	5.10	24.83	12.03
North West	3,670,000	4,420,791	5.06	5.17	20.46	8.10
Southern	3,645,000	6,001,695	5.03	7.02	64.64	47.76
South East	1,996,000	3,021,121	2.75	3.53	51.36	35.84
South West	4,590,000	5,711,758	6.33	6.68	24.44	11.68
West Midlands	6,646,000	8,338,689	9.17	9.75	25.47	12.60
Yorkshire	4,472,000	6,131,382	6.17	7.17	37.11	23.05

APPENDIX D

SUMMARY OF SUBSIDY PER HEAD BY REGION 1999-2000

(Source: Nicholas Wilson and Mark Hart: *Regional Funding Revisited: Arts Expenditure in the English Regions* (Small Business Research Centre, Kingston University, 2001)

	East England Arts	East Midlands Arts	London Arts	Northern Arts	North West Arts	Southern Arts	South East Arts	South West Arts	West Midlands Arts	Yorkshire Arts
Grant-in-aid	£1.48	£1.96	£12.85	£3.55	£2.52	£2.21	£1.44	£2.89	£2.58	£2.91
Less national cos	£1.42	£1.96	£4.44	£3.18	£2.46	£2.16	£1.40	£2.59	£2.52	£2.81
Av annual lottery awards	£1.17	£1.24	£7.76	£7.58	£3.49	£2.75	£1.81	£2.19	£4.25	£2.36
Grant-in-aid + lottery	£2.65	£3.20	£20.61	£11.13	£6.01	£4.96	£3.25	£5.08	£6.83	£5.28
Less national cos	£2.59	£3.20	£12.20	£10.76	£5.95	£4.91	£3.21	£4.78	£6.77	£5.17

Appendix D

Local authority	£2.66	£2.83	£5.38	£2.05	£2.42	£2.18	£2.87	£3.34	£2.98	£3.84
All 3 [1]	£5.31	£6.03	£25.99	£13.18	£8.44	£7.14	£6.12	£8.42	£9.81	£9.12
Business sponsorship	£0.26	£0.50	£10.99	£0.79	£0.39	£1.01	£0.81	£0.55	£1.05	£0.66
All spending [2]	£5.56	£6.53	£36.98	£13.97	£8.83	£8.15	£6.93	£8.98	£10.86	£12.82

[1] ie Grant-in-aid, lottery and local authority: including national cos
[2] Including National companies. Authors note that totals might not add up exactly because of rounding

APPENDIX E

MINISTERS AND ARTS COUNCIL EXECUTIVE 1984-2010

Arts Council: Chair
Lord Rees-Mogg: 1982-1989
Lord Palumbo: 1989-1994
Lord Gowrie PC: 1994-1998
Gerry Robinson: 1998-2003
Sir Christopher Frayling: 2004 –2009
Dame Liz Forgan: 2009 -

Arts Council: Secretary General
Luke Rittner: 1983-1990
Anthony Everitt: 1990-1994 (previously deputy Secretary general 1983-1990)
Mary Allen: 1994-1997

Chief Executive
Peter Hewitt: 1998 - 2007
Alan Davey: 2007-

Ministers for Arts
NB: From 1992 to 1997, the post was combined with the office of Secretary of State for National Heritage. The title of the post was changed to Minister for Culture in 2005, and to Minister for Culture, Creative Industries and Tourism in 2007.

Lord Gowrie: 1983-1985
Richard Luce: 1985-1990
David Mellor: 1990
Timothy Renton: 1990-1991
* David Mellor: 1992
* Peter Brooke: 1992-1994
* Stephen Dorrell: 1994-1995

* Virginia Bottomley: 1995-1997
Mark Fisher: 1997-1998
Alan Howarth: 1998-2001
Tessa Blackstone: 2001-2003
Estelle Morris: 2003-2005
David Lammy: 2005-2007
Margaret Hodge: 2007-2008
Barbara Follett: 2008-2009
Ben Bradshaw: 2009 –

* Secretary of State: Department of National Heritage

Appendix F

Arts Council Drama Advisory Panels 1984 - 2002

1984/85
Tony Church (Chair)
Robert Woof (Vice Chair)
Alun Bond
Ian Brown
Pearl Connor
Robert Fowler
Nancy Meckler
Robin Midgley
Roy Nevitt
Clive Perry
John Potts
Elizabeth Sweeting
Robert Sykes
John Wallbank

1985/86
Brian Rix (Chair)
Robert Woof (Vice Chair)
Michael Attenborough
Alun Bond
Patrick Boyd Maunsell
Robert Breckman
Ian Brown
Pearl Connor
Alan Drury
Marty Flood
Nancy Meckler
Robin Midgley
Roy Nevitt

Elizabeth Sweeting
Robert Sykes
John Wallbank

1986/87
Brian Rix (Chair)
Beverley Anderson
Michael Attenborough
Patrick Boyd Maunsell
Pip Broughton
David Conville
Alan Drury
Fiona Ellis – CoRRA advisor
Vicky Ireland
Geoffrey Joyce
Peta Lily
Genista McIntosh
Nancy Meckler
Elspeth Morrison
Professor J Mulryne
Kenneth Rea
Ian Reekie
Sylvia Syms
William Weston

Observers
Chrissie Bradwell – British Council
J R Williams – HMI

1987/88
Sir Brian Rix (Chair)
Beverley Anderson
Michael Attenborough
Patrick Boyd Maunsell
Pip Broughton
David Conville
Alan Drury
Fiona Ellis – CoRRA advisor
Vicky Ireland
Geoffrey Joyce
Peta Lily

Genista McIntosh
Nancy Meckler
Elspeth Morrison
Professor J Mulryne
Kenneth Rea
Ian Reekie
Sylvia Syms
William Weston

Observers
Chrissie Bradwell – British Council
J R Williams – HMI

1988/89
Sir Brian Rix (Chair)
Beverley Anderson
Michael Attenborough
Patrick Boyd Maunsell
Pip Broughton
David Conville
Alan Drury
Vicky Ireland
Geoffrey Joyce
Peta Lily
Genista McIntosh
Nancy Meckler
Elspeth Morrison
Professor J Mulryne
Kenneth Rea
Ian Reekie
Sylvia Syms
William Weston

Observers
Chrissie Bradwell – British Council
Ivor Davies – CoRRA
J R Williams – HMI

1989/90
Sir Brian Rix
Beverley Anderson

Michael Attenborough
Patrick Boyd Maunsell
Pip Broughton
David Conville
Stella Hall
Hugh Hudson Davies
Vicky Ireland
Geoffrey Joyce
Peta Lily
Genista McIntosh
Elspeth Morrison
Professor J Mulryne
Kenneth Rea
Ian Reekie
Sylvia Syms
Timberlake Wertenbaker
William Weston

Observers
David Evans – British Council
Ivor Davies – CoRAA
JR Williams – HMI

1990/1991
Sir Brian Rix
Beverley Anderson
Michael Attenborough
David Conville
Stella Hall
Hugh Hudson Davies
Hilary Hammond
Vicky Heywood
Peta Lily
Phyllida Lloyd
Genista McIntosh
Deborah Paige
Kenneth Rea
Timberlake Wertenbaker

Observers
Suzie Boyd – British Council
Ivor Davies – CoRAA
JR Williams – HMI

1991/1992
Brian Rix (Chair)
Paul Allen
Eileen Atkins
Roger Chapman
Hugh Hudson Davies
John Gale
Stella Hall
Hilary Hammond
Vikki Heywood
Phyllida Lloyd
Penny Mayes
Deborah Paige
Timberlake Wertenbaker

Observers
Tim Butchard – British Council
Shelia Connolly– RAB
JR Williams – HMI

1992/93
Brian Rix (Chair)
Beverley Anderson
Paul Allen
Eileen Atkins
Roger Chapman
Bush Hartshorn
Hugh Hudson Davies
John Gale
Stella Hall
Hilary Hammond
Vikki Heywood
Phyllida Lloyd
Penny Mayes
Deborah Paige
Timberlake Wertenbaker

Observers
Tim Butchard – British Council
Alannah Lucas– RAB
Roger Williams – HMI

1993/94
Thelma Holt (chair)
Paul Allen
Roger Chapman
Bush Hartshorn
Hilary Hammond
John Gale
Stella Hall
Hilary Hammond
Vikki Heywood
Phyllida Lloyd
Penny Mayes
Deborah Paige
Jenny Topper
Jatinder Verma

Observers
Tim Butchard – British Council
Brian Debenham– RAB Observer
Roger Williams – HMI Observer

1994/1995
Thelma Holt (Chair)
Paul Allen
David Brieerlye
Roger Chapman
Bush Harshorn
Hilary Hammond
Vikki Heywood
Phyllida Lloyd
Penny Mayes
Deborah Paige
Michael Ratcliffe
Jenny Topper
Jatinder Verma

Observers
Tim Butchard – British Council
Brian Debenham– RAB Observer
Michael Convey – HMI Observer

1995/96
Thelma Holt (Chair)
Paul Allen
David Brierley
Roger Chapman
Richard Cogo-Fawcett
Neil Fountain
Bush Hartshorn
Jude Kelly
Penny Mayes
Sam Mendes
Michael Ratcliffe
Jenny Topper
Jatinder Verma
Maggie Wooley

No observers listed

1996/97
Thelma Holt (Chair)
Paul Allen
David Brierley
Roger Chapman
Richard Cogo-Fawcett
Neil Fountain
Bush Hartshorn
Jude Kelly
Penny Mayes
Sam Mendes
Michael Ratcliffe
Jenny Topper
Jatinder Verma
Maggie Wooley

Observers
Simon Gammel – British Council
Brian Debenham– RAB Observer
Helen Flach - RAB
HMI Observer

1997/98
Thelma Holt (Chair)
Paul Allen
Michael Attenborough
Alan Ayckbourn
Roger Chapman
Richard Cogo-Fawcett
Keith Davies
Bush Hartshorn
Jude Kelly
Barbara Matthews
Sam Mendes
Michael Ratcliffe
Mandy Stewart
Jenny Topper
Jatinder Verma
Maggie Wooley

Observers
Shirley Campbell– RAB Observer
Mike Faulkner - RAB
Janet Mills - HMI Observer

1998/99
Graeme Morris (Chair)
Michael Attenborough
David Benedict
Gwenda Hughes
Ewan Marshall
Martin McCullum
Nancy Meckler
Indhu Rubasingham
Kully Thirai
Mandy Stewart
Adrian Vinkin

2000
Graeme Morris (Chair)
Michael Attenborough
David Benedict
Gwenda Hughes
Ewan Marshall
Martin McCullum
Nancy Meckler
Indhu Rubasingham
Kully Thirai
Mandy Stewart
Adrian Vinken

2001
Graeme Morris (Chair)
Michael Attenborough
David Benedict
Gwenda Hughes
Ewan Marshall
Martin McCullum
Nancy Meckler
Indhu Rubasingham
Kully Thirai
Mandy Stewart
Adrian Vinken

2002
Graeme Morris (Chair)
Michael Attenborough
David Benedict
Gwenda Hughes
Ewan Marshall
Martin McCullum
Nancy Meckler
Indhu Rubasingham
Kully Thirai
Mandy Stewart
Adrian Vinken
Dorothy Wilson

BIBLIOGRAPHY

Arts Council of Great Britain, *The Theatre Today in England and Wales. The Report of the Arts Council Theatre Enquiry*, (London: ACGB, 1970)
ACGB/RAA Working Group, *Towards a New Relationship* (London: ACGB, 1980)
ACGB, *The Glory of the Garden: the development of the arts in England - a strategy for a decade* (London: ACGB, 1984)
—. *A Great British Success Story: An Invitation to Invest in the Arts*, (London: ACGB, 1985)
—. *Partnership. Making Arts Money Work Harder*, (London: ACGB, 1986)
—. *Better Business for the Arts*, (London: ACGB, 1988)
—. *Glory Reflected: A Progress Report on The Glory of the Garden)*, (London: ACGB, 1989)
—. *An Urban Renaissance: Sixteen Case Studies Showing the Role of the Arts in the Urban Regeneration*, (London: ACGB, 1989)
ACE, *National Policy for Theatre in England*, (London: ACE 2000)
—. *The Next Stage: Towards a New Policy for Drama in England*, (London: ACE, 2000)
—. *A Living Theatre: Delivering a National Policy for Theatre in England*, (London: ACE, 2001)
—. *Arts in England: Attendance, Participation and Attitudes in 2001*, (London: ACE, 2002)
—. *Eclipse Developing Strategies to Combat Racism in the Theatre*, (London: ACE, 2002)
—. *Public Investment in the Arts: A Decade of Change*, (London: ACE, 2006)
—. *Theatre Assessment*, (London: ACE, 2009)
John Bailey, *A Theatre For All Seasons: Nottingham Playhouse The First Thirty Years 1948-1978 (*Stroud: Alan Sutton Publishing / Nottingham Playhouse, 1994)
Elizabeth Barry and William Boles, "Beyond Victimhood: Agency and Identity in the Theatre of Roy Williams" in Dimple Godiwala (ed), *Alternatives within the Mainstream: British Black and Asian Theatres* (Newcastle: Cambridge Scholars Press, 2006), pp.295-313

Bibliography

Michael Billington, *State of the Nation: British Theatre Since 1945* (London: Faber & Faber, 2007)

Pierre Bourdieu, *Distinction: A Social Critique of the Judgment of Taste* (Harvard: Harvard University Press, 1987)

Peter Boyden Associates Ltd, *The Roles and Functions of the English Regional Producing Theatres* (London: Arts Council of England, 2000)

Bristol Live, *Bristol Live: A Performance Culture of Ambition, A Discussion Paper*, (London: ACE, 2008)

Ian Brown and Rob Brannen "When Theatre was for All: the Cork Report, after Ten Years", *New Theatre Quarterly*, Vol. XII no. 48 (1996), pp 367-83

Ian Brown, Rob Brannen and Douglas Brown "The English Arts Council Franchise System and political theatre", *New Theatre Quarterly*, Vol. XVI No 64 (2000), pp 379-87.

Ian Brown, 'The road through Woodstock: counter-Thatcherite strategies in ACGB's drama development between 1984 and 1994,' *Contemporary Theatre Review*, Volume 17(2), 2007, pp 218-229

John Bull, *Stage Right: Crisis and Recovery in British Contemporary Mainstream Theatre* (Houndmills: Macmillan, 1994)

Marvin Carlson, "Become Less Provincial", *Theatre Survey*, XLV, No 2 (November 2004) 177-80

Claire Cochrane, *The Birmingham Rep: A City's Theatre 1962-2002* (Birmingham: Sir Barry Jackson Trust, 2003)

—. "A Local Habitation and a Name": The Development of Black and Asian Theatre in Birmingham since the 1970s', in Dimple Godiwala (ed), *Alternatives within the Mainstream: British Black and Asian Theatres* (Newcastle: Cambridge Scholars Press, 2006), pp.153-173

Richard Cogo-Fawcett, *Relationships between Subsidised and Commercial Theatre*, (London: ACE, 2003)

Sir Kenneth Cork et al., *Theatre IS for All: The Report of the Inquiry into Professional Theatre in England under the Chairmanship of Sir Kenneth Cork* (London: ACGB, 1986)

Alan Davey, *A Review of Arts Council England's Regularly Funded Organisations Investment Strategy 2007/2008*, (London: ACE, 2008)

Department of Culture, Media and Sport, *Culture at the Heart of Regeneration*, (London: HMSO, 2004)

Department of Culture, Media and Sport Select Committee, *Report on Theatre*, (London: HMSO, 2006)

Maria M Delgado and Caridad Svich (eds), *Theatre in Crisis? Performance manifestos for a new century* (Manchester: Manchester University Press, 2002)
Graham Devlin, *Keeping the Show on the Road. Touring theatre in Britain in 1985* (London: ACGB, 1985)
John Elsom, *The Theatre Outside London* (London: Routledge Kegan Paul 1971)
—. *Postwar British Theatre* (London: Routledge, 1979)
Equity, *The Theatre Commission: A Report on Subsidised Theatre in the UK* (London: Equity, 1996)
Richard Eyre and Nicholas Wright, *Changing Stages. A View of British Theatre in the Twentieth Century*, (London: Bloomsbury, 2001)
Clare Fenn & Alan Joy, *Local Authority Expenditure on Arts in England, 2002/3* (London: ACE, Research Report 39, 2005)
Grace Wyndham Goldie: *The Liverpool Repertory Theatre* (London: Hodder and Stoughton, 1935)
Clive Gray, *The Politics of the Arts in Britain* (London: Macmillan, 2000)
Jen Harvie, *Staging the UK* (Manchester: Manchester University Press, 2005)
Robert Hewison, *Culture and Consensus: England, Art and Politics since 1940* (London: Methuen, rev. ed. 1997)
Nadine Holdsworth, "They'd Have Pissed on My Grave: The Arts Council and Theatre Workshop", *New Theatre Quarterly*, 1997 15:57
Patricia Hollis, *Jennie Lee: A Life* (Oxford: Oxford University Press, 1997)
Tyrone Huggins, *The Eclipse Theatre Story* (London: Arts Council England, 2006)
Robert Hutchison, *The Politics of the Arts Council* (London: Sinclair Browne, 1982)
—. *A Hard Fact to Swallow: The Division of Arts Council Expenditure Between London and the English Regions* (London: Policy Studies Institute, 1982)
Anthony Jackson, "The Repertory Theatre Movement in England, 1960-1990", in *Englisches Theater der Gegenwart: geschichte(n) und strukturen* (Tubingen: Gunter Narr Verlag, 1993)
—. *Learning Through Theatre: New Perspectives on Theatre in Education*, (London: Routledge 1993)
—. *Theatre, Education and the Making of Meanings (*Manchester: Manchester University Press, 2007)

—. "The Dialogic and the Aesthetic: Some Reflections on Theatre as a Learning Medium.", *The Journal of Aesthetic Education* - Volume 39, Number 4, Winter 2005, 104-118

Baz Kershaw, "Building an Unstable Pyramid: the Fragmentation of Alternative Theatre", *New Theatre Quarterly*, 1993 9:36

—. "Discouraging Democracy: British Theatre and Economics, 1979-99", *Theatre Journal*, 1999 51, pp.267-283

—. (ed.), *The Cambridge History of British Theatre*, vol. 3: Since 1895 (Cambridge: Cambridge University Press, 2004)

Naseem Khan, *The Arts Britain Ignores: The arts of the ethnic minorities in Britain* (London: The Commission for Racial Equality, 1976)

Andy Martin & Helen Bartlett, *Implementing the National Policy for Theatre in England: Baseline Findings* (London: ACE/MORI: Research Report 33; 2003)

Andy Martin & Helen Bartlett, *Implementing the National Policy for Theatre in England: Case Studies 1* (London, ACE/MORI, 2004)

Francois Matarasso, *Towards a Local Culture Index* (London: Comedia, 1999)

Lord Redcliffe-Maud, *Support for the Arts in England and Wales* (London, Calouste Gulbenkian Foundation, 1976)

Brian McMaster, *Supporting Excellence in the Arts: from Measurement to Judgement* (DCMS, 2008)

John Myerscough, *The Economic Importance of the Arts in Britain.* (London: Policy Studies Institute, 1988)

National Campaign for the Arts, *The Future for the Arts Council: Report of Proceedings of Seminar 18th March, 1994* (London: NCA, 1994)

National Campaign for the Arts, *Theatre in Crisis: The Plight of Regional Theatre* (London: NCA, 1998)

North West Arts Board, *A Review of Theatre Provision in the North-West of England* (Manchester: NWA,1997)

Charles Osborne, *Giving It Away: the Memoirs of an Uncivil Servant* (London: Secker & Warburg, 1986)

D. Keith Peacock, *Thatcher's Theatre: British Theatre and Drama in the Eighties* (Westport, Connecticut, and London: Greenwood Press, 1999)

John Pick, *Vile Jelly: The Birth, Life and Lingering Death of the Arts Council of Great Britain* (Doncaster: Brynmill, 1991)

Michael Prior, *Dreams and Reconstruction: a cultural history of British Theatre 1945-2005* (Lulu.com, 2006)

Simon Reade, *Cheek by Jowl: Ten Years of Celebration*, (Bath: Absolute Classics, 1991)

Dan Rebellato, 'Playwriting and Globalisation: Towards a Site-Unspecific Theatre', *Contemporary Theatre Review*, 2006 Vol. 16.1
—. *Theatre & Globalization* (Basingstoke: Palgrave, 2009)
Redcliffe-Maud, Lord, *Support for the Arts in England and Wales,* (London: Calouste Gulbenkian Foundation, 1976)
Jo Robinson, "Becoming More Provincial? The Global and the Local in Theatre History", *New Theatre Quarterly* 23:3 (August 2007) 229-240
George Rowell and Anthony Jackson, *The Repertory Movement: a History of Regional Theatre in Britain* (Cambridge: Cambridge University Press, 1984)
Dominic Shellard, *British Theatre since the war* (New Haven & London: Yale University Press, 1999)
—. *Economic Impact Study of UK Theatre* (London: ACE, 2004)
—. *Economic Impact Study of West Midlands Theatre* (London: ACE, 2005)
—. *Social Impact Study of UK Theatre* (London, ACE, 2006)
Simon Shepherd and Peter Womack, *English Drama: a Cultural History.* (Oxford: Blackwell, 1996)
Andrew Sinclair, *Arts and Cultures: The History of the Fifty Years of the Arts Council of Great Britain* (London: Sinclair-Stevenson, 1995)
Society of London Theatre: *The Wyndham Report* (London: SOLT, 1998)
—. *After Wyndham: Key Issues in London Theatre* (London: SOLT, 1999)
Andrew Sinclair, *Arts and Cultures: the History of the 50 years of the Arts Council of Great Britain* (London: Sinclair-Stevenson, 1995)
Tony Travers, *The Wyndham Report: The Economic Impact of London's West End Theatres* (London: Society of London Theatre, 1998)
John Tusa, *Art Matters: Reflecting on Culture* (London: Methuen, 2000)
Olivia Turnbull, *Bringing Down the House: The Crisis in Britain's Regional Theatres* (Bristol: Intellect, 2008)
Richard Wilding, *Supporting the Arts: A Review of the Structure of Arts Funding* (Arts Council, 1989)
Nicholas Wilson & Mark Hart, *Regional Funding Revisited* (Small Business Research Centre, Kingston University: 2001)
Richard Witts, *Artist Unknown: An Alternative History of the Arts Council* (London: Warner Books, 1998)

CONTRIBUTORS

James Blackman is Head of Strategy and Communication at the Lyric Theatre Hammersmith and is also associate director of the Lyric's Capital project which is building the first teaching theatre for performing arts in the UK. Previously he was Co-Director of Creative Learning at the Lyric and worked in theatre education for over ten years. He has worked in a variety of settings including touring a play in Liverpool, running a Musical Theatre Academy in south-east London, on a youth theatre exchange in Texas, project managing in Switzerland, administrating in Plymouth and teaching in Nepal.

Ian Brown is a playwright, poet and freelance scholar. Formerly ACGB Drama Director (1986-94), he was, until 2002, Professor of Drama and Dean of Arts at Queen Margaret University. Currently he is visiting professor at both Glasgow and Glamorgan Universities. He publishes on theatrical, literary and cultural topics and is General Editor of *The Edinburgh History of Scottish Literature* (EUP: 2007) and joint series editor for the *Edinburgh Companions to Scottish Literature* for which he has edited volumes on the twentieth century and drama. He was founder Chairman (1973-75) of the Scottish Society of Playwrights and founding Convenor of North West Playwrights Workshop (1982-5).

Claire Cochrane is senior lecturer in Drama and Performance at the University of Worcester. She is the author of two books on the Birmingham Repertory Theatre: *Shakespeare and the Birmingham Repertory Theatre 1913-1929* (Society for Theatre Research, 1993) and *Birmingham Rep: A City's Theatre 1962-2002* (Sir Barry Jackson Trust, 2003). Her recent publications focus on developments in Black British and British Asian Theatre and she has contributed to the AHRC-funded Exeter University British Asian Theatre project. She is currently completing a book on social and economic factors in twentieth century Britsh
theatres for Cambridge University Press.

Kate Dorney is Senior Curator of Modern and Contemporary Performance at the Victoria and Albert Museum where she specialises in researching the history and practice of state subsidy and subsidised theatre. She oversees the documentation of contemporary performance, including the National Video Archive of Performance, which makes high-quality live recordings of contemporary performance, and a rolling oral history project of short interviews with practitioners, 'What is Performance?'. Kate is editor of the journal *Studies in Theatre & Performance* and the author of *The Changing Language of Modern English Drama 1945-2005*. In January 2010 she joined Arts Council England's panel of Artistic Assessors.

Gwenda Hughes was an actor in theatre and television before being awarded a Trainee Directors Grant from the Arts Council to work with Theatre Centre. Her directing career has included freelance work with M6, Red Ladder, Women's Theatre Group, The Young Vic, Oldham Coliseum, Lip Service, the National Youth Theatre and Salisbury Playhouse. She was Artistic Director of Watford Palace Theatre in Education Company for three years and Associate Director of Birmingham Rep for nine. From 1998 to 2006 she was Artistic Director and Chief Executive of the New Vic Theatre in North Staffordshire. Since stepping down from this role she has been working as a freelance director, writer and researcher. Last year, she became a poacher, turned gamekeeper, and was appointed a council member of Arts Council, West Midlands.

Anthony Jackson is Emeritus Professor of Educational Theatre at The University of Manchester and director of the Performance, Learning and Heritage research project (2005-8). A recipient of the Judith Kase-Cooper Honorary Research Award from the American Alliance for Theatre & Education (2003), his publications include, most recently, *Theatre, education and the making of meanings*. He has written extensively on regional theatre, notably, with George Rowell, *The Repertory Movement: A History of Regional Theatre in Britain*.

Ros Merkin is a Reader in Drama at Liverpool John Moores University. Her publications include *Liverpool's Third Cathedral: the Liverpool Everyman Theatre*, compiled for the 40th anniversary of the theatre and she is currently working on a book for the 100th anniversary of Liverpool Playhouse in 2011 and one on the contribution of regional theatre to the theatre ecology. She was project director for the AHRC funded Everyman Archive housed at Liverpool John Moores. She also creates and directs performances including *Suitcase* at Liverpool Street Station, to commemorate the 70th anniversary of the arrival of the kindertransport

Olivia Turnbull is a Senior Lecturer in Drama Studies at Bath Spa University. Her research interests include contemporary British and American theatre, verbatim, site specific, and experimental performance practices. Her publications include *Bringing Down the House: The Crisis in Britain's Regional Theatres*.

Glen Walford is an international theatre director well-known for her epic Shakespeare and musical productions. She was Founding Artistic Director of the London Bubble Company and the Chung-Ying Theatre Company, Hong Kong. She was Artistic Director of the Everyman Theatre in Liverpool for seven years and of the Ludlow Festival Shakespeare where she mounted five Shakespeare productions.

During her time at the Everyman, she re-visited and re-invented musicals (including *Cabaret* and *The Threepenny Opera*) and re-wrote the libretto for the opera *Tosca* which she directed and which was performed in the round by actor-musicians musically directed by Paddy Cunneen. She commissioned and directed the world premiere of *Shirley Valentine* for the Everyman in 1986 and 2010 sees her directing Meera Syal as Shirley for the Menier Chocolate Factory.

INDEX

A Hard Fact to Swallow, 82
A Policy for the Arts, 33
ABSA (Association of Business Sponsorship), 7, 15
Allen, Mary, 56
Allen, Paul, 44, 57, 232
Arnold, Matthew, 21, 32
Arts Council
  Appraisal, 39, 41
  Challenge funding, 5, 7, 89, 100
  Changing role, 97
  Christmas Cuts 1980, 34, 35, 36, 37, 43, 79
  Devolution, 38, 81, 91, 95, 98, 101, 105, 171, 172
  District Councils, 92
  Eclipse Conference, 149
  Economic Impact, 9, 125
  Enhancement funding, 5, 101
  Founding, 32
  Funding for National Theatre and RSC, 21
  Funding in the 1980s, 48
  Housing the Arts, 9, 12
  Jennie Lee, 33
  Local Authorities, 39, 43, 47, 49, 51, 52, 53, 204, 206
  Metropolitan Excellence, 33
  National Policy, 107, 197
  Panel Members, 44
  Parity funding, 5, 53, 100, 171, 172, 187, 204, 207, 225
  Poll-tax, 100
  Regional Offices, 5, 42, 43
  Relationship with regions, 32, 43, 45, 53, 54, 55, 57, 83, 85, 95, 96
  Spending in the regions, 81, 91
  Theatre Review, 221
  Theatre Today, 120
  Woodstock, 56, 57, 58, 102

Basingstoke, Horseshoe Theatre, 37, 78, 90, 112, 113, 233
Birmingham Rep, 22, 25, 103, 109, 111, 119, 142, 143, 146, 150, 152, 153, 155, 202, 208
Blackstock, Anthony, 6
Bolton Octagon, 20, 38, 81, 86, 89, 101, 102, 104, 110, 115
Booth, Peter (Merseyside Arts), 46, 47, 49, 50, 97, 114
Boyden Report, 13, 41, 51, 106, 107, 109, 116, 149, 166, 221, 227, 257
Bristol Old Vic, 48, 94, 99, 100, 101, 102, 111, 115, 150, 209, 222, 224, 225, 230, 232, 233, 237
Brooke, Peter, 99
Business Sponsorship Incentive scheme, 7
Canterbury, Marlowe Theatre, 20, 111
Cheek by Jowl, 117, 121, 122, 127, 128, 129, 130, 133, 134
Cheeseman, Peter, 19, 25, 42, 50, 51, 103, 135, 159
Cheltenham, Everyman Theatre, 12, 54, 55, 56, 90, 110, 113, 174, 233, 237
Chester Gateway, 12, 16, 37, 38, 78, 81, 86, 87, 113, 154, 233
Chichester Festival Theatre, 4, 228, 237
Colchester, Mercury Theatre, 13, 38, 90, 96, 110, 113, 233, 237, 238
Complicité, 117, 118, 120, 122, 130, 131, 132, 133
Cork, Sir Kenneth. See Theatre IS for All
Coventry, Belgrade Theatre, 12, 19, 20, 102, 142
Crewe, Lyceum Theatre, 20, 35, 81, 86, 111

Daldry, Stephen, 13
Derby Playhouse, 90, 100, 103, 108, 110, 113, 222, 233
Eastern Angles, 117, 135, 136, 137
Economic Importance of the Arts in Britain, The, 6, 15, 124, 139
ERPT (English Regional Producing Theatres), 8, 93, 106, 111, 224, 231, 233
Everitt, Anthony, 40, 45, 50, 55, 57, 101, 115, 245
Exeter, Northcott Theatre, 12, 113, 115, 222, 226, 238
Farnham, Redgrave Theatre, 12
Forced Entertainment, 118, 137
Frayling, Christopher, 56, 57, 221, 245
Gaiety Theatre, Manchester, 22
Glasgow Citizens Theatre, 18, 19, 23, 24, 29, 103
Glasgow Repertory Theatre, 22
Glory of the Garden, The, 5, 12, 18, 26, 31, 34, 37, 39, 45, 57, 59, 63, 64, 77, 87, 88, 91, 93, 112, 116, 118, 119, 126, 141, 142, 143, 152, 153, 164, 204, 221
Goodman, Lord, 84, 100
Gowrie, Lord, 7, 14, 104, 195, 245
Great British Success Story, A, 6, 8, 124, 125
Guildford, Yvonne Arnaud Theatre, 78, 113, 198, 233, 239
Half Moon Theatre, 55, 56, 110, 113, 234, 237
Hall, Peter, 4, 14, 74, 87, 92, 108, 133, 196, 200, 250
Hampstead Theatre, 4, 101, 151, 234, 237
Harrogate, White Rose Theatre, 78, 87, 95, 113, 234
Hedley, Philip, 1, 14, 42, 104, 108, 226, 232
Hornchurch, Queens Theatre, 238
Horniman, Annie, 23
Hull Truck, 12, 125, 195, 237

Ipswich, Wolsey Theatre, 96, 109, 115, 136, 137, 143, 150, 235, 238
Jackson, Barry, 23
Joseph, Stephen, 14, 25, 165, 166
Kellgren, Ian, 198, 201, 202, 204, 205
Kenwright, Bill, 49, 194, 197, 198, 199, 200, 201, 202, 203, 204, 205, 206, 207, 208, 209
Keynes, John Maynard, 5, 14, 26, 33, 60, 77
Kneehigh, 117, 133, 134, 223, 225, 226, 229
Lancaster, Duke's Playhouse, 38, 81, 86, 90, 110, 113, 234
Leatherhead, Thorndike Theatre, 12, 109, 110, 113, 125, 195, 197, 200, 207, 208, 234
Lee, Jennie, 32, 33, 35, 100, 117
Leeds Playhouse, 20
Leicester Haymarket, 89, 115, 119, 125, 152, 195, 200, 202
Liverpool Everyman, 3, 12, 18, 19, 23, 24, 47, 63, 88, 115, 234, 238
Liverpool Playhouse, 12, 47, 142, 143, 193, 202, 207
local authorities, 24, 31, 33, 37, 39, 43, 47, 48, 49, 50, 51, 53, 56, 66, 83, 84, 86, 89, 93, 95, 96, 102, 106, 113, 114, 124, 145, 160, 171, 173, 187, 198, 204, 205, 206, 212
Luce, Richard, 7, 95, 98, 99, 100, 114, 245
Lyric Hammersmith, 4, 13, 115, 214, 215, 226, 238
M6 Theatre Company, 38, 86, 90, 110, 112, 159
Mackenzie, Ruth, 38, 41, 60, 148
Manchester Royal Exchange, 4, 18, 19, 23, 24, 38, 86, 94, 98, 104, 108, 111, 115, 234, 238
Manchester, Contact Theatre, 19, 228, 237
McMaster Report, 27, 59, 222, 223, 228, 259

Mellor, David, 99
Mercury Theatre, Colchester, 13
Metropolitan County Councils,
    abolition of, 91
Myerscough, John, 6, 9, 15, 124, 139
National Lottery, 12, 21
National Theatre, 13, 19, 21, 22, 40,
    42, 82, 87, 88, 93, 94, 103, 119,
    127, 130, 131, 134, 148, 151,
    202, 224, 230, 239
Newcastle, Theatre Royal, 92
Newcastle-under-Lyme, New
    Victoria Theatre, 50, 60, 103, 238
Newcastle-under-Lyme, Victoria
    Theatre, 18, 19, 24, 42, 135
Northern Stage Company, 54, 238
Nottingham Playhouse, 18, 19, 20,
    42, 60, 87, 115, 142, 143, 144,
    145, 148, 150, 153, 154, 155, 186
Oldham Coliseum, 81, 86, 102, 115,
    234, 238
Osborne, Charles, 36
Palumbo, Peter, 55, 57, 124, 193,
    245
Policy for the Arts, A, 5
Pulford, Richard, 79
Rees-Mogg, William, 1, 14, 18, 26,
    37, 39, 40, 50, 52, 58, 77, 79, 87,
    88, 90, 110, 113, 245
Regional Arts Associations, 5, 31,
    32, 34, 37, 38, 39, 42, 43, 44, 45,
    46, 49, 50, 51, 52, 53, 54, 55, 56,
    57, 58, 78, 80, 81, 82, 83, 84, 85,
    88, 89, 90, 91, 92, 94, 95, 96, 97,
    98, 100, 101, 111, 235
    Conference of Regional Arts
        Associations, 82, 85
    Standing Conference of Regional
        Arts Associations, 82, 84
Regional Arts Boards, 32, 55, 56, 97,
    99, 104, 165
Renton, Tim, 99
Rittner, Luke, 6, 7, 45, 46, 50, 84, 86,
    87, 88, 98, 119, 123, 245

Rix, Brian, 16, 44, 48, 52, 54, 57, 58,
    102, 104, 205, 247, 248, 249,
    250, 251
Robinson, Kenneth, 14, 34, 108, 109,
    164, 245, 260
Royal Court Theatre, 40, 126, 202,
    230, 237
Royal Shakespeare Company, 7, 8,
    21, 22, 40, 92, 93, 94, 102, 103,
    105, 125, 126, 133, 134, 151,
    195, 196, 200, 239
Salisbury Playhouse, 18, 23, 115,
    169, 170, 171, 173, 179, 183,
    187, 189, 190, 191, 202, 238
Scarborough, Stephen Joseph
    Theatre, 4, 90, 239
Shared Experience, 118, 121, 137,
    223
Sheffield Crucible, 4, 7, 12, 52, 87,
    89, 103, 111, 112, 209
Shellard, Dominic, 9, 21, 25, 59
Southampton, Nuffield Theatre, 38,
    90, 115, 238
Southend, Palace Theatre, 38, 90,
    110, 113, 235
Tara Arts, 42, 48, 89, 123, 142, 147
Temba, 38, 110, 113, 118, 141, 146
Theatre IS for All (The Cork Report),
    9, 41, 42, 47, 53, 61, 89, 93, 119,
    121, 122, 129, 130, 135, 138,
    172, 189, 196
Theatre Royal Stratford East, 4, 42
Theatre Royal, Plymouth, 8, 36, 51,
    102, 105, 110, 133, 239
Towards a New Relationship, 43, 45,
    80, 82, 83, 111
Tricycle, 4, 37, 78, 113, 149, 151,
    235, 239
TyneWear Theatre Company, 54
Venables, Clare, 27, 40, 52, 59
Verma, Jatinder, 40, 42, 252, 253,
    254
Watford, Palace Theatre, 38, 96, 102,
    108, 110, 115, 239
West Yorkshire Playhouse, 3, 12, 25,
    53, 58, 60, 104, 106, 115, 239

Westcliff-on-Sea, Palace Theatre, 16, 96, 101
Wilding, Richard, 55, 56, 85, 91, 94, 95, 96, 97, 98, 99, 100, 101, 102, 113, 114, 204
Worcester, Swan Theatre, 8, 10, 11, 12, 16, 110, 113

Worthing, Connaught Theatre, 78, 90, 113, 235
York Theatre Royal, 16, 53, 95, 115, 129, 239
Young Vic, 4, 19, 24, 115, 222, 235, 239